A Handbook for African Mother-Tongue Bible Translators

Isaac Boaheng

University of the Free State, South Africa

Series in Language and Linguistics

VERNON PRESS

Copyright © 2022 Vernon Press, an imprint of Vernon Art and Science Inc, on behalf of the author.

www.vernonpress.com

In the Americas:
Vernon Press
1000 N West Street, Suite 1200
Wilmington, Delaware, 19801
United States

In the rest of the world:
Vernon Press
C/Sancti Espiritu 17,
Malaga, 29006
Spain

Series in Language and Linguistics

Library of Congress Control Number: 2021942687

ISBN: 978-1-64889-382-7

Also available: 978-1-64889-293-6 [Hardback]; 978-1-64889-329-2 [PDF, E-Book]

Cover design by Vernon Press. Cover image by Aaron Burden on Unsplash.

A Handbook for African Mother-Tongue Bible Translators is an engagingly written, hands-on study of the art and science of Bible translation written by an African scholar primarily for an African audience. It provides a very thorough presentation of the essential principles, methods, processes, and intricacies of Bible translation from beginning to end, including pre-project planning and final draft testing. The various stages of this vital interlingual communication process are carefully and clearly explained in a sequence of logically arranged major sections and individual chapter units. In this book, Boaheng not only takes his readers on an engaging tour of the social and linguistic challenges facing African Bible translators (as they move between linguistic and cultural traditions to make the Bible accessible to people in the language they best understand), but he also provides a practical guide for navigating these troubling and tempestuous waters in Bible translation. Helpful thought-provoking review exercises are also supplied at the end of each chapter to test and encourage the progressive learning process.

The fact that an experienced African Bible translator has authored this book makes the text especially relevant for the continent of Africa, where so much translation and revision work is currently either underway or being planned. To this end, I can heartily recommend this book as an essential resource. It would also serve as an excellent introduction to this subject in Universities, theological schools and seminaries. How I wish I had this systematic guide available for service in the field some years ago when I was serving as a United Bible Societies Translation Consultant in Southeastern Africa! All African Bible translators and Translation Consultants working today will certainly benefit by having this *Handbook* close at hand! Boaheng needs commendation for such a resourceful piece.

Prof. Ernst R. Wendland, PhD

Stellenbosch University, South Africa & South Africa Theological Seminary
Retired Translation Consultant, United Bible Societies

This book is a useful guide for people who would like to serve in the ministry of Bible translation. It also provides vital information for those who would like to learn about the theory and practice of Bible translation or who are studying translation in the academy. It introduces the rudiments of Bible translation in readable style and offers very useful suggestions, particularly regarding how to translate idioms, figures of speech and other cultural features in the mother-tongue context. It fairly accounts for the necessary theoretical considerations of Bible translation and proceeds to highlight specific contextual matters that frequently prove challenging in any mother-tongue translation exercise. Another useful feature of this book is that it comes from someone who is currently an active member of his own mother-tongue translation team, working hard to reduce the word of God into his own mother-tongue. This makes Boaheng's book unique as he addresses issues he himself is confronted with daily in the translation exercise. Written specifically with the African context in mind, this book seeks to address the numerous challenges involved in transferring Judeo-Christian concepts, thought categories and ideas from the Bible into various African mother-tongues with the intention of facilitating translation. The book is highly recommended.

Rev. Dr. Frederick Mawusi Amevenku, PhD

Senior Minister, Evangelical Presbyterian Church, Ghana,
Senior Lecturer (New Testament Studies) & Director of Graduate Studies,
Trinity Theological Seminary Legon-Accra, Ghana

Bible translation is critical to the Christian faith because Christianity is a religion whose authenticity is not limited to a particular language. This makes the field of Bible translation very critical in academia and world Christianity. It is the translation of the Bible that led to the establishment of Christianity in territories outside Palestine, where the faith began. For the gospel to be understood rightly and applied appropriately, one has to read it in a language he/she understands. In that regard, Lesslie Newbegin stated that "if the gospel is to be understood, if it is to be received as something which communicates truth about the real human situation... 'make sense,' it has to be communicated in the language of those to whom it is addressed and has to be clothed in the symbols that are meaningful to them" (Newbegin 1989:41). This calls for principles and guidelines for mother-tongue biblical translation for translators.

In the book *A Handbook for African Mother-Tongue Bible Translators*, Isaac Boaheng critically and convincingly examined issues at the heart of mother-tongue Bible translation in general and in the African context in particular. The work looked at how various genres, idiomatic expressions, figures, etc., ought to be translated and interpreted to communicate meaning to African Christians. A reflexive study of the book brings to mind the core duty of the early church fathers when they were faced with translating the Bible from its initial languages of Hebrew, Aramaic, and Greek to communities not familiar with the biblical languages (Aryeh 2014: 281-301). Boaheng clearly pointed out that mother-tongue biblical translation is not limited to merely replacing terms in the Source Language with terms in the Receptor Language but the dynamic translation that focuses attention on the Receptor Language and culture that does not conflict with the message of the Bible (Nida 2003:77).

A Handbook for African Mother-Tongue Bible Translators is a significant response to challenges of mother-tongue Bible translation that many African scholars such as B. Y. Quarshie, John D. K. Ekem, and Howell A. Allison, among others have cogently mentioned (Quarshie 2002: 4-14; Ekem 2010: 34-37; Allison 2010: 21-33). Boaheng analyzed the need for sign language mother-tongue translation principles that are not deeply harnessed in Africa. I recommend this book to biblical scholars and students to further explore sign language mother-tongue biblical translation in Africa. The book is a Competent Based Training (CBT) module for mother-tongue Bible translators and biblical studies students. The format is simple, such that non-theological clergy could adapt it for use during missions. I commend Isaac Boaheng for such a groundbreaking work to sustain the scholarly discussion concerning mother-tongue Bible translation and for pointing out novel areas for further consideration in the academy.

Rev. Dr. Daniel Nii Aboagye Aryeh, PhD

Senior Lecturer (New Testament Studies) & Rector,
Perez University College, Winneba, Ghana

I am grossly limited by words to concisely describe the practical resourcefulness of the book in your hands. However, to put it mildly, without any form of exaggeration, the book *A Handbook for African Mother-Tongue Bible Translators* brings to the reader scholarly insights and discussions about key issues in Bible translation viewed from an African perspective in particular. The fact that this book has been written by someone who is a Bible translator himself makes it a very important document that will contribute immensely to the development of the academic field of Translation Studies in Africa and beyond. I am sure that both present and future generations will benefit greatly from this excellent piece. I wish this book to be not only in the hands of Bible translators and translation consultants but also of all students of the Bible. It will serve as a handbook to the Translator for sure, an additional help to the Consultant, and a reliable Commentary to the Christian Scholar. I highly recommend this book to everyone who desires to understand God's word and apply it appropriately.

Apostle Monty Abraham

Epie Bible Translator
Bible Society of Nigeria

As an African mother-tongue Bible translator, I understand the need for a resource material aimed at addressing the challenges associated with Bible translation in Africa and beyond. Rev. Isaac Boaheng has responded to this need by his well-researched publication, *A Handbook for African Mother-Tongue Bible Translators,* which provides vital data to educate readers on the theory and practice of Bible Translation. The book traces the history of Bible translation from the Septuagint to modern translations. An African mother-tongue Bible translator himself, Rev. Boaheng pays particular attention to the African context and deals adequately with most of the key challenges that confront African translators daily with particular reference to cultural idioms, proper names (places, peoples), units measures (weights, length, heights), figurative language (metaphor, simile) and others. He cites concrete and relevant cases from various parts of Africa to illustrate the principles taught. A unique feature of the book is the chapter on sign language Bible Translation. Not much has been published in this area with reference to the African situation, and I hope readers will take the opportunity to learn from this book. There are thought-provoking exercises at the end of each chapter to help the reader review carefully what has been taught in a particular chapter before proceeding to the next. This is a valuable resource of knowledge for pastors, missionaries, laymen, and Bible translators, translation consultants and lecturers in the field of translation studies. I do not only recommend this book but also commend my good friend, Rev. Boaheng, for such a bold step in producing a one-stop source for Bible translation, particularly in Africa.

Mrs. Magdalena Shilongo

Oshindonga Bible Translator
Bible Society of Namibia

I wholeheartedly dedicate this book to The Very Rev. Prof. John David Kwamena Ekem, Kwesi Dickson-Gilbert Ansre Distinguished Professor of Biblical Exegesis & Mother Tongue Hermeneutics (Trinity Theological Seminary, Legon, Ghana), Translation Consultant (Bible Society of Ghana) and Vice-Principal (Methodist University College, Accra, Ghana).

Table of contents

Foreword

Translation is an ancient activity. It is as old as the beginnings of human language diversity. As long as human language diversity has existed, the need for communication across human cultures and languages has been both necessary and real. Humans are social beings who are ever desirous of communication among themselves and of bridging the barriers across their various communities, cultures and languages. Unfortunately, the existence of these barriers across the diverse human communities and their often mutually unintelligible languages poses an apparently insurmountable obstacle. Admittedly, the need to surmount the obstacle is overwhelming. Reasons for this need are numerous and diverse—economic, religious, educational, cultural, political, and so on.

We see this need exemplified in the first recorded translation of the Hebrew Bible (or the Old Testament) from the original source language (Hebrew) into ancient Greek, which was at the time the widely spoken and written language of the Mediterranean world. This was some 200 or so years before the birth of Christ. There was the need to have the Hebrew Bible available in translation in the famous library of Alexandria. However, there was an even greater need to have the Jews in the Greek diaspora, who could no longer read their religious book in its original Hebrew. This reality led to the need to have the Hebrew Bible translated into ancient Greek. The resulting translation was the Septuagint.

Interestingly, the translators of the ancient Greek Septuagint and other major Bible translations that followed, such as Jerome's Latin Vulgate, Martin Luther's German Bible, or the Authorized King James Bible were not done by professional translators. The professionalization of translation is a recent phenomenon. It was part of the development of translation studies as an academic field of study driven by the urgent needs for translation and interpretation in business, industry, education, government, religion, medicine, politics, travel and tourism, and so on.

The professionalization of translation studies has led to the growth of translation research and study, and to the development of specialized knowledge, and as well to the training and formation of translators, and to the publication of studies and books on the subject. Translation studies has developed into a highly specialized multi-disciplinary field of study and activity, drawing on such other inter-disciplines as linguistics, literary studies, cultural studies, social anthropological studies, sociology, psychology, philosophy, historical studies, subject related studies, which includes biblical studies, individual language studies, among others.

Translation is currently carried out everywhere and in every field and activity. Bible translation is part of the ongoing global translation enterprise. There are Bible translators in every country and on every continent. Languages with millions of speakers to languages with a few thousand speakers are all a part of this global translation enterprise. The goal of Bible translation is to contribute to the dream of seeing everyone hear God speak their own languages.

My good friend Rev Isaac Boaheng is to be congratulated for taking the time to share with the reader some of the insights and key principles of the art and science of Bible translation, and specifically Bible translation in Africa. His book *A Handbook for African Mother-Tongue Bible Translators* is simply and clearly written. Its main focus is Bible translation in African languages. Isaac is not an ivory tower writer contributing to an area where he lacks practical hands-on experience and know-how. On the contrary, Isaac is himself a Bible translator in one of the Ghanaian mother tongues (the Bono dialect of the Akan language). He is widely read and well-trained in translation theory and practice. He has participated over time in the well-planned and well-equipped, international United Bible Societies Translation workshops and seminars manned by first-class translation scholars and facilitators. Isaac has not only benefitted from these seminars and workshops; he brings on board his experience as a translator.

It has been my honor and privilege to know Isaac, and I do not hesitate to commend this well-written book to a wider audience and readership.

Aloo Osotsi Mojola, PhD

Professor, Philosophy and Translation Studies,
St. Paul's University, Limuru, Kenya
Honorary Professor, Faculty of Theology and Religion,
University of Pretoria, Pretoria, South Africa
Retired Translation Consultant and former Africa Translation
Coordinator, United Bible Societies

Preface

The Christian Church exists to fulfill the Great Commission of making disciples of all nations (cf. Matt. 28:19-20 and its parallels). This is a cross-cultural activity involving one's encounter with different cultural and linguistic traditions. Since language is the main vehicle of communication, an effective cross-cultural mission requires the translation of the Bible into the language of the audience. Vernacular Bible translation is, therefore, imperative for a successful missionary enterprise.

I was appointed a Bible translator in October 2017. In addition to other training programs, I had a two-year Translators' Training Program at the St. Paul's University (Limuru, Kenya) comprising the following courses: Biblical Hebrew, Biblical Greek, Translation Theory & Practice, Old Testament & New Testament in their Cultural Settings, Old Testament Interpretation & New Testament Hermeneutics, Linguistics & Translation, and Discourse Analysis of Old Testament & New Testament Texts. I was privileged to study at the feet of seasoned United Bible Societies Global Translation Advisors, including Dr. Misheck Nyirenda (from Zambia), Dr. Samy Tioye (from Burkina Faso), Rev. Dr. Brigitte Rabarijaona (from Madagascar), Dr. Lénart de Regt and Dr. Marijke de Lang (both from the Netherlands) and Prof. Elizabeth Mburu of International Leadership University, Africa International University and Pan-Africa Christian University in Nairobi, Kenya and the Africa Regional Coordinator for Langham Literature. I also had the opportunity to interact with Prof. Aloo Osotsi Mojola (retired Translation Consultant and former Africa Translation Coordinator, United Bible Societies) and Rev. Dr. Kees de Blois (United Bible Societies Translation Consultant and Interregional Consultant for Computer-assisted Translation and Publishing). It was a great privilege to study together with over sixty Anglophone Africa Translators from Ghana, Nigeria, Liberia, Sierra Leone, Zambia, Sudan, Namibia, Uganda, Tanzania, Kenya, Zimbabwe, and others.

As I interacted with my lecturers and fellow African translators, I became convinced that even though there are various publications on Bible translation from which one could make a choice, most existing publications on the subject of Bible translation fail to address practical challenges that confront the African mother-tongue Bible translator. This situation served as the immediate impetus for writing *A Handbook for African Mother-Tongue Bible Translators*, a concise, systematic, logical, and thorough presentation of the essential principles, methods, processes, and intricacies of Bible translation in Africa that seeks to address the social and linguistic challenges facing African Bible translators in their quest to transfer God's message from the biblical languages into various African languages.

This book is an introductory study that examines key theoretical and practical issues to equip readers with the basic skills required to translate the Bible naturally, accurately, faithfully and clearly into their mother tongues. Since proper translation enhances the interpretation and application of Scripture, the book will also improve the hermeneutical ability of the reader. The twenty-chapter book is divided into two parts: the first part deals with theoretical issues related to Bible translation in general (with the African context in focus), whereas the second part focuses on key practical matters in translation. The choice of the issues discussed and the mode of discussion were informed by my experience as a translator and a researcher. Going through the stages of drafting, harmonization, external review and Consultant's checks, I have encountered a lot of challenges which many translators also encounter in their projects. In each case, I paid critical attention to the nature of the challenge and the way it was eventually resolved. I discuss some of these practical issues in part two of this book, with the hope of addressing others in subsequent publications.

The book begins with a general introduction which sets the tone for the discussions in the chapters that follow. Chapter two focuses basically on what characterizes a good Bible translation and what errors one needs to avoid in Bible translation. Chapter three deals with pre-translation activities (such as the formation of the translation team, preparation of a translation brief), the stages involved in the actual translation work and publication of the text. The fourth chapter introduces the reader to the Bible by examining such issues as the attributes, canonization and inspiration of the Bible and how a proper understanding of the nature of the Bible should inform Bible translation activities. The next two chapters deal with the history of Bible translation. Chapter five considers this history globally, starting from the first Bible translation project, which took place in Alexandria (in Egypt), to modern versions of the Bible. It begins with a brief discussion of the emergence and development of the subject of Translation Studies and then continues to consider the major epochs in the development of Bible translation. In chapter six, attention is given to the African story of Bible translation. The first part deals with Bible translation projects that took place in Africa before missionary Christianity was introduced to the continent. The second part accounts for Bible translations into major African mother tongues starting from the missionary period.

The seventh chapter focuses on three major theories of translation, namely: linguistic approaches, equivalence theories and functional theories. There are many other theories of translation; I considered these three theories because of their huge influence on Bible translation in Africa as compared to the other philosophies. Guidelines are given to the reader to know the appropriate approach to use in translating a given text. Chapter eight deals with textual criticism, the process involved in determining as close as possible the original biblical text. The chapter shows the need for textual analysis of biblical manuscripts to arrive at the original text. The focus of the ninth chapter is the place of hermeneutics/exegesis and intertextuality in Bible translation. The chapter contends that "while a good exegete does not automatically make a good translator, a good exegetical skill is an indispensable tool for making a high-quality translation." Among other things, intertextuality helps the translator to (at least partly) determine the meaning of a text based on its use in another literary document. In chapter ten, the book considers the linguistic aspects of Bible translation, while the next chapter highlights strategies that can be employed in making ambiguous texts clearer for the reader without compromising meaning. The issue of explicitation and structural adjustment is the subject of chapter eleven. In some cases, the translator finds no lexical equivalence for a biblical expression. The question of whether to use an approximate local expression or to adopt the foreign term in the translating text becomes crucial in such situations. The twelfth chapter, through a critical discussion on the concepts of foreignization, domestication and cultural adaptation, gives some guiding principles for dealing with such cases.

The next seven chapters deal with selected practical issues in Bible translation, namely the challenges associated with and strategies for translating cultural idioms, proper names (places, peoples), units measures (weights, length, heights), figurative language (metaphor, simile) and others. Illustrations are taken from various parts of Africa to cater for the need of different African societies. The twentieth chapter takes up the challenge of sign language translation, focusing on the need, challenges, and prospects of sign language Bible translation in Africa. The book concludes with a recap of the major points discussed as well as recommendations for the development of translation studies.

I have avoided the use of many technical terms; those which are used have been explained to enhance comprehensibility. Almost every chapter includes an introduction outlining the main issues in the chapter, illustrative texts with translations, chapter summary and review exercises that help the reader revise the work before proceeding to the next chapter. It is hoped that African

Bible translators, translation consultants, biblical exegetes, undergraduate and postgraduate students and everyone who desires to know more about the Bible and its translation will find this work worth reading.

Isaac Boaheng

June, 2021
Sunyani, Ghana

Acknowledgments

Foremost, I thank God for his grace throughout my life. Coming from a less endowed family, I did not imagine I will get this far. All glory to the LORD for picking me from the pit and placing me where I am today. I am indebted to many scholars whose works were consulted in preparing the manuscript.

I owe an enormous debt of gratitude to Prof. Aloo Osotsi Mojola (Retired Translation Consultant and former Africa Translation Coordinator, United Bible Societies) for writing the foreword to the book after a critical study of the manuscript. Prof. Mojola worked as Africa Area Translation Coordinator of the United Bible Societies from 2000 to 2006, during which he oversaw the work of about thirty biblical/linguistic/translation consultants working in over two hundred Bible translation projects in Sub-Saharan Africa. He supervised various translation projects under the care of these consultants, in their various locations in Senegal, Gambia, Mali, Liberia, Sierra Leone, Ivory Coast, Ghana, Nigeria, Burkina Faso, Togo, Benin, Cameroon, Democratic Republic of Congo (former Zaire), Eritrea, Ethiopia, Kenya, Uganda, Tanzania, Seychelles, Mauritius, Madagascar, Mozambique, Malawi, Zambia, Zimbabwe, Namibia, Angola, Botswana, and South Africa. He has participated as a Translation Consultant of the United Bible Societies in the translation of over 61 Bibles and New Testaments in different African languages. He has about eighty publications in the field of Translation Studies, Philosophy, Linguistics and others. Prof. Mojola has recruited, trained and mentored several Translators and Translation consultants; no wonder some people call him "the ancestor" of Bible Translation in Africa. He has participated in Bible Translation conferences, consultations and missions around the globe in all the continents, including most countries in Africa and several countries in Europe, Asia, North America and South America. To have a person of this stature critically study your manuscript and write a foreword to it is a great honor. The positive comments he made about the manuscript served as additional motivation to get the manuscript published. I have learnt a lot through my interactions with him. Prof. Mojola, may God bless you with more years and good health.

Prof. Ernst R. Wendland (also Retired Translation Consultant, United Bible Societies) is acknowledged for writing an endorsement for me. We met this year (2021) at an e-conference organized by the South African Theological Seminary on the Fourth Gospel, and afterward, I approached him to evaluate my manuscript and write an endorsement for me. He readily did so despite his tight schedules. I am very grateful to you, Prof. Wendland. May God continue to keep you healthy and strong. Rev. Dr. Frederick Mawusi Amevenku (Senior Lecturer in New Testament Studies & Director of Graduate Studies, Trinity Theological Seminary Legon-Accra, Ghana), my lecturer, mentor and friend, played a key part in this work, from drafting to publication. He is acknowledged for his contributions toward this and other publications. Rev. Dr. Daniel Nii Aboagye Aryeh of Perez University College (Winneba, Ghana) critically evaluated the book and contributed an endorsement. May God richly bless you! Apostle Montgomery Abraham of the Bible Society of Nigeria and Mrs. Magdalena Shilongo of the Bible Society of Namibia are also appreciated for recommending this book to public readership.

The Very Rev. Prof. John D. K. Ekem is appreciated for his mentoring role and for his contributions toward the development of my ministry and translation work. I am particularly grateful to The Rt. Rev. Daniel Kwasi Tannor, the Bishop of the Sunyani Diocese of the Methodist Church Ghana, for his fatherly counsel and support. Dr. Misheck Nyirenda, Dr. Samy Tioye, Rev. Dr. Brigitte Rabarijaona, Dr. Lénart de Regt, Dr. Marijke de Lang, Prof. Elizabeth Mburu and Rev. Dr. Kees de Blois are appreciated for directly or indirectly shaping the materials presented in this book.

I owe profound gratitude to my parents, Mr. Noah Nti (posthumously) and Mad. Mary Ampomah, for their care, love and support. I pray that my mother will enjoy the fruit of her labor. May God richly bless my siblings, Yaw Boahen, Kofi Boachie, Samuel Boahen, Hayford Ampaabeng-Kyeremeh, Racheal Oforiwaa, Collins Frimpong, Solomon Amo, for their encouragement and support. My in-laws need a special mention at this point for their unfailing love and support. Mr. Adu Ofori and Mad. Mary Twenewaa, may you live longer than you expect. My brothers-in-law, including Isaac Adu-Ofori, George Adu Prempeh, Seth Adu-Ofori and Samuel Adu Gyamfi, have supported me in diverse ways and need to be acknowledged in a special way. Mr. Anthony Asiedu and his family (Berekum) contributed immensely to my ministerial formation and must be appreciated for their benevolence.

I thank my wife and children for their love, support and patience that contributed to the success of this research. My dear wife, Gloria Adu-Agyeiwaa, and lovely children, Christian Adom-Boaheng, Benedict Adu-Boaheng, Julia Ampomah-Boaheng and Kalix Ohene-Boaheng; this is how far your sacrifice, encouragement and prayers have brought this work. I really appreciate your efforts.

I am extremely grateful to my friends and colleagues in the various institutions in which I serve for the impact of their interactions and help in the process of writing this book. To the staff of Vernon Press, I say God richly bless you. Amen!

Introduction

In this book titled *A Handbook for African Mother-Tongue Bible Translators*, Rev. Isaac Boaheng, an enterprising Ghanaian biblical scholar and systematic theologian, has prepared a commendable manual for Bible translators and Bible translation administrators in Africa. Rev. Boaheng brings on board a solid background in theology and Bible translation, acquired from his studies in Ghana, Kenya and South Africa, as well as from his association with the Bible Society of Ghana for the past four years as one of three translators assigned to the Bono Bible Translation Project. This rich exposure has, by divine providence, gifted him with the rare ability to skillfully articulate pertinent issues of contextual theology in the Ghanaian/African setting. The book handles an important subject matter that can be placed under the umbrella of African biblical hermeneutics. It throws light on the key principles required for translating and rooting the Judeo-Christian Scriptures (i.e. the Bible) on African soil. It also highlights procedures for organizing Bible Translation Projects right from their inception through to their completion. Such an approach carries the obvious advantage of facilitating an appreciation of processes involved in the translation of the Bible into various African languages. Apart from ushering us into the rudiments of Bible translation for the hearing and reading audiences, the author admirably devotes a chapter to a discussion of translation principles for the non-hearing community via the art of Sign Language. This is indeed a most welcome development, because Sign Language Translation in Africa— which addresses the needs of an otherwise "forgotten" audience—can be viewed as being in its infant stages. The latter observation powerfully reminds us that Bible translation is an artistic exercise that ought to be carefully balanced with its scientific component of critically engaging texts, using a variety of interpretative approaches, including the conventional historical-critical methodology. It is an undeniable fact that Bible translation work in Africa stands to gain from the disciplines of biblical studies (including a mastery of source texts in Hebrew, Aramaic and Greek), African linguistics, cultural anthropology and translation studies. Boaheng's book demonstrates an awareness of these vital components. There is a sense in which we can make a case for the book as a noble attempt to build on the classic works of Bible translation experts such as Eugene Nida, Kathy Barnwell, Ernst Wendland, Aloo Mojola, Lynell Zogbo and Jean-Claude Loba-Mkole, to mention but just a few.

Rev. Isaac Boaheng belongs to the younger generation of Bible translators whose passion for the provision of life-transforming mother-tongue Scriptures for their communities propel them to make their voices heard in a constructive manner. Our young, enterprising author leaves no stone unturned in ensuring that what he produces meets acceptable standards required by the Forum of Bible Agencies. The book is presented in a user-friendly format and promises to be of great benefit to all categories of Bible translators and Bible translation administrators. It showcases the fundamental hermeneutical principles of understanding, analyzing and re-packaging texts for particular audiences, conscious of the fact that layers of interpretative tradition that have, since ancient times, characterized biblical texts, ought to be transposed into fresh contexts, including those from present-day Africa. Precisely, we need to acknowledge the fundamental fact that texts have always been undergoing a metamorphosis in response to changing circumstances. This point throws into question the myopic approach of handling ancient biblical texts as if they were "fossilized documents" that have fallen, so to speak, from the skies, and simply need to be drilled into the *tabula rasa* minds of receptor audiences.

For one thing, Bible translation and interpretation are done by people of flesh and blood who are presented with fresh opportunities to contextualize and re-semanticize biblical texts in response to the religio-cultural, economic, social and political exigencies of their time. This does not in any way overlook the key issue of divine inspiration. That God has always been speaking to people throughout the ages in languages that they can understand is dynamically demonstrated through the Incarnation whereby according to the Prologue of John's Gospel, the Christologically re-interpreted Logos became flesh and pitched his tent (dwelt) among us: *Kai ho logos sarx egeneto kai eskēnōsen en hēmin* (John 1:14a). The history of Bible translation and interpretation shows consistently that no meaningful communication can take place without this incarnation principle where divinity condescends to reach out to humanity in ways that can be best understood by the latter, our limitations notwithstanding. This calls for deep humility even as we interact with biblical texts. We need to be conscious of the divine-human engagement which involves God's use of frail human interpreters, who are limited by their circumstances, to make his purposes known from generation to generation. The ministry of Bible translation implies, therefore, that translators are expected to engage texts critically with lenses from their own contexts, while at the same time acknowledging that God, who once upon a time, spoke to ancient peoples via their languages and culture (in the case of the Bible, via ancient Hebrew, Aramaic and Greek languages embedded in Ancient Near Eastern, Hebrew, Hellenistic/Graeco-Roman cultures), still has a word for us via our current life-settings. Herein lies the validity of considering Bible translation as a comprehensive spiritual exercise supported by its artistic and scientific dimensions.

Boaheng's book comes at a time when many African communities await translation of the Judeo-Christian Scriptures (the Bible) into their languages. Bible Societies and sister organizations are being called upon to make judicious use of such an opportunity. This unfinished task of Bible translation in Africa requires the recruitment and training of qualified translators and reviewers. I have no doubt at all that these will benefit immensely from the insights offered by this book. It is hoped that the exercises provided in *A Handbook for African Mother-Tongue Bible Translators* book will facilitate effective mother-tongue interactions with the Bible and positively impact receptor communities.

John D K Ekem, Dr. Theol

Translation Consultant, The Bible Society of Ghana

Kwesi Dickson-Gilbert Ansre Distinguished Professor of Biblical Exegesis & Mother Tongue Hermeneutics, Trinity Theological Seminary, Legon, Accra, Ghana

23rd July 2021

Part I:
Theoretical Issues in Bible Translation

Chapter 1

Introductory Matters

One of the main reasons why the Christian church exists is to fulfill the Great Commission of making disciples of all nations (cf. Matt. 28:19-20 and its parallels). In the vision of the global Church before the throne of God, John saw the redeemed from "every nation, tribe, people and language" (Rev. 7:9). The process of making disciples of all nations is a cross-cultural activity involving an encounter with different languages. One's own language—the language which forms part of one's everyday experience— serves as the most efficient medium for understanding and applying Scriptures. Yet, many societies still do not have the Bible in their language. The United Bible Societies' report for 2015 indicates that of the approximately 7,000 languages of the world, only 563 (corresponding to 5.1 billion people) have full Bibles, while a further 2372 have portions of it. This leaves about 3952 languages without Bibles.[1] The need for more translation projects is obvious. Without the translation of the Bible, the word of God cannot be transmitted effectively.

In order to make the word of God accessible to Africans, many translation projects have been or are being undertaken in various parts of the continent to have the Bible in various African indigenous languages. Bible translation began in Egypt in the third century BCE, when Hebrew Scriptures were translated into Greek. Since then, Bible translation projects have been undertaken all over the world to facilitate the proper understanding of and appropriate response to God's word by the receptor community. In Africa (and many other parts of the world), pioneer missionaries from Europe (and later America) worked tirelessly first to reduce major African languages into writing, and then to translate the Bible into these mother tongues. One of the most evident results of this enterprise is the preponderance to theologize in the mother tongue as part of the assimilation of Christianity in Africa. However, like any human endeavor, African Bible translation has brought in its wake numerous challenges, which various translation agencies continue to grapple with in their quest to give the best version possible to their audience. Africa has played an impressive role in the history of Bible translation since

---

[1] United Bible Societies 2015. Global Scripture Access Report. 2015 Annual Progress. Accessed from https://www.unitedbiblesocieties.org/wp-content/uploads/2016/03/GS AR15_A4_ENG_12pages.pdf, (Accessed: 23/03/2020).

the event of the Septuagint, and there is still a lot that Africa can contribute to global Bible translation theory and practice. Africa's efforts to make God's word accessible to every African society and make a substantial contribution to global Bible Translation studies may not be fruitful if key challenges that confront African Bible translators are not adequately addressed. *A Handbook for African Mother-Tongue Bible Translators* has been published to address some of these challenges to enable translators to do their work with the highest degree of naturalness, accuracy and faithfulness.

What is Bible Translation?

Etymologically, "to translate" means "to carry across." In context, "to translate" could mean "to carry across a message" or "a text". Generally speaking, the term translation may refer to three things: an academic field of study, a process, and a product. As a field of study, translation (or translation studies) refers to the academic discipline concerned with "problems raised by production and description of translations."[2] It also deals with the history and theory of translation.

As a process, translation may be defined as the process of transferring information from a source language to a translating language, taking into consideration the specific socio-cultural context of the receptor community.[3] Source Language refers to the language from which a translation is made (the text being translated). Translating Language, on the other hand, refers to the language into which a translation is made. It is also referred to as the receptor language. Translation may be defined differently as conveying "meaning of a text in one language (the 'source text') and the production, in another language, of an equivalent text (the 'target text,' or 'translation'), which ostensibly communicates the same message."[4] Katharine Barnwell defines translation as "re-telling, as exactly as possible, the meaning of the original message in a way that is natural in the language into which the translation is being made."[5] Roman Jakobson distinguished between three types of translation as follows:

---

[2] Sugeng Hariyanto, *Website Translation: with special reference to English – Indonesian language Pair* (Malang: CV Transkomunika Kencana, nd), 19.
[3] Basil Hatim and Jeremy Munday, *Translation: An Advanced Resource Book* (London: Routledge, 2004), 6.
[4] Bill Ashcroft, Gareth Griffiths and Helen Tiffin, *Post-Colonial Studies: The Key Concepts* (New York: Routledge, 2007), 215.
[5] Katharine Barnwell, *Bible Translation: An Introductory Course in Translation Principles* (third edition) (Texas: SIL International, 1999), 8

i. *Intralingual translation or Rewording:* Translation within a language which would involve explaining it in words of the same language.

ii. *Interlingual translation or Translation proper:* Translation from one language into another language.

iii. *Intersemiotic translation or Transmutation:* Translation from one linguistic system to another or the transference of meaning from a verbal to a non-verbal system or from one medium to another.[6]

From Jakobson's distinction, one knows that translation can take place within the same language and that it is referred to as intralingual translation. This involves rewording or paraphrasing, summarizing, expanding or commenting within a language. The intralingual kind of translation is often ignored in translation discourses. Interlinear translation involves the reinterpretation of the message in another linguistic code, that is, an interpretation of verbal signs using another language. An example is the translation of a message in the Swahili language into the Zulu language or the interpretation of a message from the Igbo language into the Luganda language. Intersemiotic translation, or translation between media or sign systems, happens when some ideas expressed verbally are translated into images and/or movement. This is usually used in film, theatre and the visual arts, as well as image design and advertising.

As a form of communication, it involves a sender and a receiver. The sender sends a message that is coded in a certain way, and the receiver decodes it to have the message sent. The communicative aspect of translation means that it involves two languages in which the translator acts as a mediator. As in any other form of communication, translation does not guarantee that the receiver decodes the sender's message in the way the sender intended. In every aspect of translation, the translator acts as an agent of change and transformation.[7] The translator is one who has "an active hand in the intercultural process" because "language is always embedded in cultural and ideological structure."[8] About the process involved, Snell-Horby writes, "The

---

[6] Roman Jakobson, "On Linguistic Aspects of Translation" In *Language in literature*. Eds. Krystina Pomorska and Stephen Rudy, pp. 428–435 (Cambridge, MA: Belknap Press, 1987), 429.

[7] Maria Tymoczko, *Enlarging Translation, Empowering Translators* (Manchester: St Jerome, 2007).

[8] Jacobus Marais, "The Language Practitioner as Agent: The Implications of Recent Trends in Research for Language Practice in Africa," JNGS 6/3 (2008): 35-47, 35.

translator starts from a present frame (the text and its linguistic components); this was produced by an author who drew from his own repertoire of partly prototypical scenes. Based on the frame of the text, the translator-reader builds up his own scenes depending on his own level of experience and his internalized knowledge of the material concerned."[9] In the process, the translator influences and is influenced by the environment because "a translation cannot travel to new surroundings without adapting to its new environment, on the one hand, and, on the other hand, a translation will influence its new surroundings."[10]

Therefore, translation is an operation performed on languages or the act of replacing a text in one language with a text in another language. In other words, translation is "the replacement of textual material in one language by equivalent textual material in another language."[11] In this sense, translation is solely a process of transcoding. As a transcoding process, translation presupposes a "one-to-one correspondence between form, code and message of the ST [source text] and that of TT [translating text]."[12] Therefore, the core of translation is transforming a message, meaning or idea from a source language to a target one. As a form of communication, translation involves three factors: the source, the message (in terms both of form and content), and the receptor (or receptors). The process of translation can be represented as shown below.

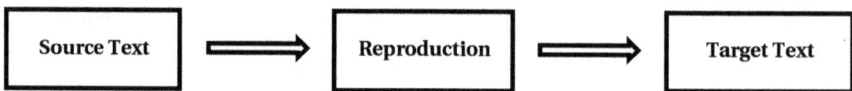

Fig. 1.1 The process of translation.

As a product, translation is the outcome of transferring information from one language to another. It is a written or verbal expression of the meaning of a text in another language. It is tangible, usually in the form of a book or other printed material, visual and/or audio material that comes out of the process of translation.

---

[9] Mary Snell-Horby *Translation Studies: An integrated approach* (Amsterdam-Philadelphia: John Benjamin Publishing Company, 1988), 81.

[10] Cynthia L. Miller-Naudé And Jacobus A. Naudé, "The Translator as an Agent of Change and Transformation: The Case of Translating Biblical Proverbs," *OTE* 23/2 (2010): 306-321, 306.

[11] Clifford as cited in Hariyanto, *Website Translation*, 20.

[12] Hariyanto, *Website Translation*, 20.

Based on the ongoing discussions, Bible translation may be considered as the rewriting of a biblical text from the source language (which includes Hebrew, Greek and Aramaic) to another language, re-packaging the original message for the receptor community. In this regard, Bible translation is the vehicle for communicating the message of the Bible from the original text to a target audience. The goal of the Bible translator is to produce "a version that is an accurate rendering of the text written in such a way that the Bible retains its *literary beauty, theological grandeur*, and, most importantly, its *spiritual message*."[13] In other words, Bible translation must allow the receptor language reader to understand God's word as nearly as possible in the same sense as those who received it in the source language. Such a task requires the translator to mediate between two cultures, namely the biblical culture and the receptor culture. The mediation involves "re-packaging the thought embedded in an 'original revelation/message' for speakers of other languages, taking cognizance of relevant theological, linguistic and cultural factors"[14] purposely to suit the targeted audiences and readers according to their generation needs and interests. To sum up, Bible translation is the process of rendering a biblical text from the source language to any other language, taking into consideration the religio-cultural and linguistic contexts of the people for whom the translation is done.

Ideally, a translation establishes equivalence between the biblical text and the target text. Four types of equivalence are known in Bible translation, namely, linguistic equivalence (similarity between words of the source language and translating language); paradigmatic equivalence (similarity between grammatical components); stylistic equivalence (similarity in the meaning or impact of the expressed text/message) and textual (syntagmatic) equivalence (similarity in the structure and form of the texts). However, differences between languages and historical backgrounds of the source and receptor worlds (among other factors) make it impossible to achieve equivalence in most cases. In spite of this challenge, the translator is expected to "reproduce in the receptor language the *closest natural equivalent* of the message in the source language," first of all equivalence in meaning and secondly in literary form.[15] Some situations may require that the translator

---

[13] G. G Scorgie as paraphrased in Andreas J. Köstenberger and Leonard Scott Kellum, *The Cradle, the Cross, and the Crown: An Introduction to the New Testament* (Nashville: B&H Publishing, 2009), 36. Italics original

[14] John D. K. Ekem, "Interpreting the Lord's Prayer in the Context of Ghanaian Mother-Tongue Hermeneutics," *Journal of African Christian Thought* 10 (2007): 48–52, 48.

[15] Nida, *Bible Translating*, 289-90, original italics.

changes the literary genre, but the meaning of the receptor text must always be the same as that of the source text. Thus, in translation, one is permitted to alter the literary form, provided the meaning of the text remains the same.

Why the Need for African Mother-Tongue Scriptures?

According to John D. K. Ekem, "The varied mother tongues of Africa have a lot to offer by way of biblical interpretation in Ghanaian/African languages as viable material for interpretation, study Bibles and commentaries."[16] Similarly, Kwame Bediako states that "God speaks into the African context in African idioms, and that it is through hearing in African mother tongues 'the great things God has done' (Acts 2:11), that African theology emerges to edify not only the African church but the church worldwide."[17] There are good reasons why the Bible needs to be translated into various languages. A few of these reasons are outlined below.

The most important reason why the Bible has to be translated into other languages is that it is the word of God intended for the salvation of all people; as such, it must be heard by all in a language they best understand. Bediako therefore rightly opines that "the ability to hear in one's own language and to express in one's own language one's response to the message which one receives, must lie at the heart of all authentic religious encounters with divine realm."[18] It is through the translation of the Bible that people whose native languages are different from the biblical languages can have access to the word of God in a way they can best understand and apply.

Aside from this, Bible translation leads to the development of vernacular languages. The translation process includes the development of linguistic materials such as vernacular alphabets, grammars, dictionaries and vocabularies of the language that serve as the foundation for language development. The literature that is published (for example, literacy primers) as a result of language development helps preserve the language, identity, philosophy and worldview of the receptor community.

More so, the translation of the Bible into vernacular languages catalyzes church-planting activities. Language development and Bible translation

---

[16] Ekem, *"Interpreting the Lord's Prayer in the Context of Ghanaian Mother-Tongue Hermeneutics,"* 47.

[17] Kwame Bediako, *Jesus in Africa: The Gospel in African History and Experience* (Akropong: Regnum Africa, 2000), vii.

[18] Bediako as cited in Moses O. Biney, *From Africa to America: Religion and Adaptation among Ghanaian Immigrants in New York* (New York: New York University Press, 2011), 91.

greatly facilitate the planting and expansion of the Christian faith as it offers people the opportunity to use mother-tongue Scriptures to construct oral theologies. Mother-tongue Scriptures give people the chance to express their faith in their everyday lives. In Africa, some people sleep with their Bible under their pillow; others place it in their car; still others write (in their vernaculars) expressions such as "The Lord is my Shepherd", "God is good," or "The Lord is my light and my salvation" on their vehicles, kiosks or doorposts. In times of difficulties, many Africans turn to the Bible for guidance. All these are indications that the indigenous Bibles are firming the faith planted.

Again, Bible translation into vernacular languages contributes to mass evangelization. Many people read the Bible to know how God speaks their own language, and in the end, get converted. As more people access the Bible, God's Word reaches more people, and the church grows and spreads to many places. Such mass evangelism, like any other kind of evangelism, must be followed by carefully planned discipleship lessons to help build the faith of converts.

Further still, Bible translation into African vernacular languages leads to religious emancipation. When people read the Bible in their mother tongue, they discover some discrepancies that existed between what God actually says in the Bible and what the others preach to them. In Africa, mother-tongue Bibles (especially those produced in the missionary era) empowered people to critique missionary teachings on several points and to contend for the validity of their traditional institutions. This became a platform upon which Africans later demanded independence from the religious imperialism of Western extra-biblical ideas.

Another fruit of mother-tongue Scriptures is popular biblical interpretation. In a community where vernacular Bibles do not exist, the prerogative of interpreting the Bible belongs to the clergy and few others who can read the Scriptures in other languages. However, once the vernacular Bible is available to the laity through mother-tongue Bible translation projects, the laity do not only read it but, more so, interpret it in their own way irrespective of what church leaders teach. The participation of the laity in church activities helps the church grow both spiritually and numerically.

Conclusion

I have explained the concept of Bible translation and justified the need for mother-tongue Bible translation projects. In fact, translation is arguably the life wire of the Church. This is the reason why all efforts must be made to ensure that every community gets its own version of the Bible. Where do we start in the process of getting the Bible is one's language? Who and who are to be involved in the process? What quality control measures are to be put in place to ensure that God's word is delivered accurately to every community? What challenges usually confront (African) mother-tongue Bible translators, and how are these challenges to be addressed? In the chapters that follow, I will attempt to answer these and other questions related to Bible translation with particular reference to the African context.

Review Exercise

1. In your own words, explain what is meant by Bible translation.

2. To what extent do you agree to the assertion that "translation is the life wire of the Church"?

3. Convince a funding agency about the need to support Bible translation projects in your country.

4. In what two ways can mother-tongue Bibles be used to promote literacy projects in your society?

5. To what extent do you consider the translator as a mediator between two linguistic traditions?

Chapter 2

Quality Control in Bible Translation

In this chapter, I take the reader through the key features of a good translation and also outline some common errors in translation which must be avoided at all costs. The discussions in this chapter will help equip (African) mother-tongue Bible translators with the necessary skills required to produce a faithful and accurate translation of God's sacred word. To this end, I will engage two key questions: what characterizes a good translation? What common translation errors are to be noted and avoided?

Features of a Good Translation

As mentioned earlier, translation is the vehicle for exchanging ideas and cultures between two languages. The translator negotiates between two cultures by forming texts with culture-specific items and linguistic elements like idioms, proverbs, metaphors and collocations. The process requires the translator to be conversant with the cultural, grammatical and linguistic features in the source text in order to produce a text that is natural to its readers. A good Bible translation is one that gives the readers the actual message of the source text— no more, no less. Such a translation is characterized by at least three basic features, namely, accuracy, clarity and naturalness.[1] To these three qualities, Anderson adds a fourth, namely, "the criterion of perceived authenticity."[2] The translator's task is to try as much as possible to reconcile all these qualities (accuracy, clarity, naturalness and authenticity). However, if it is not possible to maintain all of them, priority should be given to accuracy. I proceed to discuss each of these features briefly below.

Accuracy

A translation is accurate if it reflects the meaning of the original text as closely as possible. An accurate translation takes contemporary readers of the Bible back to the world of the Bible so that they can hear the biblical message just as the original audience heard it. To be accurate, the translator has to study the

---

[1] Barnwell, *Bible Translation*, 23.

[2] T. David Anderson, "Perceived Authenticity: The Fourth Criterion of Good Translation," *Notes on Translation* 12(3) (1998): 1-3.

meaning of lexicon, cultural elements, communication contexts and grammatical form of the source language and then reconstruct the same meaning of these elements in the receptor language.[3] A good translation maintains as much as possible the genre of the source text. For example, a translation of a New Testament epistle should resemble a first-century Greco-Roman letter. However, if it is not possible to achieve accuracy in both meaning and genre, the translator must maintain the meaning and change the genre in the receptor language. A translation is inaccurate if part of the original meaning is lost (missing meaning), if something is added to the original meaning (added meaning) or if the original meaning is changed (changed meaning). The translator must try as much as possible to avoid any of these shortfalls. Larson suggests a test for the accuracy of a translation by following these steps:[4]

    i.   compare the translation result with the source text at several points in the total project during the translation process,

    ii.   after the comparison is complete, do one more careful comparison,

    iii.   when checking for equivalence of information context, make sure that the information is included–nothing omitted, nothing added, and nothing different,

    iv.   after checking to be sure that all of the information is there, make another comparison of the source language and target language text.

Larson further argues that maintaining the dynamics of the original source text means that the translating text must evoke the same reaction as the source text attempted to evoke.[5]

Clarity

In any given language, there may be more than one way of expressing a particular idea. The translator's aim is to translate the meaning in the clearest way possible. By clarity, we mean the translation must be coherent and understandable. Clarity is achieved by avoiding the use of obscure and awkward expressions. Obscurity in translation makes the text foreign to the

---

[3] Larson, *Meaning-Based Translation.*
[4] Larson, *Meaning-Based Translation*, 3.
[5] Larson, *Meaning-Based Translation*, 6.

reader and also moves the reader away from the author's intended meaning of the text. One way to achieve clarity is to make what is implicit in the source text explicit in the translating text. For example, the opening phrase of Luke 1:26, "In the sixth month . . ." can be misunderstood if it is translated as it is. The question that arises is: Is this the sixth month of the year or the sixth month of Elizabeth's pregnancy? Though the answer is clear when the text is read in its immediate context, a reader could easily be confused and miss the point. The verse may be clarified by translating it as, "In the sixth month of Elizabeth's pregnancy" (as in Today's NIV, NLT, and GNT). By adding the expression "of Elizabeth's pregnancy," the implied information is made explicit so that the reader can easily understand the text.[6]

The translator must endeavor to make his/her translation comprehensible by discovering and eliminating expressions that can easily be misunderstood and those so difficult and "heavy" (whether in vocabulary or grammar) and hence have the potential of discouraging readers. A translation that is misunderstood by a high percentage of readers is not a legitimate one. The translator must endeavor to make the receptor text as clear as possible to enhance comprehension.

Naturalness

A translation may be clear and accurate and yet not natural. Naturalness implies accessibility. A natural translation uses expressions that reflect everyday usage in the receptor language and hence sounds like not a translated work. Naturalness simply means the natural usage of grammar and lexis in a way that readers of the translating text do not realize that it is a translated version. The translator must use the common grammar and language structure, common lexis that sound natural to his/her audience. Naturalness is what is missing when readers of a translation say, "we understand the translation but this is not how we say it." The lack of naturalness in a translation can have a negative impact on the entire translation project and even lead to the rejection of the translated text by the receptor community on account of difficulties they may encounter in reading and comprehending it. An unnatural text, if not rejected, may be misread and consequently misinterpreted and inappropriately applied.

Few illustrations of the above points are appropriate at this point. The literal translation of the Greek text of Acts 22:11 is "but the word was heard into the ears of the church, the one being in Jerusalem . . ." The text is translated

---

[6] I shall return to explicitation later in the book.

various as: "The report of this came to the ears of the church in Jerusalem" (ESV); "News of this reached the ears of the church at Jerusalem" (Today's NIV). Though one would understand what the text means, the Greek idiom "the ears of the church" does not sound naturally in English. That is not to say the expression is not natural in Greek. Rather, a natural Greek expression has been rendered in a manner that is not natural in English. A natural translation of this idiom is achieved in the NTL's translation, "When the church at Jerusalem heard what had happened."

Translators must always ensure that their translation is natural. It is, however, sometimes difficult to maintain both accuracy and naturalness due to factors like "the communicative concepts, cultural concepts, figures of speech, fixed expressions, expressive values, writer's style, and the language system."[7] Nida outlines three key areas that contribute to the naturalness of the translated text: the receptor language and culture as a whole, the context of the particular message, and the receptor language audience. For any rendering to be stylistically acceptable, it must conform to the receptor language and culture as a whole. Frere explains the quality of naturalness, stating, "the language of translation ought, we think, ... be a pure, impalpable and invisible element, the medium of thought and feeling and nothing more; it ought never to attract attention to itself... All importations from foreign languages...are...to be avoided."[8]

Translators usually make adjustments in grammar and lexicon to make their text natural. Grammatical adjustments (such as changes in word order, use of verbs to replace nouns, and substitution of nouns for pronouns) are made to make translating texts conform to the structure of the receptor language. Lexical adjustments require considerations at three levels.[9] The first level involves terms which have parallels in the receptor language. Examples are river, sky, stone, clay and others. This level does not usually pose problems in translation. The second level comprises terms which refer to culturally different objects with similar usage. For instance, in many African societies, the term "book" (Akan of Ghana: *nwoma*) refers to an object with pages put together into a unit, but in biblical terms, it is a long parchment or papyrus

---

[7] Adham Mousa Obeidat, Ghada Rajeh Ayyad and Tengku Sepora Tengku Mahadi, "The Tension Between Naturalness and Accuracy In Translating Lexical Collocations In Literary Text," *Journal of Social Science and Humanities* 17(8), (2020):123-134, 124.

[8] Frere as cited by Eugene A. Nida, "Principles of Correspondence," *The Translation Studies Reader*, Edited by Lawrence Venuti (London and New York: Routledge, 2004), 136.

[9] Nida, "Principles of Correspondence", 136-137.

rolled up in the form of a scroll. Terms in this category can create confusion in the translating text. The translator deals with such terms by either using another term that maintains the form of the referent, though not the function, or that has the same function though not the same formal identity. Thirdly, there are terms that identify cultural specialties, including synagogue, denarius, shekel, cherubim, and jubilee. It is difficult to avoid the "foreign associations" when translating terms in this category. Translators are to find the best possible way to deal with such terms.

Differences in source and receptor cultures may also affect naturalness. Cultural differences usually make certain basic themes and accounts impossible to be "naturalized" by the process of translation. For example, in many West-African societies where the path to be walked on or ridden over by a king is expected to be thoroughly tidy, the behavior of Jesus' disciples in spreading leaves and branches in his way as he rode into Jerusalem (Matt. 21:8) is unacceptable. Many West Africans will consider spreading the leaves on Jesus' way as tantamount to insulting him. The translator may therefore have to insert a footnote to put such behavior or practice in its right cultural perspective.

In addition, the issue of naturalness is a problem of co-suitability on at least four key levels—word classes, grammatical categories, semantic classes and cultural contexts.[10] There are situations where the receptor language lacks the word class of a particular word in the source language. An example could be the lack of the noun form of the word "love" in one's language. In this case, one must often say, "God loves" instead of "God is love". On grammatical categories, one could cite the example of languages in which predicate nominatives must always agree in number with the subject such that the expression "the two shall be one" has to be "the two persons shall act just as though they are one person."[11] With regards to semantic classes, offensive words in "a language may be based upon the perverted use of divine names, but in another language may be primarily excremental and anatomical."[12] On discourse types languages may differ as to whether one has to use, for example, a direct quotation or an indirect one. Cultural contexts also affect naturalness; for example, in many cultures, the New Testament practice of reclining at tables (Matt. 9:10) is strange, if not unacceptable. Differences in culture must be catered for as the translator tries to make the translated text as natural as possible.

---

[10] Eugene Albert Nida, *Toward a Science of Translating: With Special Reference to Principles and Procedures involved in Bible Translating* (Leiden: Brill, 1964), 168.

[11] Nida, *Toward a Science of Translating*, 168.

[12] Nida, *Toward a Science of Translating*, 168.

The use of anachronisms may also violate the rule of co-suitability of message and context and hence affect naturalness. For example, replacing the expression "heaven and earth" (Gen. 1:1) with "universe", though technically correct does not adequately deal with naturalness within the context of the text.[13] Nida identifies two sources of anachronism as the use of "contemporary words which falsify life at historically different periods, e.g., translating 'demon possessed' as 'mentally distressed,'" and the use of "old-fashioned language in the receptor language and hence giving an impression of unreality."[14] Naturalness is one of the key factors that makes translations acceptable by the receptor community. The concept of acceptability is discussed briefly below.

Authenticity or Acceptability

The three qualities (accuracy, clarity and naturalness) outlined above are well-known in the field of Bible translation. These qualities employ translation principles, linguistics, theology, and communication theory in the exegesis of the source text and the production and testing of the translated text. The fourth criterion (namely, "the criterion of perceived authenticity") shifts attention to the audience's assessment of the translated text. The first three qualities are objective ways of judging a translation; the fourth measures the subjective quality of a translation in terms of the audience's perception of it. Anderson, relating this criterion to the other three, defines "perceived authenticity" as "the receptor audience's perception that the text is an authentic and trustworthy version of the original message."[15] The fourth criterion is built on the premise that many issues and debates about translation (including controversies about literal translation versus dynamic equivalence) are really issues about authenticity expressed in terms of accuracy. In Anderson's view, whether a receptor community will accept or reject a translating text depends on the community's perceived authenticity of the text. Thus, the receptor community has a significant role to play in judging a text as an accurate and meaningful expression of the source text in their own language.

Anderson must be commended for his bold step in adding a fourth dimension to a quality translation. The word "authentic" primarily means "genuine, of undisputed origin or authorship" and secondarily "trustworthy, reliable." Anderson's failure to distinguish between these two senses of "authenticity" seems problematic. One can infer from Anderson's analogy of a letter to the

---

[13] Nida, *Toward a Science of Translating,* 169.
[14] Nida, *Toward a Science of Translating,* 169.
[15] Anderson, "Perceived Authenticity," 1.

bank with his signature that he had the primary sense of "authenticity" in mind. The primary sense of "authenticity" requires the translated text to be original, written by the biblical author. However, the Bible translator cannot be the original biblical author. Therefore, it is impossible to achieve authenticity in the primary sense of the word in a Bible translation project. Certainly, a copy of a written text presents the same text as the original author wrote, though it is written by a different person (who is not the original author). One can therefore talk of the originality of the copied text. However, in Bible translation, the words used and the context in which they are used differ from those of the original text in such a way that it is impossible to apply authenticity to a translated text in the primary sense of the word.

If "authenticity" is taken in the secondary sense, that is "trustworthy", then one may ask: What makes a translation trustworthy? Trustworthiness depends on one's view of translation, tradition, and expectations. The community's trust in the translation team will encourage them to trust the translated text. One may trust the KJV because they believe the KJV renders the source text in the closest possible way in English. The secondary meaning of authenticity is close to acceptability. In the light of this argument, one may refer to Anderson's "criterion of authenticity" as "the criterion of acceptability." Larson's assertion that "acceptability should be a major concern to translators" because the lack of acceptability could lead to the rejection of a translation project is a statement about the relevance of acceptability.[16] I prefer "acceptability" to "authenticity" because it seems clearer than "authenticity." Whatever one's position, what is important is that the quality of a good translation also depends on the perception of the receptor community about it. For a translation to be good, it must be perceived to be of good quality by the receptor community.

To facilitate acceptability, the translation team and the receptor community (represented primarily by reviewers and opinion leaders) must have frequent interactions. The Bono Bible translation team (of which I am a member), for example, usually visits various traditional councils and communities to update them on the project and to seek their opinions on key issues related to it. Literacy programs, seminars, community durbars and other activities are also organized to enhance this interaction. In the process, it sometimes becomes necessary to adjust the translation to meet the expectations of the recipient readership. As part of these interactions, the team gets the opportunity to test their translated text within the receptor community and receive feedback from the people. It is, therefore, important that translators organize Scripture-use activities within the receptor community right from

---

[16] Larson, *Meaning-Based Translation*, 44.

the beginning to the end of the project. The time allocated to each activity depends on the size of the receptor community, the mission history in the community, the strength of the church in the community as well as the presence and activities of other Christian-based organizations in the community. Most of the African societies in which Bible translation projects are carried out have some church presence already, and hence most of the people are familiar with a Bible translation in a colonial language (English, French, Portuguese, Arabic, and others) or an indigenous language (Swahili, Igbo, Ga, Xhosa, Ewe, and others). The receptor community would often want their Bible to be similar to the one they are used to. For example, if the Bible they are used to was translated in a predominantly literal manner, the receptor community for the new project would expect the same from the translating team, even if there are good reasons to avoid a literal translation. To produce a meaning-based Bible for a community which is used to literal translation requires thorough education as to why the community must accept this "new" type of translation. Without adequate education, there is a very high tendency that the receptor community will reject the Bible after the project is completed. Among other things, there is the need to explain that the meaning-based translation will make reading and listening more enjoyable, will enhance understanding and offer a more accurate message from the original text. By explaining the benefits of the meaning-based translation to the receptor community, one helps change their perception and expectation, thus changing their initial rejection into acceptance of that same translation.

The first three qualities may be considered as the legs of a three-leg stool, with the fourth as the seat. Authenticity rests on accuracy, naturalness and clarity. To sum up, a translation must make sense, carry the spirit and manner of the original text, have a natural and easy form of expression, and produce the same response as that which the original text produced in the original audience.

Common Translation Errors

Quality control is important in any project, more so, Bible translation. In the process of translation, some errors may occur to undermine the quality of the translating text. An error in translation (translation error) refers to "any lack of congruence between the source text and the target text which includes dis-congruities in meaning and failures in the use of the target language according to standard norms, as interpreted by the evaluator."[17] These are

---

[17] Telejumba Kennedy Salano, *An Analysis of Semantic and Lexical Errors of Translating the New Testament from English into Kiswahili: A Case Study of biblia Ya Mafunzo Ya Uzima* (Masters of Arts Thesis: University of Nairobi, 2018), 43.

anomalies that occur in translation when a source text is mistranslated or mismatched in the process of rendering it into another language. They may result from non-equivalence between the source and target languages. Christine Nord, from a functionalist's perspective, defines translation error as anything that prevents a translating text from achieving the purpose for which it is produced.[18] For Nord, translations should not be judged so much by intrinsic criteria such as correctness but by their ability to meet the expectations and needs of the target audience.

The categorization of translation errors has been approached differently by different scholars. For example, Waddington categorizes translation errors into three:

i) Inappropriate renditions, which affect the understanding of the source text; these are divided into five categories; addition, omission, unresolved extra-linguistic references, loss of meaning, inappropriate linguistic variation (register, style dialect, etc.).

ii) Inappropriate renderings, which affect expression in the target language; these are divided into five categories; spelling, grammar, lexical items, text, and style.

iii) Inadequate renderings, which affect the transmission of either the main function or secondary function of the source text.[19]

Nord, on the other hand, has four categories of translation errors: pragmatic, cultural, linguistic, and text-specific.[20] Pragmatic errors are those caused by failure to deal adequately with pragmatic challenges like the lack of receiver orientation. For Nord, translation means translating meaning; therefore, anything short of that constitutes a pragmatic error. A translator's failure to carefully consider language use (including such issues as the intention of the sender, the understanding and interpretation of the receiver, the pragmatic situations of the language at that time, among others) can easily lead to pragmatic errors.

---

[18] Christiane Nord, *Translating as a Purposeful Activity: Functionalist Approaches Explained* (Manchester: St. Jerome, 1997), 74.

[19] Salano, *An Analysis of Semantic and Lexical Errors of Translating the New Testament from English into Kiswahili,* 43-44. C. Waddington, "Different Methods of Evaluating Student Translations: The Question of Validity," *Meta: Translators' Journal* 46(2), (2001): 311-325.

[20] Nord, *Translating as a Purposeful Activity,* 75-76.

Cultural errors in translation are due to inadequate decisions in the reproduction or adaptation of culture-specific conventions, which depend on the influence they have on the function of the target text. A translator will commit cultural error if the influences of his/her own native culture make him/her misunderstand the culture in the source language and consequently renders the text wrongly. Aside from cultural misreading, cultural translation errors, cultural default (that is, the absence or lack of relevant cultural background knowledge shared by the author and his/her target reader) may also affect translation. Bible translation is an interlingual and inter-cultural communication; unfortunately, the target audience may lack key cultural information that the original author shared with the original audience. Failure to make implicit key cultural elements explicit in the translating text for the benefit of the target readership would result in cultural errors.

Linguistic errors result from the translator's failure to use target language structures in transferring the meaning and sense of the source text. They may arise at the word level (for example, using the wrong word), phrase level or sentence level. For example, the Hebrew text of Genesis 1:1 reads literally "In the beginning created God the heavens and the earth." The sentence structure does not agree with that of the English language, and so the sentence has to be rearranged in English as "In the beginning, God created the heavens and the earth." Similar adjustments are required in most African languages, which do not have the same sentence structure as the Hebrew language. Failure to make such required adjustments will lead to linguistic errors.

Text-specific errors are those that undermine the suitability of the translation for the target readers. A text to be translated may be descriptive, narrative, argumentative or expositive, based on the content and how a writer uses it. In addition, each text has its own style, diction and a particular way of expressing it. A translator commits text-specific errors if these issues are overlooked.

Conclusion

The discussions in this chapter have highlighted certain foundational truths about Bible translation which need a recap. First of all, the term translation may refer to an academic field of study, a process and a product. Secondly, the need for the Bible to be translated into all languages was established; the most important reason for this is that the Bible is God's word for all people and hence needs to be translated into other languages, else it will remain God's message to only those who have knowledge of biblical languages. Again, the four main features of a good translation, namely, accuracy, clarity, naturalness and acceptability have been outlined. The last part also dealt with common errors in translation. I now proceed to consider the translation process in the next.

Review Exercise

1. In your own words, explain the following terms as applied to Bible translation.
    a) Accuracy b) Clarity
    c) Naturalness d) Acceptability

2. What strategies may be used to achieve faithfulness and accuracy in Bible translation?

3. To what extent do you agree with the assertion that "The Bible must remain in the original languages because translating it into other languages tends to introduce errors into God's word?"

4. With two relevant examples, explain how over-literalness in Bible translation may affect naturalness.

Chapter 3

An Overview of the Translation Process

The Bibles most people use are the product of a series of processes that happened behind the scenes. Most readers are completely ignorant about the events and processes that yielded their Bibles. This chapter is a journey through the various stages and processes involved in the pre-translation planning, drafting, checking and publication of the Bible in languages other than the biblical languages.

Socio-linguistic Survey

The translation process begins with the identification of the need for the Bible to be translated into a particular language. The translating agency responsible for the project then conducts a socio-linguistic survey to know the social-cultural context within which the project will take place. This survey brings out more about the culture of the receptor community for sponsoring agencies and other parties who have an interest in the project. The survey also reveals the specific target audience for the translation and the kind of translation (for example, literal translation or free translation) necessary for the community. The population that speaks the language in question, the existence of sub-dialectical differences and other issues are also considered in the survey. Thus, the outcome of the survey is a major player in decisions regarding the project.

Composition of the Translation Team

Bible translation is teamwork; it is not a one-man show. Therefore, it requires people who can work with others. The translation team comprises a number of individuals who work together to undertake a translation project. Each member of the terms has special qualifications and skills for a particular task. The diverse gifts and graces are used to achieve the common goal of producing a faithful, natural, accurate and acceptable translation. In almost all cases, a translation team comprises a Translation Consultant, a Computer-Assisted Publishing (CAP) officer, an exegetical advisor, a team of translators, and a review team. I discuss each party briefly below.

Translation Consultant

The translation department is headed by a Translation Consultant (TC)/Translation Officer (TO) who exercises general oversight of the various operations involved in a project. The Consultant is well-versed in the biblical languages as well as the theory and principles of translation. The consultant must have "advanced knowledge of linguistics, of the principles of translation, of biblical languages, and of other biblical studies."[1] According to the United Bible Societies' standard, a TC must be a PhD holder and should have been given further training to equip him/her for the job. The Jerusalem Centre for Bible Translators (JCBT) is one of the global institutions that train Mother-Tongue Bible translators and translation consultants for Bible translation agencies such as Biblica, Bible League, Institute for Bible Translation (IBT), Nigeria Bible Translation Trust (NBTT), Summer Institute of Linguistics (SIL), The Seed Company (TSCO), United Bible Societies (UBS), Word for the World and Wycliffe, as well as sign language agencies like Deaf Missions and Deaf Opportunity OutReach (DOOR).

The responsibilities of the Consultant include organizing training workshops for translators, discussing translations problems with translators and suggesting solutions to them, checking the quality of translations, and helping translators to ensure their manuscript is up to the publisher's standard.[2] The Consultant checks for accuracy in exegesis and accuracy in transferring the source text into the target language. Moreover, the Consultant ensures that Bible translation principles and standards are duly followed. In this light, the Consultant draws attention to any errors or inconsistencies in the translating text to ensure that they are corrected. In all these, the Consultant is expected to build consensus with the team of translators rather than imposing his decisions on them.

Computer Assisted Publishing (CAP) Officer

The translation team also has a Computer Assisted Publishing (CAP) Officer/Manager who checks manuscripts and prepares them for typesetting and publishing. The CAP officer also plans the workflow and budgets for the translation department. The CAP officer must be well-versed in ParaText (a software designed for Bible translation projects) and also have good computer, linguistic, manuscript proofreading and editing skills. The CAP officer is given regular training and refresher courses by the UBS and other agencies.

---

[1] Barnwell, *Bible Translation*, 223.
[2] Barnwell, *Bible Translation*, 223.

Exegetical Advisor

Bible translation requires exegetical analysis. Before a text can be rendered appropriately, some degree of exegesis must be done. Translators are therefore expected to have some exegetical skills. However, the exegetical analysis done by the translators can be supplemented by a professional biblical exegete who is appointed as an exegetical consultant/advisor for the project. The exegete may be someone appointed within the translation team or an outsider.

Among other things, the exegete participates in preparing the text, revising, preliminary exegetical checking, and TC checking sessions. The required expertise includes advanced skills in biblical exegesis, in-depth knowledge of the source text and languages, a good understanding of language and culture acquisition, sociolinguistics, syntax, semantics, discourse, translation principles and cultural anthropology, among others. The exegete must ensure that the source text meanings are clearly understood throughout the translation process. According to SIL policy, exegetical advisors are to undertake these courses (or their equivalents): Cultural Anthropology, Language and Culture Learning, Language and Society, Introduction to Language Development, Morphology and Syntax, Semantics and Pragmatics, Translation Principles, Theory and Practice, Biblical Backgrounds and Discourse Analysis.[3] It is important for each project to have an exegete; however, financial constraints and/or non-availability of qualified exegetes make it impossible to have an exegete for every project.

Team of Translators

The team of translators comprises people responsible for drafting and revising receptor texts. A team of translators (usually not less than three) is formed from the native speakers of the receptor language. One has to be an active believer and a member of a church to qualify as a Bible translator. The translator also needs to have a correct understanding of the source text. This requires knowledge of biblical languages, strong Bible knowledge and exegetical skills. Bible translation also requires a correct understanding of the target language and culture. The translator needs to have translation skills (including intuitive and analytical knowledge of translation principles) to be able to transfer a text from one language to another. He/she also needs administrative and technical skills to process materials in an orderly way from the first draft to the ultimate publication of the Scriptures. This requires team

---

[3] Retrieved from https://www.sil.org/training/translation on 7th April, 2021.

building, training, management, as well as administrative, keyboarding, and computer and financial management skills.

External Review Team

A team of reviewers comprising selected native speakers of the receptor language who can read and write well in the language is formed to help review the draft prepared by the translators. Ideally, each project has about fifteen to twenty external reviewers. They must be people of different denominations (Methodists, Presbyterians, Charismatics, Pentecostals, Catholics, Lutherans, and so on), from different localities within the receptor community, and of different educational backgrounds and levels. This team represents the entire receptor community, so they must help the translators shape their translation to make it accessible and acceptable to the receptor community.

Translation Brief

A translation brief is a set of instructions or specifications indicating (among other things) how a translation project is to be carried out, what must be achieved and the key beneficiaries of the translation. It is a statement of the standards for the project indicating the source texts to be used, the specific audience, intended use(s) of the translation, and so on. Setting these principles out at the beginning will help the translation team work together toward the common goal of their project.

Ideally, the brief must be prepared and approved before the actual translation work starts. The brief is done in consultation with church and community leaders, other agencies and partner organizations involved in the project. It serves as a guide for the project so that by working according to it, the set goals can be achieved. A translation brief usually covers the following areas:

Sociocultural frames

The sociocultural frame of a translation project deals with the audience (for example, the Bono people of Ghana), producers (for instance, Bible Society of Ghana), social goals (usefulness of the project to the Bono community), religious goals (what the church hopes to do with and benefit from the project). The following questions/issues are dealt with under this section:

a)   Who will use this translation?

b)   Who initiated this translation project?

c) Describe the church context of this translation project. Here one must account for the cosmology of the people and how that may inform certain decisions in the translation process. In most African societies, the traditional religious context basically comprises African Traditional Religion.

d) What are the goals and functions of this translation project?

e) What is the relationship between the proposed translation and existing translations?

To use the Bono Bible Translation Project as an example, the following (social and religious) benefits can be noted. The project will elevate the Bono dialect to the level of a developed language to increase its strength among other languages. The project will include the development of literacy materials and classes for both adults and children. Though there are some sharp sub-dialectical differences among various Bono communities, it is hoped that language development, literacy, and translation will lead to the emergence of a "unified" Bono dialect which in the end will serve to strengthen the bond that holds the Bono people together. Religiously, the Bono Bible Translation Project will lead to spiritual transformation as the community interaction with the translated text. All those involved in the project will experience a transformation of attitudes, values, and behaviors in genuine and profound ways. Three aspects of transformation, namely identity, evangelism (conversion), and liberation, are anticipated. The project will result in the merger between the Bono identity and the Christian identity to make people experience the two identities in a hybrid form. The project will also promote evangelism in the Bono community. As people read the Bible in their own language, they will hear God speak to them directly without the need for preachers to mediate the divine-human communication. This will lead to mass conversion, resulting in the expansion of the church. The translation will help legitimize the Bono as a viable and strong ethnic group in Ghana and hence liberate them from negative perceptions about them.

Organizational Frames

The following issues/questions are considered:

a) What are the partner organizations of this translation project? This has to do with the church that initiated the project, the receptor community, and the translation agency or agencies undertaking the project. If the project does not belong to a particular denomination, then all the denominations that have at least one active congregation in the receptor community are actives stakeholders.

b) Describe the role of each partner organization with regard to its contributions and decision-making process.

c) Provide the translators' profiles (full names, church affiliation, and academic qualifications).

The Bono Bible Translation Project is again used as an example. In the translation project, six main traditional areas in the Bono community are considered: Dormaa-Ahenkro, Berekum, Sunyani, Techiman, Wenchi and Nkoranza. The team of translators is unique with respect to denominational diversity, diversity in their working experience and expertise, and educational background. They are Rev. Daniel Asomah Gyabaa, who (before becoming a translator) was the Duayaw Nkwanta district minister for the Presbyterian Church of Ghana, Rev. Isaac Boaheng, who was at that time the minister in charge of the Asikasu Section of the Dormaa-Ahankro Circuit of the Methodist Church Ghana, and Mrs. Afia Aframa, a member of the Seventh Day Adventist Church and a teacher by profession. Rev. Gyabaa hails from Danyame in the Dormaa-Ahenkro traditional area; he schooled in Berekum for two years and worked at Wamfie as a teacher for eight years. He also worked at Nkwabeng in the Nkoranza district as a pastor for four years. Rev. Boaheng comes from Busunya near Nkoranza but was born and raised at Odumasi in the Sunyani-West municipality, whilst Mrs. Aframa is a native of Techiman who schooled in Sunyani and Berekum during her secondary and tertiary education. She worked briefly in Wamfie (in the Dormaa traditional area) and was working in Sunyani when she was appointed as a translator. Rev. Boaheng worked in Berekum as a teacher at Berekum Senior High School for eight years. Reverends Gyabaa and Boaheng are theologians, and Mrs. Aframa is a linguist. These diverse backgrounds are very helpful in the translation project.

Objectives of the Publishers

This part of the brief focuses on the following issues.

a) Translation type (literal, common language, interlinear, etc.)

b) Name of the source-text (Hebrew, Greek, Aramaic)

c) Linguistic and cultural directives (e.g., the policy in place for transliterating proper names, measurements, etc.)

d) Additional materials (introductions, cross-references, glossary, index, etc.)

e) Other related products (e.g., portions and Bible-based literacy material)

f) Media format (e.g., print, audio, video, digital, oral performances, etc.)

g) Implementation plan and communication lines during the life span of the project

h) Means of communication (e.g., emails, Skype, Zoom, Send/Receive)

Stages in Bible Translation

With the above sections as background, I now discuss the various stages involved in the actual translation work, from pre-drafting preparation to publication.

Preparation

Once the translation team is formed, there is the need to prepare the translators for the task ahead. They must receive adequate training in areas such as linguistics, theology (including working knowledge in biblical languages, Hebrew, Greek and Aramaic), hermeneutics, exegesis, theory and practice of Bible translation, Information and Communications Technology, among others. Translators need to have adequate knowledge of the various cultures of Hebrew and Greek settings related to the Bible (for example, the general culture of the Ancient Near East). They also need to develop the skill of sympathy to differing views, especially when working as a team. Enough resources must also be available to them to enhance quality and timely delivery. The preparation phase will also include a thorough analysis of the language and culture of the community for which the translation project is undertaken. A standard orthography[4] for the language in question must be prepared (if one does not exist), or an existing one may be adopted (and revised/modified). After the necessary preparation is done and adequate logistics obtained, the translation work proper begins. The processes involved in UBS translation projects may be summarized as follows:

---

[4] In linguistics, orthography means the various conventions for writing a language, including rules of spelling, hyphenation, capitalization, stress, and punctuation, among others.

Exegesis

The first stage of the actual translation process involves an exegetical study of the text to be translated. By exegesis, I mean the process of discovering the meaning of a text within its original context.[5] Drafting a text requires discovering the meaning of the text (exegesis) and re-expressing the meaning in the receptor language (actual drafting). Therefore, the drafting of the book into the translating language can only begin after adequate background study of the book in question and the source text has been done.[6] Background information about a text may be obtained from any good Bible commentary, Bible dictionaries, theological dictionaries, and Bible encyclopedias, among others.

The following steps are involved in the preparation.[7] (a) Read through the entire section to be translated in the source language (if the translator has working knowledge in the source language) or in a model text (say NRSV, GNB, ASV, or NIV). Because most translators lack adequate knowledge in the biblical languages, most translation projects use, say, an English version as the model text from which translation is done. The problem with this approach is that one's translation becomes a translation of a translation. Inaccuracies in the model text get their way into the new translation. The good news, however, is that the TC checks the translated text against the biblical text in its original language and, in the process, deals adequately with such inadequacies. (b) Determine the meaning of the passage by identifying the controlling theme of the section (what the section is about), noting alternative interpretations through the comparative study of various versions, and noting down places with ambiguous meanings or places which pose translation difficulties. Use the following methods to resolve the difficulty.

i.   If the meaning of the verse is not clear, read it in other Bible versions. It may also be helpful to read other passages of Scripture related to it and use the cross-references as well.

ii.   If the meaning of a word is not clear, look up the word in a Bible/theological dictionary or any appropriate resource.

iii.   Use your Bible dictionary or any other resource to handle issues related to Jewish culture or religion.

---

[5] I shall treat exegesis again later in the study.

[6] According to UBS standards, there are a number of verses to be drafted each day depending on what is referred to as the degree of difficulty of the book.

[7] Adapted with slight modifications from Barnwell, *Bible Translation*, 182.

iv.   Try rewriting the verse in the receptor language using simple words and expressing the meaning in a way that makes it natural, clear and accurate.

v.   Refer to a commentary or Translator's Handbook for notes on the book and passage in question.

vi.   If any challenge still remains after exhausting all these methods, consult your exegete or consultant for clarification.

Drafting

The drafting stage refers to the phase of preparing the first-draft translation. Usually, each translator in the team is assigned a book or a set of books to work on. Asking a translator to draft a complete book is necessary for ensuring uniformity of style. However, where there's a major break in the topic or organization of the text, drafting may be divided between two translators.

After adequate background and exegetical study, the translator then thinks through the translation of the entire passage, writes down the translation and reads through the translation to make the necessary revisions before passing it on to other team members for their review. Before doing the actual translation, it is important to decide what local expressions you will use to translate certain key terms. For example, in drafting Acts 16:16–40, one may have to decide how the following key terms/expressions could be translated into the receptor language: slave-girl, spirit of divination, fortunes telling, Most High God, way of salvation, authorities (v.19), magistrates, prison, jailer, earthquake, chains, sword, foundations, baptize, police, Roman citizens, etc. Prepare the first draft one section at a time together with section headings, footnotes, cross-references and glossary entries (if applicable).

After this, the translator types the draft translation into ParaText Translation and Publishing software. The ParaText Translation and Publishing software comprise software programs developed jointly by the UBS and SIL International, which allows the translator to input, edit, check and publish a translation based on the original biblical texts and modeled on versions in major languages. Different versions of ParaText are available, ParaText 9 being the latest version at the time of writing this book (December 2020).

Check for naturalness; that is, whether the translation is smooth and whether each sentence connects well with the other sentences to form a unit. Check also for clarity, making sure that there is nothing in the translation that could be misunderstood and/or confuse readers. In addition, check for accuracy by comparing every bit of your translation with the source text to find out if nothing has been left out, added or changed. Further still, check for formats such as correct spellings, tone markers, special character marks such as dots under some vowels, proper use of capital letters, correct use of punctuation marks (including commas, full stop, question marks, quotation marks, parentheses), chapter and verse (inserting missing ones). Spelling mistakes, wrong punctuations, wrong use of tone markers, and others can result in misunderstanding and misapplication of text. The effect of the position of a comma on the meaning of a text is evident in Luke 23:43. If the text is translated as "Jesus answered him, 'Truly I tell you, today you will be with me in paradise'" the meaning is different from when it is translated as "Jesus answered him, 'Truly I tell you today, you will be with me in paradise.'" The focus is on whether the comma in Jesus' statement is to be placed before or after the word "before." In the first instance (where the comma is placed before "today"), it means Jesus is promising that his addressee will be with him in paradise on the same that he was speaking to him (the addressee). In the second case (where the comma comes after "today"), it means the word "today" is in reference to the day that Jesus was speaking and not the day that his addressee will be with him in paradise. The second translation gives room for the doctrine of soul sleep, that is, the human soul becomes unconscious after death and before the resurrection. The first translation, however, contradicts the doctrine of soul sleep. From the example given, it is clear that the translator should be careful not to take things for granted at all, else he/she will distort God's message.

In addition, the draft must be checked thoroughly against the original text to eliminate any possible errors, ambiguities, and omissions. The duration for this initial phase is informed by many factors, including the translator's knowledge about source and receptor languages and the level of knowledge in the use of the translation software, among others. However, in general, the drafting is expected to be done faster (with improved quality) as translators receive more training and gain more experience.

Modern translators have access to various training workshops that equip them for their task. They use modern technology to ensure that the text is edited to the highest standard. There are resources such as exegetical notes, maps, background literature, source language texts, illustrations, parallel and cross-references which can be used to enhance the quality of translation. Lynell Zogbo offers useful insight on this:

> Bible translation teams are also now equipped with new technology. Computers enable translators to bypass the numerous hand-written drafts of the past. Through innovative programs such as Paratext (a program designed by UBS and supported by SIL), translators can have instant access on their screens to dozens of Bible versions, including

the source texts, as well as to dictionary definitions and parsing of Hebrew and Greek forms. Manuscript spelling and punctuation checks, which in the past took months of tedious work, are today carried out in far less time, with the assistance of computer programs. Though attempts at machine translation and adaptation have produced uneven results in the first instance, or controversial versions in the second, new technology has given Bible translation teams around the world a new sense of autonomy.[8]

Team Review (Harmonization)

This stage requires the team of translators to review and revise the draft manuscript produced by each translator. The key checks at this stage include naturalness check, exegetical check, proper names check, biblical key terms check, and others. The team sits together to read the first draft, discuss suggestions and adopt those which improve the translation (in terms of spelling, grammar, use of figures and others) to produce a second draft. It is advisable to read each verse aloud at this stage in order to test the text for the reading community. It is also helpful to compare the draft with one or two translations, discuss exegetical choices (together with the exegetical advisor, if the project has one) that have been made in the translation, identify possible exegetical mistakes in the translation and any missing verses or sentences. In the Bono Bible Translation Project, we normally compare our draft with translations in other Akan dialects like Fante, Akuapem and Asante and make any necessary adjustments. The team must check that proper names have been dealt with (translated or transliterated) according to rules set out in the translation brief. It is also important to check and ensure that capitalization has been done correctly and consistently. Also, check the consistency of the Biblical key terms used in the passage with the terms documented in the Biblical terms Tool (in Paratext).

From this point on, an individual translator cannot alter the work; only the full team can negotiate further revision(s). Having checked the translation for exegetical faithfulness, places that are still problematic may be marked out and discussed with the Consultant for settlement. The translation may be tested further at this stage by reading it to people who have not been exposed to it before. This step will help to test for naturalness and build people's confidence in the outcome of the project.

---

[8] Lynell Zogbo, "Bible, Jewish and Christian," *Routledge Encyclopedia of Translation Studies* edited by Mona Baker, pp. 21-27 (London: Routledge, 2003), 24.

External Review

Each translation project has an external team of reviewers selected from different denominations and locations who are "usually educated people, church leaders, and others who have been appointed by the local churches to help in checking the translation."[9] The reviewers are people with keen interest in the translation project and they must be selected from a cross-section of the people (including men and women, well-educated and less educated, Bible scholars and non-Bible scholars) and well versed in the receptor language.[10] These people must receive some training to enable them perform their task well.

The external review stage typically involves extensive testing of the work which has been reviewed by the translators in order to determine whether the translation communicates accurately, clearly and naturally. The team checks spellings, grammar, archaism (outmoded terminologies), dialect use, style and translation approach, making sure the translation brief is reflected in the translation. Copies may be sent to individual reviewers who read through the draft and write down their comments for consideration by the team. Or the reviewers may meet together and do this checking together through a verse-by-verse analysis of the text. The use of a slide projector is useful if reviewers come together and do the review as a group.

Consultant's Check

At this stage, the work is brought before the TC who examines the exegesis, the translation approach, the content and the presentation of supplements. If the Consultant understands the translating language, there will be no need for a back-translation of the translated text. On the contrary, if he/she does not understand the translating language, then a back-translation of the work will be done verbally by one of the translators, or the back-translation of each text will be written down for the Consultant to check. The Consultant goes through the text verse by verse, chapter by chapter and book by book, comparing what has been translated to the source text to ensure accuracy and conformity of the translation to the source text before it can be published. The nature of the task requires high competence in source knowledge and experience in translation work. The Consultant, therefore, uses a lot of resources. Formerly, consultants used to turn up with piles of books, but today

---

[9] Barnwell, *Bible Translation*, 192.
[10] Barnwell, *Bible Translation*, 221

a laptop with enough resources installed on it is enough for the task. In the COVID-19 defined society and beyond, TC checking may be done virtually.

Publication

At every stage of work, the manuscript must be checked for typographical accuracy, consistency and completeness, making sure that all intended revisions have been incorporated. After the necessary revisions prompted at the TC checking are done, the work goes to the CAP officer, who checks the quality of the manuscript and gets it ready for publishing. The process includes checking for consistent use of key biblical terms, consistent translation of parallel passages in the gospels, consistent formatting, and selecting supplementary material such as footnotes, illustrations and maps. The ParaText software is designed to assist in these and other checks. The team of translators must proofread the document after this stage before it is finally sent for publication.

Conclusion

It is clear from this chapter that what readers have in their hands as the Bible is the process of a complex process involving many people of diverse backgrounds. The translator works with God in the divine "laboratory" where the word is analyzed, processed and brought out for consumption. In the process, there are a lot of choices the translator makes, each of which affects the translation in one way or the other. It is important, therefore, that translators go through well-structured serious training to be equipped for the task. The translator's relationship with Christ is crucial to the success of every translation project; therefore, Bible translators must be spiritual, not carnal, people. Translators must endeavor to build their spirituality to enhance the spiritual task they perform. The Bible is a spiritual document and must be treated as such. In the next chapter, I discuss the spiritual nature of the Bible without ignoring its human dimension.

Review Exercise

1. Explain the role of each member of the Bible translation team.

2. What is meant by the term "first draft"? Explain how one can draft accurately, naturally and clearly.

3. What role does background study play in Bible translation?

4. Who is a Translation Consultant? What is his/her role in the translation process?

5. What is a translation brief? How useful is it to the work of the translator?

6. Prepare a sample translation brief for a project to be done for your community.

7. Why is the spiritual life of the Bible translator so crucial?

8. Critically appraise the various stages that the translating text passes through before it is finally published. What additional measures do you want to be put in place to ensure the work is done perfectly?

9. Draw a curriculum for training Bible translators in your country.

10. Explain how you will recruit people for Bible translation project in your community. Your recruitment should cater for every aspect of the translation process starting from planning to publication.

Chapter 4

The Bible

The English word "Bible" refers to the canonical collection of sacred writings of Judaism and Christianity. In Judaism, it is often referred to as the *Tanak*. The *Tanak* or the Hebrew Bible corresponds to the Christian Old Testament. The Bible is a unique book written over a period of 1,500 years by about 40 authors of diverse backgrounds— including kings, philosophers, fishermen, farmers, poets, statesmen and scholars— and from different places (mostly within the Jewish nation). All the authors of the Bible are Jews except those of Luke-Acts and the Gospel according to Mark. This chapter introduces the reader to aspects of the Bible which I consider very important to be known by every translator before even beginning the actual translation work.

Dual Nature of the Bible

The Bible has a dual nature, divine and human nature.[1] The Bible was composed by humans to be understood by people. This assertion has certain implications. First of all, each biblical text was written by someone to specific hearers or readers in a specific historical-geographical situation for a specific purpose. In other words, biblical passages are contextually informed because they were prompted by the prevailing situation at the time of their writing. Secondly, every biblical text is culturally conditioned. That is to say, each biblical text was couched in the cultural setting of the times in which it was written. Thirdly, biblical authors used everyday language and followed normal grammatical meanings, including figurative language. For this reason, the Bible contains every literary genre and stylistic device that was present in ancient Israel and the Greco-Roman world, including simile, metaphor, poetry, proverbs, narratives, laws, prophecy, wisdom literature, epistles, and others. Therefore, each biblical text must be understood according to the basic principles of logic and communication.

The second aspect of the nature of the Bible is the divine aspect. As a divine book, the Bible contains mystery. There are certain aspects of the Bible that are plain; others are just mysteries (Deut. 29:29). The Bible contains unity; its

---

[1] I have gleaned most of my data in this section from Clinton Lockhart, *Principles of Interpretation*, 2nd ed. (Fort Worth: S. H. Taylor, 1915), 18-31.

message is from one source (that is, God). Therefore, it does not contradict itself; each part is expected to complement the other. Finally, the Bible contains progression. It was progressively revealed by God. Therefore, it is important to consider the entire teaching of the Bible on a particular issue before drawing conclusions.

Inspiration of Scripture

The doctrine of the inspiration of scripture refers to the fact that the books of the Bible were written under the influence of the Holy Spirit (See Job 32:8 and 2 Tim. 3:16). Inspiration deals with the objective text of the Bible, not the objective intention of the writer.[2] In other words, inspiration refers to "that controlling influence which God exerted over the human authors by whom the Old Testament and New Testament were written."[3] The Bible in totality is God's word, not part of it. We must therefore believe all that it contains or disbelieve all. Because the Bible was produced under supernatural influence, the message in it is infallible. This does not mean, as I have discussed earlier, that there are no human factors that contributed to the writing of Scriptures. The divine influence did not remove the human nature of the authors; rather, it complemented human nature and made sure the message received from God was accurately transcribed.[4] Inspiration differs from revelation in that revelation deals with material or content by which God is disclosed, while inspiration has to do with how that content was recorded. Finally, inspiration can only be predicated on the original writings, not on copies or translations.

Attributes of the Bible

What the Bible teaches about itself can be categorized into four major attributes (characteristics): (1) the authority of Scripture; (2) the clarity of Scripture; (3) the necessity of Scripture; and (4) the sufficiency of Scripture. The Bible is authoritative in that all that it contains are the words of God in such a way that anyone who disbelieves or disobeys any word of Scripture disbelieves or disobeys God. The authority of the Bible is grounded in the concept of inspiration. Biblical data on its authority are abundant. For example, the introductory formula "Thus says the LORD" found in many parts of the Bible underscores the fact that what was said came from God (see, for

---

[2] Norman L. Geisler and William E. Nix, *A General Introduction to the Bible* (revised edition) (Chicago, IL: Moody Press, 1968), 36.

[3] Lewis Sperry Chafer, *Systematic Theology Vol. 1* (Dallas, TX: Dallas Seminary Press, 1947), 61.

[4] As cited in Roy B. Zuck, *Basic Bible Interpretation* (Colorado Springs, CO: Victor, 1991), 33.

example, Isa. 44:2, 6; Jer. 9:7, 15, 17). There are many instances where God is said to have spoken to prophets (1 Kings 14:18; 16:12, 34; 2 Kings 9:36; 14:25; Jer. 37:2; Zech. 7:7, 12). This means that what the prophet says is what God says. The extent of divine authority in Scripture includes all that is written (2 Tim. 3:16), even the very words (Matt. 22:43; 1 Cor. 2:13), tenses of verbs (Matt. 22:32; Gal. 3:16) and even the smallest parts of words (Matt. 5:17–18).

The second attribute is the clarity (or perspicuity) of the Bible which is the idea that the message of the Bible can be understood by all who desire to understand it. In other words, God's Word has been given to us in such a way that everyone, who is willing, can understand it. This means that God's Word was never intended to be esoteric, dark, enigmatic, obscure, inscrutable, ambiguous or vague. Rather, it is a perfect, clean and true light, illuminating the character and plan of God. The idea of clarity of the Bible is an encouragement for all Christians to study and apply Scriptures to their lives. Moses alluded to the clarity and comprehensibility of Scripture when he told Israel that God's word is not far from them and that they have it and can obey it as well (see Deut. 30:11-14). Paul told the Corinthian church that his letters have been straightforward and that there is nothing written between the lines and nothing we can't understand (2 Cor. 1:13-14; see also Phil. 3:15-16; 2 Tim. 3:14-17). Though not unclear, the word of God can be incomprehensible to us because of cultural, geographical, and time gaps between our world and the Bible world. We therefore need the illumination of the Holy Spirit together with serious studies to be able to understand Scripture properly.

The necessity of Scripture refers to the affirmation that Scripture is necessary for genuine knowledge about God. It refers to humankind's absolute dependence on God's special revelation in the Scriptures in order to obtain a true knowledge of God, his gospel and his plan of salvation, which cannot be obtained through the general revelation of nature and conscience. We exist as humans to have a relationship with God in which we live according to his will and purpose. To know God's will and purpose, one has to search the Scriptures because it is in it that he has revealed himself in a special way. Jesus taught the necessity of Scripture when he said, "Man shall not live by bread alone but by every word that proceeds from the mouth of God" (Matt. 4:4; cf. Deut. 8:3). Scripture is a necessary document for the remedy of humankind's sinful situation. It is also necessary because of God's incomprehensibility. Without it, there is no way we can understand God. General revelation is insufficient and lacks what it takes to bring about salvation. The necessity of Scripture is the fact that the Scripture is necessary for our salvation. Certainly, there can be no question that Scripture is necessary.

The fourth attribute of Scripture is sufficiency, meaning, what God has revealed in the Bible is sufficient for us to know all things that is necessary for the proper understanding of who God is, who we are, how God has acted in the past, and what God expects from us. Simply put, the Bible contains all that humans need to know for salvation. This means that we do not need anything else to be revealed about God or his plan for the human race before we can be saved. God has given us sufficient information in the Bible and what we need to do is to search for it. It is, therefore, wrong for people to assume or claim that they have new revelations which are required to be known before one can be saved. What God does in our time is giving us illumination of what has been revealed previously. Illumination helps us to have a better understanding of Scripture, not to have a completely new revelation. Jesus came as the perfect and final revelation of God (Heb. 1:1-3).

These attributes of Scripture have some implications for the task of translation. Aware of the fact that the Bible is the word of God, the translator should endeavor to carry out his/her task in such a way as not to alter God's word by adding to it or removing something from it. As God's word is meant to be understood by people of all places, the translation of the Scripture must be clear to facilitate the needed understanding. Translators must therefore work diligently to preserve the content of the biblical text. The need to avoid obscurity in translation is grounded in the doctrine of clarity of the Bible. If God gave a clear message to his people, then the translator should also ensure that what he/she gives to the receptor community is also clear.

The Biblical Canon

The word "canon" comes from the Greek term *kanōn* (meaning measuring rod). In this book, I use it to refer to the list of books that are accepted as authoritative and part of inspired Scriptures. The term **canonization** refers to the process by which the church recognized each Bible book as divinely inspired and hence, part of God's authoritative Word. Or canonization is the process of measuring and singling out books that were composed under divine inspiration to become part of God's authoritative word.[5] Protestants and Catholics do not agree on the number of books that make up the Old Testament canon. Both traditions agree on thirty-nine books, with the Catholics including seven additional books: Tobit, Judith, 1 and 2 Maccabees, the Wisdom of Solomon, Ecclesiasticus (Wisdom of Jesus ben Sirach) and Baruch, as well as extra material in the books of Esther and Daniel.

---

[5] Emmanuel Owusu Bediako, *History of the Bible* (Accra: Advocate Publishing Limited, 2008), 61-62.

Protestants refer to these books as Apocryphal (hidden) books, but Catholics call them Deuterocanonical (second-canon) books.

The Hebrew Canon

The Hebrew Bible has three main divisions, namely, the Pentateuch (*Torah*), the Prophets (*Nevi'im*) and the Writings or Hagiographa (*Kethubhim*). The development of the Hebrew canon took place over a long period of time. The biblical text was not written as the events happened. Usually, an event occurred, people talked about it and transferred the facts orally across generations before they were finally written under the guidance of the Holy Spirit. Some of the earliest compositions include Miriam's song (Exod. 15:1-18) and Deborah's song (Judg. 5)—probably not later than the 12th century BCE—, and the Decalogue, which was written not later than the 12th to 11th century BCE. It was God himself who wrote his commandments on two stone tablets (Exod. 31:18). Later, Moses' composition, which was to be placed beside the Ark of the Covenant (Deut. 31:24–26), was added to the earlier writings. Joshua, Moses' successor, also added to the collection of written words of God (Josh. 24:26).

The next stage of the composition of Jewish sacred writings took place during the time of the prophets. Not all prophets documented events that took place during their time. Those who wrote include Samuel, who wrote the rights of the people and duties of the kingship in a book (1 Sam. 10:25), Nathan, and Gad (1 Chron. 29:29). In addition, the records of the event of other leaders were documented and kept in the Temple. The content of the Old Testament canon continued to grow until the latest books, such as Daniel and Esther, were written by the 2nd century BCE and the Apocryphal books, like 2 Maccabees and Wisdom of Solomon, were completed by 100 BCE.[6]

The canonization of the Hebrew Bible took place through three stages. The first stage was the **collection of the *Torah*** which included the expansion of the Hebrew law codes preserved in the Pentateuch (which include the Decalogue of Exod. 20:1-7, the Covenant Code of Exod. 20:22-23:19, and religious Code of Exod. 34:11-26) to include the creation stories, legends of the Patriarchs, and stories of early history and origins of people. In about 622 BCE, Hilkiah found a law book (which probably forms the core of Deut. 12-26) in the Temple (2 Kings 22:8ff). This was revised and later (in 444 BCE) accepted officially as God's Word for the nation, as Ezra and his

---

[6] Raymond F. Collins, "The Canon of the Old Testament," *The New Jerome Biblical Commentary* (Englewood Cliffs, NJ: Prentice-Hall, 2011), 1037.

contemporaries read and explained it to the post-exilic community (Neh. 8:1-10:39). Some contemporary scholars opine that the Pentateuch was essentially completed by about 1000 BCE but was revised in minor ways until the time of Ezra. Whatever the case, our conviction is that by the 3rd century BCE, the *Torah* was fully composed, divided into five books of the Pentateuch published and read in various synagogues.[7]

The second stage of the canonization process was the **collection of the writings of the Prophets** and **the history** of the period in which the prophets lived and ministered. This stage was completed about two centuries after the canonization of the Torah.[8] Records from the Apocryphal book of Ecclesiasticus (the Wisdom of Jesus the Son of Sirach), a second-century BCE book, points to three divisions of the Hebrew Scriptures that existed at that time. They include the Law and the Prophets and "the other books of our fathers", including the "Former Prophets" or Deuteronomistic history (Joshua, Judges, Samuel, Kings) and the "Latter Prophets" (Isaiah, Jeremiah, Ezekiel, the Twelve [Minor Prophets]). Undoubtedly, many of these books had been recognized as authoritative for a long time before their collection.

The final stage involved the collection of miscellaneous Writings or sacred writings (**Kethubhim**) or **Hagiogragpha**, including books from Psalms to Chronicles in the Hebrew Bible. Unlike the Law and the Prophets, which consist of final editions of particular literary genres presumably meant for canonization, the Writings were made up of ten literary works which had to achieve independent canonical status through circulation and wide acceptance by the people of God.[9] Three major factors governed the canonicity of the *Hagiographa*, namely the survival of the book, anonymous authorship and time of writing. The survival of a book was proof that it was always in demand by the people of God such that various copies of it were produced to ensure its survival. Ancient Jewish writings were characteristically anonymous; it was only at the time that people began to question the inspiration of these books that Jewish writers identified themselves in their documents. Apart from the prophets, who put their public addresses together, only one ancient Jewish writer attached his name to his book[10] (Ecclus. 50:27-29). Jewish tradition holds that prophetic inspiration ended soon after the time of Ezra. Therefore, no book (written after Ezra's time) was considered for canonicity. Flavius

---

[7] Robert H. Pfeiffer, *Introduction to the Old Testament* (New York: Harper and Brothers Publishers, 1948), 58.

[8] Pfeiffer, *Introduction to the Old Testament*, 58.

[9] Pfeiffer, *Introduction to the Old Testament*, 62.

[10] Pfeiffer, *Introduction to the Old Testament*, 62.

Josephus gives the earliest witness to the Jewish theory of inspiration and canonicity. He divided sacred Scriptures into three parts, five books of the *Torah*, thirteen books of the Prophets, and four books of hymns.[11] Josephus further noted that books to be considered for canonization had to be written by inspired prophets during the prophetic age, which according to him, ended with Artaxerxes (in the Persian period).[12] Other criteria for canonicity included wide acceptance among God's people, consistency with revealed word and character of God, prophetic authorship and so on.

Three factors—namely, the destruction of Jerusalem by the Romans in AD 70, the threatened extinction of Judaism, and the rise of Christianity with literature that was regarded by Jewish leaders as heretical—necessitated the gathering of some Jewish rabbis at a town in south-western Judah, called Jamnia, to brainstorm prayerfully whether or not to include some of "the Writings" (especially such books as Ecclesiastes and the Song of Solomon) in the Hebrew canon. The status of the other books was not reviewed because they had been in existence for several centuries and had gained status as authoritative writings. Post-Jumnia debate centred on the status of Esther and parts of Ezekiel. By the middle of the second century AD, these books were accepted as canonical. Thereafter, the canon was fixed permanently. In all the processes, God was actively present; canonicity is determined by God.

The New Testament Canon

Both Protestants and Catholics accept the 27 books in the New Testament canon, comprising four Gospels (Matthew, Mark, Luke, and John), one historical book, twenty-one letters (Pauline epistles, Johannine epistles and general epistles) and one book of prophecy. When Christianity began, the Old Testament, oral traditions about Jesus Christ and proclamation of the apostles were the main sources by which knowledge about God was obtained.[13] The apostles felt reluctant to write about the person and works of Christ because they thought his Second Advent was at hand. They were, therefore, interested in preaching about him, not writing about him. Later, when some of them started dying, the surviving ones realized the need to document Jesus' life and ministry.

---

[11] Flavius Josephus, *The Complete Works of Flavius Josephus* translated by William Whiston (Nashville: Thomas Nelson Inc., 1998), 929.

[12] Josephus, *The Complete Works of Flavius Josephus*, 929.

[13] Robert H. Gundry, *A Survey of the New Testament*, 5th edition (Grand Rapids, MI: Zondervan, 2012), 102. See also Philip Schaff, *History of the Christian Church Vol. 1* (Grand Rapids, MI: Wm. B. Eerdmans Publishing Company, 1910), 571.

In the first 100 years of the Christian faith, a number of documents began to circulate among the churches, including epistles, gospels, memoirs, apocalypses, homilies, and collections of teachings. Documents like the Pauline letters and the four historical accounts of Jesus (the Gospels) were written, copied and circulated throughout the churches for use in teaching.[14] The earliest New Testament literature to be circulated among Christian communities were the Pauline epistles. This took place as early as the late 40s (AD). The gospel of Mark was composed some years later (in about 65AD). Not long after their circulation, the Pauline epistles and the Gospels were accepted as Holy Scripture, of equal importance (or more, in the eyes of some people) as the Jewish Scriptures. They became known as the *homolegoumena*, meaning "confessed."

The process of discernment and discrimination lasted about 200 years. The need for canonization was prompted by at least three factors. First, Christians needed to refute heresies that were being preached. For example, Marcion, a gnostic, taught that the God of the Old Testament as a wrathful God incompatible with the loving God of the New Testament. He opined that the Old Testament was contradictory and barbaric and that the true Gospel was not at all Jewish, but that Jewish ideas had been imported into New Testament texts by interpolators, and only Paul's teachings are true. Marcion provided a list of books which he considered as sacred writing, including a truncated version of Luke's gospel and ten Pauline letters.[15] In the midst of such a situation, Christians needed to come out clearly on which books they considered authoritative and hence could be used for formulating and defending church doctrine. Secondly, the persecution of Christians in the Roman Empire (including the martyrdom of people in possession of Christian literature) made it necessary to define the Christian canon so that one would know which books were worth dying for. The third factor is that in the second century, people began to produce writings and associated them falsely with the twelve Apostles.[16] Christians, therefore, needed to determine the writings that were truly connected with the apostolic tradition.

Initially, Jesus' sayings of Jesus and the writings of the apostles were often quoted alongside the Old Testament Scripture as having a similar authority but not as themselves constituting Scripture. The fact that Paul commanded his audience to read his epistles in the congregation (1 Thess. 5:27; cf. Col

---

[14] Schaff, *History of the Christian Church I*, 571.

[15] Mark Allan Powell, *Introducing the New Testament* (Grand Rapids, MI: Baker Academic, 2009), 52.

[16] Powell, *Introducing the New Testament*, 53.

4:16) underscores the fact that he considered his letters to have scriptural status. A similar claim is made about the book of Revelation (Rev. 1:3; 22:18-19). In 2 Peter 3:16, Paul's epistles are actually called "Scriptures," and the gospel is identified as "the Scripture" in 1 Timothy 5:18.

Most of the New Testament books were established as early as 200 AD. The earliest Christian lists New Testament books come from the Muratorian fragment which contained 22 out of the 27 books of the present New Testament canon. It refers to Luke as the third Gospel, then lists John, Paul's 13 letters, Jude, two epistles of John and Revelation as Scripture. By the end of the second century, the term "Scripture(s)" was commonly used to denote New Testament writings, including the four Gospels, Acts, thirteen epistles of Paul, 1 Peter and 1 John. The remaining seven, so-called *"Antilegomena,"* were only finally included at the end of the fourth century. In the early third century, Origen used the same twenty-seven (27) books as in the present New Testament canon, though there were still lingering disputes over Hebrews, James, 2 Peter, 2 and 3 John, and Revelation. Eusebius gave a record of all the New Testament books except James, Jude, 2 Peter, 2 and 3 John, which he says were disputed by some people, but recognized by the majority.[17] He divided religious literature into three classes: *Homologoumena*, or compositions universally accepted as sacred, *Antilegomena*, or contested writings; these, in turn, are of the superior and inferior sort. The better ones are the epistles of James and spurious (*notha*). Athanasius, Bishop of Alexandria, (in his Easter letter in 367AD) gave a list of exactly the same books as what would become the twenty-seven-book New Testament canon. Finally, in Carthage in 397 AD, the church in the West as a body approved the twenty-seven books alone as authoritative and inspired.

Biblical Languages

A biblical language is any language in which the original text of the Bible was written. There are three such languages, namely, Hebrew, Aramaic and Koine (common) Greek. The Hebrew language was/is the language spoken by the people of Israel. The Old Testament was originally written in Hebrew. Scholars usually refer to the kind of Hebrew used to document the biblical message as Biblical Hebrew to distinguish it from the Modern Hebrew. The fact is that Modern Hebrew is different from the Hebrew language with which the biblical text was written. The Old Testament (except few areas, such as a portion of Daniel and Ezra) was written in biblical Hebrew. Ancient Biblical Hebrew words were built using only consonants, without vowels, and the resulting text

---

[17] Eusebius, *The Church History: A New Translation with Commentary* translated by Paul L. Maier (Grand Rapids, MI: Kregel Publications, 1999), 115.

was called Unpointed text. This does not mean that ancient Hebrew words did not have vowel sounds. Rather, it means ancient Hebrew did not write their vowel sounds. The people of ancient Israel achieved correct pronunciation based on an oral tradition that was handed over from generation to generation. They supplied fixed vowel sounds in their reading and conversation based on their knowledge of the language. As a rule, all verbs (with few exceptions) used the "a" sound while their noun equivalent used the "e" sound in the first vowel position.

Later, certain Hebrew consonants (א, ו , ה and י) were used to represent vowel sounds. Around 500 AD, a group of Jewish scholars called Masoretes realized the need to add vowels to written Hebrew so that they could maintain correct pronunciation that had been transmitted orally across generations. In order to maintain the length of each word after the introduction of the vowel, the Masoretes decided to use pointings or marks (mostly dots and dashes) that were placed around the consonants. The Biblical text that resulted from the pointing system came to be known as the Masoretic Text (MT). This text has served as the source text for major Jewish and Christian translations, and today, its latest complete edition, the *Biblia Hebraica Stuttgartensia*, serves as the primary source text for Bible translation throughout the world.

Aramaic was the spoken language of the Near East from the sixth to fourth century BCE. It belongs to the Semitic subfamily of the Afroasiatic language family. It was the language that Babylonians spoke until their conquest by Alexander the Great, when Greek became their official language. Aramaic became the language of exilic Jews during their stay in Babylon. Later, when Persia conquered Babylon and then allowed the Jews to go back to Israel, they returned with Aramaic as their second language, and many of them had even lost the Hebrew tongue altogether. It was the language Jesus spoke. Parts of Old Testament books of Ezra (4:8-6:18; 7:12-26) and of Daniel (2:46-7:28) were written in Aramaic. New Testament expressions such as *talitha cumi* (Mark 5:41), *ephphatha* (Mark 7:34), *Eli Eli, lama sabachthani* (Mark 14:36) are Aramaic expressions.

Greek is an Indo-European language spoken primarily in Greece. The history of the development of the language is divided into four phases: the Ancient phase, which is subdivided into a Mycenaean period (characterized by texts in syllabic script attested from the 14th to the 13th century BCE) and the Archaic and the Classical periods (beginning with the adoption of the alphabet, from the 8th to the 4th century BCE); Hellenistic and Roman phase (4th century BCE to 4th century AD); Byzantine phase (5th to 15th century AD); and a Modern phase. Through Hellenization, Greek became the official language in the Greco-Roman world. Scholars agree that the New Testament was originally written in Greek, specifically Koine Greek, even though some authors often included translations from Hebrew and Aramaic texts. Koine Greek emerged in the fourth century BCE and was used until about the sixth century.

The fact that Jesus spoke Aramaic but his teachings were originally written in Greek underscores the fact that what we have as our original New Testament text is somehow a translation of Jesus' teachings from Aramaic into Greek. This situation sometimes poses some challenges for us. The expression "If your hand is...." (cf. Matt. 5:30), for instance, is an Aramaic expression that means "If you are a thief...." The meaning of this idiom in Greek may not bring out its Aramaic usage and meaning.

Conclusion

The fact that the Bible is the word of God makes it imperative for the translator to give the best representation in meaning and form for the receptor community. Any misrepresentation will destroy God's message to his people. Bible translation must therefore be done with the greatest care so that the contemporary reader gets exactly the message that God wants him/her to get. Having discussed relevant portions of the subject of Bibliology (the doctrine of the Bible), I now shift attention to the history of Bible translation in the next chapter.

Review Exercise

1. Why is it necessary for translators to study biblical languages?

2. Write short notes on each of the three biblical languages.

3. Critically examine the processes by which New Testament writings became Scriptures.

4. To what extent do you agree that vernacular Bibles are inspired?

5. What does it mean to say that the Bible is sufficient?

6. Are there lost books of the Bible? Explain your answer.

7. Discuss how the Hebrew canon was formed.

8. If the Bible is clear, how come people find it difficult to understand its message?

9. "If the Bible has human nature, then it is not a divine document." Discuss.

10. To what extent do you agree that the Bible has authority?

Chapter 5

History of Global Bible Translation

This chapter considers Bible Translation from a historical perspective. Time and space limitations will not allow me to conduct an exhaustive study of the history of Bible translation. Therefore, I offer highlights of major developments that have taken place in the history of translation. I begin with a brief discussion of the emergence and development of the subject of Translation Studies and then move to discuss the major epochs in the development of Bible translation briefly.

What is Translation Studies?

The expression "Translation Studies" is used to refer to translation-related theory and practice. Translation Studies is the field of study that deals with the theory, description, phenomenon and application of translation.[1] A multilingual and interdisciplinary subject, Translation Studies requires knowledge from diverse fields, including comparative literature, cultural studies, gender studies, computer science, communication, history, linguistics, philosophy, rhetoric, education, cognitive science, comparative literature, literary discourse, philosophy, semiotics, film studies, folklore and popular culture studies. Translation activities have a long history, but translation as an academic discipline is relatively new. Translation Studies deal with the systematic examination of translation not only as an applied practice but also as a means of understanding the transfer of meaning across diverse languages and cultures. The practical experiences of the translator, the theoretical and methodological perspectives of the history and philosophy of translation, as well as present trends in the field of translation, all form an integral part of this discipline. It explores issues related to culture, economics, politics, gender, ethics (and others) which affect translation. Translation Studies also develops the analytical, practical, evaluative, aesthetic, and expository skills required to address challenges in translation. Lastly, it includes the development of research skills, practical translation skills, and

---

[1] Jeremy Munday, *Introducing Translation Studies Theories and Applications* (London: Routledge, 2001), 1.

the ability to develop strategies for managing complex linguistic and cultural issues related to translation.

Emergence and Development of Translation Studies

Throughout human history, written and spoken translations have played a significant role in inter-human communication. Cicero and Horace (first century BCE) and Sophronius Eusebius Hieronymus (ca. 342–420 AD), also known as Jerome (fourth century AD), are among the early scholars in translation.[2] Nonetheless, the study of translation as an academic subject is relatively new (as noted earlier). From the late eighteen century to the 1960s, the grammar-translation method dominated language learning in secondary schools. This method was derived from the classical method of teaching Greek and Latin. It focuses on teaching grammatical rules and structures and then applying those rules by translating sentences between the receptor language and the native language. In this period, translation was perceived as a way of learning a new language or a way of reading a foreign language text. Therefore, once adequate skills were obtained for reading a foreign language, the student went no further.

A shift from the grammar-translation method to the direct method or communicative approach to language teaching occurred in the 1960s. The direct method, which emphasizes students' natural capacity to learn a language, is characterized by teaching concepts and vocabulary through real-life objects and other visual materials, teaching grammar through an inductive approach, the centrality of spoken language (including a native-like pronunciation) and a focus on question-answer patterns. The introduction of this method made people abandon translation in language learning. It was only in the higher-level and university language courses and professional translator training that translation was taught.[3]

The publications of scholars like Jean-Paul Vinay and Jean Darbelnet (in 1958), Alfred Malblanc (in 1963), George Mounin (in 1963) and Eugene Nida (in 1964) contributed to the development of Translation Studies in this period.[4] Nida is credited for developing a sociolinguistic approach to translation. However, it was James S. Holmes' 1972 paper, "The name and nature of translation studies", which served as the point of origin for the

---

[2] Munday, *Introducing Translation Studies Theories*, 7.
[3] Munday, *Introducing Translation Studies Theories*, 8.
[4] Munday, *Introducing Translation Studies Theories*, 9-10

recognition of Translation Studies as an academic discipline.[5] Holmes divided the field of Translation Studies into two major areas: translation theory and descriptive science on the one hand and applied Translation Studies on the other hand. His framework for Translation Studies comprised: (1) translator training: teaching methods, testing techniques, curriculum design; (2) translation aids: such as dictionaries, grammars and information technology; (3) translation criticism: the evaluation of translations, including the marking of student translations and the reviews of published translations; and (4) translation policy: the place of translation in society and the language teaching and learning curriculum.[6]

The second phase of the linguistic-oriented approach to translation emerged in the 1970s and focused on text linguistics. The new approach focused on the text itself, which was regarded not only as an isolated verbal construct but also as an attempt at communication that functions in a certain way, in a certain situation or culture and may not work with the same degree of success in another situation or culture. Text linguistics, therefore, gave a much-needed functional dimension to the analysis of the translation process and of translated texts. Scholarship in Translation Studies since the 1970s has focused on one or more aspects of Holme's framework.

According to Munday, the prominence of Translation Studies in the past few decades could be attributed to at least two reasons.[7] The first reason is the "proliferation of specialized translating and interpreting courses at both undergraduate and postgraduate level."[8] For example, in the 1960s, the first specialized postgraduate programs in translation and interpretation were set up in institutions in the United Kingdom. After this, various institutions rolled out translation programs and established Centers for Translation. The other factor has to do with the various conferences and (books and journals) publications on translation across the globe. Three of these conferences were very influential. The first took place in Leuven in 1976, the second in Tel Aviv in 1978 and the third in Antwerp in 1980. The outcome of the first conference was published as *Literature and Translation* (Holmes, Lambert and Van den Broeck 1978), that of the second conference was published in a special issue of the journal *Poetics Today* (vol 2, no. 4, 1981, edited by Even-Zohar and Toury), and that of the third in the Michigan-based semiotics journal *Dispositio* (vol. 7, nos. 19-21, 1982,

---

[5] E. Gentzler, Contemporary translation theories (second edition) (Clevedon: Multilingual Matters Ltd, 2001), 92.

[6] Munday, *Introducing Translation Studies Theories*, 12.

[7] Munday, *Introducing Translation Studies Theories*, 6.

[8] Munday, *Introducing Translation Studies Theories*, 6.

edited by Lefevere). These programs and publications urged a lot of people to pursue transition studies. Today, Translation Studies is recognized as a discipline in its own right, and like all other disciplines, it has its own set of terms to denote various aspects of the process. African institutions such as Stellenbosch University and the University of the Free State, South Africa, Akrofi-Christaller Institute of Theology, Mission and Culture, Ghana, and St. Paul's University and African International University, Kenya, are among those which offer undergraduate and graduate programs in Translation Studies.

Major Epochs of Bible Translations

In this section, I consider key Bible translation projects that have taken place globally since the first translation project took place in the ancient world till today. For convenience, I have divided the history of Bible translation into four periods as follows: The first period includes the translation of Scriptures into the dominant languages of the ancient world; the second focuses on translation into Latin and other European languages prior to the Reformation; the third is the missionary era, when pioneer translators undertook the preparation of renderings into various languages and dialects, in many of which there was previously often not even an alphabet; and the fourth stage is the stage where indigenous people paly key role in the translation process.

The First Great Age of Bible Translation (200 BCE-400 AD)

The First Great Age of Bible translation marks the period between 200 BCE and 400 AD when Hebrew Scriptures were translated into Greek and Aramaic.[9] Initially, the Jews stayed in Palestine, their native land and spoke their native language. Later (in 586 BCE), they went into Babylonian exile and lost their sovereignty as a nation. Living in Diaspora, the Jews acquired Aramaic and Greek languages. Hellenism that resulted from the rule of Alexander the Great made Hellenistic Jews in the Diaspora so familiar with the Greek language that a Greek translation was needed to facilitate the spread of the Hebrew sacred text among them and to help them participate fully in Jewish religious worship.

The first Bible translation took place in Alexandria (Egypt in North Africa), in about the third century BCE (circa 250 BCE), when Jewish Scriptures were translated from Hebrew to Greek. The translation was started under Ptolemy II of Egypt and was executed by seventy people in about 300 years. The resulting translation became known as the Septuagint (Latin: *septuaginta* = 70,

---

[9] H. Orlinsky and R. G. Bratcher, *A History of Bible translation and the North American contribution* (Atlanta, GA: Scholar Press, 1991), 1.

LXX) because of the involvement of seventy scholars in the project. The LXX was, therefore, a Greek Hebrew Bible for Greek-Speaking Jews. The Greek language of the LXX is Jewish Hellenistic Greek. The translators of the LXX rendered the Hebrew text literally, employing legitimate Greek vocabulary and grammatical constructions to suit the needs of their audience. The LXX employed both free (or even sometimes paraphrastic) translations (for example, for books such as Job, Proverbs, Isaiah, Daniel, and Esther) and literal translations (for example for books like Judges, Psalms, Ecclesiastes, Lamentations, Ezra-Nehemiah, and Chronicles).[10]

The arrangement of books and the number of books in the LXX vary from those of the Hebrew Bible. The LXX had additional books like Tobit, Ecclesiasticus, Wisdom of Solomon, 1, 2, 3, and 4 Maccabees, and others. The LXX also had supplemental materials that are not found in the Hebrew Bible. For example, the Greek form of the Book of Esther, which in Hebrew contains 167 verses, has six more sections, an additional 107 verses. The Book of Daniel has three supplements; the English Apocrypha of the King James Version refers to these as the History of Susanna, Bel and the Dragon, and the Song of the Three Holy Children.

At the same time, the LXX lacks some materials found in the Hebrew Bible. For example, the LXX version of the Book of Job is about one-sixth shorter than what appears in the Hebrew Bible, and the Book of Jeremiah lacks about one-eighth of the material in the Hebrew text. The reason for this may be that the translators of the LXX used Hebrew versions that differed slightly from what later became the traditional Masoretic Text.[11] The LXX abandoned the traditional division of the Hebrew Bible into the Law, the Prophets, and the Writings and arranged biblical books according to their literary character: (1) Pentateuch and historical books, (2) poetical and sapiential books, (3) prophetical books.

The LXX later became the received text of the Old Testament in the early church and the basis of its canon. In producing the LXX, the translators had to interpret the source text. The rendering of the Hebrew word for "young woman" as "virgin" in the LXX (Isaiah 7:14 cf. Matt. 1:23), for instance, points to interpretation involved in the process. The approach used by the translators varies from near wooden literalism in some places to virtual paraphrase in others. For example, a word-for-word translation of Genesis 6:6 would be "God repented (*nacham*) for having made human beings." However,

---

[10] Bruce M. Metzger, *The Bible in Translation: Ancient and English Versions* (Grand Rapids, MI: Baker Academic, 2001), 17.

[11] Metzger, *The Bible in Translation*, 18.

the LXX avoids a literal translation and renders it "God took it to heart ..." In Exodus 24:9-10, the Hebrew text, literally reads "Then Moses, Aaron, Nadab, Abihu and seventy of the elders of Israel went up the mountain again, and **they saw the God** (*ra'ah Eloyhim*) **of Israel**...." The translators of the LXX, informed by the Jewish tradition that no one can see God and live (Gen. 32:30 cf. Exod. 33:20), renders this text as "They saw the place where the God of Israel stood."

The LXX became a very important version for the New Testament writers. Not only is it the earliest biblical version, it is also the most valuable of ancient biblical versions. About 75 percent of Old Testament citations in the New Testament were quoted from the LXX. The Church Fathers also placed much value on the LXX and quoted extensively from it in their preaching and theological publications. The LXX was a major medium through which Hebrew religious traditions spread to the world outside Israel. It was also the basis for the Old Latin, Coptic, Gothic, Armenian, Georgian, Ethiopic, Christian Palestinian Aramaic, Syriac, Arabic, and Slavonic versions of the Hebrew Bible. To this day, the LXX is the authoritative biblical text of the Old Testament for the Greek Orthodox Church. F. C. Conybeare and St. George Stock, in their *Grammar of Septuagint Greek*, make the following observation which explains the extent of the influence of LXX on Christianity:

> St. Augustine remarks that the Greek-speaking Christians for the most part did not even know whether there was any other word of God than the Septuagint (*C.D.* XVIII, 43). So when other nations became converted to Christianity and wanted the Scriptures in their own tongues, it was almost always the Septuagint which formed the basis of the translation. This was so in the case of the early Latin version, which was in use before the Vulgate; and it was so also in the case of the translations made into Coptic, Ethiopic, Armenian, Georgian, Gothic, and other languages. The only exception to the rule is the first Syriac version, which was made direct from the Hebrew.[12]

Targums

Another ancient translation that took place in this period was the Jewish Aramaic version of the Hebrew Bible (called Targums, literally "translation") which was produced mainly for the Jews who were in the Asian Diaspora. Targums were ancient Aramaic paraphrase or interpretation of all the books of

---

[12] Frederick C. Conybeare and George Stock, *Grammar of Septuagint Greek* (Eugene, OR: Wipf&Stock, 2014), 19-20.

the Hebrew Bible (with the exception of Ezra, Nehemiah, and Daniel). This translation was needed at the time when Hebrew was ceasing to be a spoken language among the Jews. Aramaic became the spoken language of the Jews in the first century BCE; Jesus also spoke Aramaic (as noted earlier). The Targums were produced from around the first century BCE, while the LXX was translated between 250 and 100 BCE. The Targums were read in the synagogue. Three Targumic versions emerged in the synagogue:[13] The predominantly literal Targum Onqelos was composed in the first or second century AD by Judeans, and this was adopted and revised by Babylonian Jews. The second one is the Palestinian Targum which was composed in Galilee by the early third century AD. It was also literal and had additional comments; it had a wide circulation. The largest of the Palestinian Targum is Targum Neofiti (or Targum Neophyti) which consists of 450 folios covering all books of the Pentateuch. The third version, which was composed some centuries later, is Targum Pseudo-Jonathan which merged Onqelos's translation, the Palestinian Targums' additions, and additional material of its own.

Translators of the Targums added glosses to the translated text (a) "to resolve textual difficulties by interpreting obscure words or simplifying syntax," (b) "to harmonize conflicting texts," (c) "to reconcile the biblical text with accepted tradition," (d) "to incorporate specifics of Pharisaic-rabbinic Judaism into the text," (e) "to provide specificity to historical, juridical, or religious allusions," and (f) "to either strengthen or mitigate the force of a scriptural passage."[14] Some examples of targumists' interpretive expansions (and interpolations) are the following:

i. And whatever Adam called a living creature **in the language of the sanctuary** that was its name. (Targum Neofiti 1, Gen. 2:19)[15]

ii. Behold, **I have given them the span of** one hundred and twenty years **(in the hope that) perhaps they might repent, but they have not done so.** (Targum Neofiti 1, Gen. 6:3)[16]

---

[13] I gleaned what follows from Martin McNamara and Paul V.M. Flesher "Targum" (Retrieved on 15th June, 2021 from https://www.oxfordbibliographies.com/view/document/obo-9780195393361/obo-9780195393361-0187.xml)

[14] Metzger, *The Bible in Translation*, 21.

[15] Kevin Cathcart, Michael Maher and Martin McNamara (eds.), *Targum Neofiti 1: Genesis* (Collegeville: The Liturgical Press, 1992), 33.

[16] Martin McNamara, *Targum and New Testament: Collected Essays* (Tubingen: Mohr Siebeck, 2011), 281.

iii.   And he [Moses] reached the mount, **above which the Glory of
          the Shekinah of the Lord was revealed** Horeb. (Targum Neofiti
          1, Exod. 3:1)[17]

iv.   And when the Canaanite, the king of Arad, who dwelt in the
          south heard **that Aaron, the pious man for whose merit the
          clouds of the Glory had led forth Israel had died (lit.: had
          been taken up), and that Miriam the prophetess, for whose
          merits the well used to come up for them, had died (lit.: had
          been taken up)**, that Israel had reached the way by which the
          spies used to come up (HT: the way of Atharim), he waged war
          on Israel and took some of them captive (Nf Num 21:1).[18]

v.   May Reuben live **in this world**, and not die **in the second
          death, in which the wicked die in the world to come.**[19]
          (Targum Neofiti 1, Deut. 33:6). (Boldened texts are the
          interpolations from targumists, emphasis mine)

The Targum version of Genesis 4:8 gives an extraordinarily expansive
paraphrase which supplies the reason why Cain killed his brother, Abel. The
reason, according to the Targumist, is a disagreement over the theological
subject of the relationship between God's attributes of mercy and justice.

> **Cain said to Abel his brother**, "Come, let us both go out into the field."
> And it came to pass, when they had gone out, both of them, into the
> field, that Cain spoke up and said to Abel, "I perceive that the world has
> been created through mercy, but it is not governed according to the
> fruit of good deeds; and there is partiality in judgment. Therefore, your
> offering was accepted with favor, but my offering was not accepted
> from me with favor." Abel answered and said to Cain, "The world was
> created with mercy, and it is governed according to the fruits of good
> deeds, and there is no partiality in judgment. It is because the fruit of
> my deeds was better than yours and more prompt than yours that my
> offering was accepted from me with favor." Cain answered and said to
> Abel, "There is no judgment, no judge, no other world; there is no fair
> reward given to the righteous nor punishment exacted from the

---

[17] Cathcart, Maher and McNamara (eds.), *Targum Neofiti 1*, 33.
[18] Cathcart, Maher and McNamara (eds.), *Targum Neofiti 1*, 33.
[19] Klaas Spronk, *Beatific Afterlife in Ancient Israel and in the Ancient Near East* (Neukirchen-Vluyn: Neukirchener Verlag, 1986), 14.

wicked." Abel answered and said to Cain, "There is judgment, there is a judge, and another world; there is fair reward given to the righteous and punishment exacted from the wicked." On account of these matters, they were quarreling in the open field. **And Cain rose up against Abel his brother**, and drove a stone into his forehead, and killed him.[20] (Emphasis mine).

There are instances where the Targum contradicts the Hebrew text because of the addition or deletion of the negative particle or the change of a negative particle to a positive one and vice versa. The Targum of Exodus 33:3 reads, "I will not remove **the Glory of my Shekinah** from among you" (the emphasized portion is an addition by the targumist), whiles the Hebrew text actually reads, "I will not go up among you." The Targum records Cain's cry, "Behold, you have driven me this day from upon the land, but it is not possible for me to be hidden from you," but the Hebrew text reads, "Behold, you have driven me this day from the land, and from your face I shall be hidden" (Gen. 4:14). The changes were motivated by the targumist's unwillingness to accept the seeming limitedness of God's presence and power.[21]

Some biblical texts were purposely not translated in public. The story of Reuben and Bilhah (Gen. 35:22), the story of Tamar (Gen. 38:13ff.), the account of the golden calf (Deut. 9:12–21), the account of David and Bathsheba (2 Sam. 11:7–17), and the story of Amnon (2 Sam. 13:1ff.) were not translated because they were considered offensive; also, the Priestly Blessing (Num. 6:24–26) was not translated due to its sacrosanct status.[22] The Targum also sometimes softened anthropomorphic expressions. The high reverence the targumists had for God came to play in how they dealt with God's immanence. For example, they referred to the Deity using such terminologies as "Word" (*memra*), "Glory" (*yeqara, iqar*), or "Presence" (*shekinah, shekinta*).[23] The use of surrogates in dealing with the Deity is evident in Genesis 1:17, where Targum Neofiti 1 reads, "the **Memra of the** Lord created the two luminaries (Gen 1:16) ... and the **Glory of the Lord** set them in the firmament" (Gen 1:17).[24]

---

[20] Metzger, *The Bible in Translation*, 23.
[21] Metzger, *The Bible in Translation*, 23.
[22] Metzger, *The Bible in Translation*, 21.
[23] Metzger, *The Bible in Translation*, 21.
[24] Cathcart, Maher and McNamara (eds.), *Targum Neofiti 1*, 36.

Other Ancient Versions

Christianity was born in a Greek-speaking society, and the New Testament was consequently written in Greek. However, as Christianity spread beyond the confines of the Hellenistic world, the need to translate the Bible into other languages became obvious. Later, other Greek translations were made in the early period by Aquila (ca. 130 AD), Symmachus and Theodotian (late 2nd century AD). Aquila's translation was so literal that Greek speakers found it difficult to understand it.[25] The translations of Symmachus and Theodotian were relatively less literal and more comprehensible.

In the second and third centuries (when Christianity had been introduced into Syria), churches and individual Christians in North Africa and Italy, and Egypt, needed copies of the Scriptures in their own languages. The demand for mother-tongue scriptures led to the production of versions in Syriac, Latin, and other dialects of Coptic used in Egypt. The Syriac version served newly converted Jews and/or new Christians living in the Mesopotamian region (Syria).[26] The revised Syriac Bible, known as the Peshitta (Aramaic means "Straight"), became the standard version of the Bible for churches in the Syriac tradition, including the Maronite Church, the Chaldean Catholic Church, the Syriac Catholic Church, the Syriac Orthodox Church, the Syro Malankara Catholic Church, the Assyrian Church of the East and the Syro Malabar Catholic Church.

These were followed in the fourth and succeeding centuries by other versions in Gothic, Armenian, Georgian, Ethiopic, Arabic, and Nubian in the East Old Church Slavonic, and (much later) Anglo-Saxon in the West. Two factors, namely, the degree of the translator's familiarity with the source biblical language and the receptor language as well as the attention devoted to the task of making the translation, were two major factors that determined the reliability of the translation produced.[27]

The early Middle Ages saw the production of The Gothic translations of the Bible. The Gothic language was spoken by the Goths who lived in Eastern Germany north of the Black Sea.[28] The Goths entered history in the third

---

[25] Kevin G. Smith, *Bible Translation and Relevance Theory the Translation of Titus* (Unpublished Doctorate Dissertation: University of Stellenbosch, 2000), 9

[26] Zogbo, "Bible, Jewish and Christian", 22.

[27] Bruce M. Metzger, *A Textual Commentary on The Greek New Testament: A Companion Volume to the United Bible Societies' Greek New Testament* (fourth revised edition) (Deutsche Bibelgesellschaft: D-Stuttgart, 2002), 4

[28] Metzger, *The Bible in Translation*, 38

century AD and soon split into two after their settlement. The Visigoths or West Goths moved farther westward due to the pressure of the advancing Huns, and the Ostrogoths settled in Pannonia. The Ostrogoths later (in 458 AD) went to Italy, defeated and killed the Italian king and established their kingdom with Ravenna as their capital. The Ostrogothic kingdom was defeated in the sixth century resulting in the gradual loss of identity of the Ostrogoths.[29] The Gothic Bible was the first literary work in any Germanic dialect. Ulfilas (c. 311–383 AD) was the son of a Cappadocian captive and a Gothic father, who was also known by his Gothic name Wulfila ("Little Wolf"). He encountered the Visigoths in Moesia and Dacia (modern Bulgaria and Romania) in the fourth century. He was a missionary and a Bible translator who created an alphabet (using Greek and Latin characters as well as elements of Gothic runes) and translated the Scriptures into his native tongue, Gothic.[30]

Ulfilas completed his translation two or three years before he died in 383 AD, and this translation was used by Goths who migrated to Spain and Italy. The Gothic language was influential in those days, and many copies of the Gothic Bible were made. Metzger lists the following surviving fragments of codices of the Wulfila Bible which date from the sixth to eight century: (a) Goth Codex Argenteus, which contains part of the four gospels (Matthew, John, Luke, and Mark); 6th century AD; (b) Goth Codex Ambrosianus A-E containing Pauline epistles; c. 6th-11th century; (c) Goth Codex Carolinus containing Romans 11-15; 6th or 7th century; (d) Goth Codex Vaticanus Latinus 5750 which is a commentary on John's gospel; 6th century: (e) Goth Codex Gissensis on Luke; 5th century.[31]

The Second Great Age of Bible Translation (400AD-1500AD)

The Second Great Age of Bible Translation was between the fourth century AD and 1500 (the Middle/Dark Ages).[32] Three phases—namely, translate into Latin, the second phase into English and the third phase into dialects of German, Dutch, French, Italian and Spanish—are involved in this period. Jerome's Latin Vulgate, which was produced by Jerome and others (in the years before and after 400 AD), became a major Bible translation in this era.

---

[29] Metzger, *The Bible in Translation,* 38
[30] Metzger, *The Bible in Translation,* 38.
[31] Metzger, *The Bible in Translation,* 39-40
[32] Orlinsky and Bratcher, *A History of Bible translation and the North American contribution,* 19.

The Vulgate was not the first Latin translation[33]; it was actually a revision of the existing Latin version using Greek and Hebrew as source texts. Several different editions, known collectively today as the "Old Latin," existed before Jerome's Vulgate. These versions might have originated from Latin-speaking Christians who lived outside Rome.[34] One reason for this was because the Church at Rome used Greek for official communication until the middle of the third century.[35] The Old Latin version existed before the beginning of the third century, and one finds North-African Church Fathers like Tertullian (ca. 150–ca. 220 AD) and Cyprian (ca. 200–258 AD) quoting from it. The same text differed in different copies of the Old Latin version, suggesting that different translators worked on it.[36] The Old Latin version usually agrees with the Greek text of Codex Bezae and the Old Syriac.[37] The arrangement of the Gospels in the Old Latin New Testament is Matthew, John, Luke, and Mark.[38]

Numerous versions of the old Latin version were produced. So many Latin manuscripts of the New Testament existed by the close of the fourth century, creating a confusing diversity that prompted the following lament by Augustine:

> Those who translated the Scriptures from Hebrew into Greek can be counted, but the Latin translators are out of all number. For in the early days of the faith, everyone who happened to gain possession of a Greek manuscript [of the New Testament] and thought he had any facility in both languages, however slight that might have been, attempted to make a translation.[39]

The need for a scholarly, authentic and authoritative standard Latin version of the Bible for enhancing the church's missionary and teaching activities was obvious. In Jerome's time, "Men read their Old Testament in the recension of Lucian, if they lived in the North, Asia Minor, or Greece; in that of Hesychius, if they belonged to the Delta or the valley of Nile; in Origen's Hexaplaric edition, if they were residents at Jerusalem or Caesarea."[40] The diversity of Latin translations resulted in the emergence of three types or families of texts,

---

[33] For example, Cicero (106-143 BCE) produced a Latin translation from the Greek version before Jerome's work

[34] Metzger, *The Bible in Translation*, 30.

[35] Metzger, *The Bible in Translation*, 30.

[36] Metzger, *The Bible in Translation*, 30.

[37] Metzger, *The Bible in Translation*, 30.

[38] Bediako, *History of the Bible*, 169.

[39] Augustine as cited in Metzger, *The Bible in Translation*, 31.

[40] Swete as cited in Geisler and Nix, *A General Introduction to the Bible*, 534.

namely, Cyprian (d. 258 AD) representing the African family, Irenaeus (ca. 130—ca. 200 AD) of southern Gaul representing the European family, and Augustine (d. 430) the Italian family.[41] Each text group was characterized by choice of words. For instance, the Greek word *phōs* ("light") appeared in the African text as lumen and in the European text as *lux*; also, the Greek term *dokimazō* ("to test," "to examine," "to prove", "to inspect") was rendered *clarificare* in the African text and *glorificare* in the European.[42]

Obviously, there was the need for a consistent, thorough revision and correction of the translation from the original sources. This situation prompted Bishop Damasus's selection of Jerome in 382 AD,[43] the most learned Christian scholar at the time, to produce a revised version of the Latin Bible so that Latin-speaking Christians could have an accurate, faithful and dependable Bible to use. Jerome was born to Christian parents in Stridon, Dalmatia, where he received his basic education until he went to Rome at age twelve. In Rome, he studied Greek and Latin for eight years and became a Christian at age nineteen. Having been baptized by the bishop of Rome, Jerome devoted himself to the service of the Lord and to a life of rigid abstinence. Between 374 and 379 AD, he worked for a Jewish rabbi as a Hebrew teacher. Jerome became a presbyter at Antioch and then went to Constantinople, where he became a disciple of Gregory Nazianzen. He became the secretary to Bishop Damascus of Rome. He had extensive knowledge of Greek and Hebrew.

Initially, Jerome was hesitant to undertake this project. He explained his hesitancy to the Bishop as follows:

> You urge me to revise the Old Latin version, and, as it were, to sit in judgment on the copies of the Scriptures that are now scattered throughout the world; and, inasmuch as they differ from one another, you would have me decide which of them agree with the original. The labor is one of love, but at the same time it is both perilous and presumptuous—for in judging others I must be content to be judged by all. . . .. Is there anyone learned or unlearned, who, when he takes the volume in his hands and perceives that what he reads does not suit his settled tastes, will not break out immediately into violent language and call me a forger and profane person for having the audacity to add anything to the ancient books, or to make any changes or corrections in

---

41 Metzger, *The Bible in Translation*, 31.
42 Metzger, *The Bible in Translation*, 31-32.
43 Geisler and Nix, *A General Introduction to the Bible*, 531.

them? Now there are two consoling reflections which enable me to hear the odium—in the first place, the command is given by you who are the supreme bishop; and secondly, even on the showing of those who revile us, readings at variance with the early copies cannot be right.[44]

Jerome finally resolved to undertake the project and completed the project in 405 AD.[45] Jerome started his project by translating the Psalms from the Septuagint into Latin. The Latin Vulgate became very useful because it was done more carefully than other Latin versions. Jerome revised the Old Latin version of the gospels and completed it in 383 AD. He did not do much revision on the rest of the New Testament. His interest in Hebrew grew along the line, and so he focused his attention on the Old Testament rather than thoroughly working on the rest of the New Testament.

The approach used was sense-for-sense rather than word-for-word. Jerome, in a letter to Pammchius entitled "The best kind of translator", made a distinction between word-for-word translation and sense-for-sense translation. This letter is considered "the founding document on Christian translation theory."[46] Robinson summarizes a famous quote from this document:

> In his letter to Pammachius (395 AD) Jerome... launched a divergent and more conflicted attack on literalism, coining the term sense-for-sense translating for a faithful middle ground between... literalism ... and ... free imitations ... but also, problematically, defending literal translations of Scripture, "where even the word order holds a mystery."[47]

The Vulgate was criticized on the basis of inconsistency. Some of the criticisms against Jerome's translation are as follows:[48]

    i.   In Matthew 4:3, Jerome replaced *panem nostrum cotidianum* (our daily bread) with *panem nostrum supersubstantialem* (our bread that sustains us) but failed to use the same expression in Luke 11:3.

---

[44] Jerome as cited in Geisler and Nix, *A General Introduction to the Bible*, 531.

[45] Geisler and Nix, *A General Introduction to the Bible*, 531.

[46] D. Robinson, *Western translation theory from Herodotus to Nietzsche* (Manchester and Northampton, MA: St. Jerome, 1997), 23.

[47] D. Robinson, "Literal translation," *Routledge Encyclopedia of Translation Studies* edited by Mona Baker (London: Routledge, 2003), 125.

[48] Orlinsky and Bratcher, *A History of Bible translation and the North American contribution*, 13-14.

ii.   In Matthew 4:5, Jerome changed *pinnam* (parapet) to *pinnaculum* (highest parapet) but did not do the same in Luke 4:9.

iii.   In John 17, the Greek word *doxazein* (glorify) is best represented in Latin by *glorificare* (glorify); Jerome, however, let *clarificare* stand, because of his desire to avoid avoidable changes.

There is no scholarly consensus regarding the text type used for Jerome's project. In the case of the Gospels, opinions are divided between Alexandrian and Byzantine text types. In spite of the numerous errors in the process of transmission and the criticisms that followed, Jerome's Vulgate still became the Official Bible of the Roman Catholic Church. The official commissioning of the Vulgate by Bishop Damasus (366-384 AD) and the fact that many more people at the time spoke Latin than Greek made the Vulgate have wide acceptance in the Church and a huge influence on culture. It served as reference material for the Armenian, Georgian, Ethiopic, Arabic, Persian and Gothic Bible translations, which took place later. The Vulgate "signaled a Romanisation of the faith, an inculturation or contextualization into the cultures and language of the new imperial Roman power."[49] Metzger affirms this point by asserting that "Whether one considers the Vulgate from a purely secular point of view, with its pervasive influence on the development of Latin into Romance languages, or whether one has in view only the specifically religious influence, the extent of its penetration into all areas of Western culture is almost beyond calculation."[50]

In the fourteenth century, John Wycliffe (c. 1330–1384 AD) and associates produced the premier English version of the Bible into English. Wycliffe became the king's chaplain in about 1366 AD and a holder of a doctorate degree in Theology in 1372 AD.[51] In 1374 AD he was sent to France to meet with papal authority and negotiate peace regarding church appointments in England.[52] The source text used for his translation was the contemporary manuscripts of the Latin Vulgate, and so his Bible included the Old Testament apocryphal/deuterocanonical books. Wycliffe's translation was motivated by his conviction that the Bible is to be applied to all aspects of people's life and hence must be available in all languages. He argued as follows:

---

[49] Mojola, *Issues in Bible Translation*,
[50] Metzger, *The Bible in Translation*, 29.
[51] Geisler and Nix, *A General Introduction to the Bible*, 547.
[52] Geisler and Nix, *A General Introduction to the Bible*, 547.

Christ and his Apostles taught the people in the language best known to them. It is certain that the truth of the Christian faith becomes more evident the more faith itself is known. Therefore, the doctrine should not only be in Latin but in the vulgar tongue and, as the faith of the church is contained in the Scriptures, the more these are known in a true sense the better. The laity ought to understand the faith and, as doctrines of our faith are in the Scriptures, believers should have the Scriptures in a language which they fully understand.[53]

In his Prologue, Wycliffe describes the four stages of his approach to translation. They include: (1) a collaborative effort of collecting old Bibles and glosses and establishing an authentic Latin source text; (2) a comparison of the versions; (3) counseling "with old grammarians and old divines" about hard words and complex meanings; and (4) translating as clearly as possible the "sentence" (that is, meaning), with the translation corrected by a group of collaborators.[54] Though it is difficult to ascertain if Wycliffe himself took part in the translation, it is clear that he was the brain and motivator behind the production of the Bible that became known as the Wycliffe Bible. The work was completed by his students and colleagues, John Purvey and Nicholas of Hereford, who produced two handwritten English versions of the Bible after his death. The first version came out in 1382 AD based on a very strict literal translation philosophy, while the second was produced in 1388 AD with free renderings where appropriate.[55] The second version replaced most of the Latinate constructions with natural English idioms, thereby reducing papal influence over the English people. The two versions of the Wycliffe Bible, first and second (or early and late), represent logical phases in the production of a vernacular Bible. "The Wycliffe Bible", then, refers to the Bible versions that resulted from efforts by a group of scholars of whom Wycliffe was the leading figure if not the chief executant.

The literal approach of Wycliffe's Bible is underlined by the following quote by F. F. Bruce: "the earlier Wycliffe version is an extremely literal rendering of the Latin original. Latin constructions and Latin word-order are preserved

---

[53] Cited in Christopher K. Lensch, "The Morningstar of the Reformation: John Wycliffe," *WRS Journal* 3(2), (1996): 16-22, 5.

[54] Susan Bassnet-McGuire, *History of Translation Theory BBT Book Production Series Volume 2: Readings in General Translation Theory*, pp. 5-29 (Stockholm: N.p, 1997), 11.

[55] Metzger, *The Bible in Translation*, 57.

even where they conflict with the English idiom."[56] The following text from the letter to the Hebrews illustrates this point:

> [1] Manyfold and many maner sum tym God speakinge to fadris in prophetis, at the [2] laste in thes daies spak to us in the sone: whom he hath ordeyned eir of alle thingis, and by whom he made the worldis. [3] The which whanne he is the schnynge of glorie and figure of his substaunce, and berynge alle thongs bi word of his vertu, makyng purgacioun of synnes, sittith on the righthalf of mageste in high thingis; [4] so moche maad betere than aungelis, by how moche he hath inherited a more different, or excellent, name bifore hem (Hebrews 1:1-4).

The Latin version is as follows:

> [1] *Multifariam et multis modis olim Deus loquens patribus in prophetis* [2] *novissime diebus istis locutus est nobis in Filio quem constituit heredem universorum per quem fecit et saecula* [3] *qui cum sit splendor gloriae et figura substantiae eius portansque omnia verbo virtutis suae purgationem peccatorum faciens sedit ad dexteram Maiestatis in excelsis* [4] *tanto melior angelis effectus quanto differentius prae illis nomen hereditavit.*

A comparison of this text with the Latin version shows how faithful Wycliffe was to the Latin text. Bruce observes as follows:

> Word for word the Wycliffe version corresponds to the Latin, even at the expense of natural English word-order, as in the last clause of verse 2, on "by whom he made and the wolrdis" (the idiomatic Latin *et* before *saecula* being represented literally by the unidiomatic English *and* before the *worldis*). Again, when a particle occurs in the Latin text, itis rendered by a particle in English, although English idiom very often prefers a subordinate clause to a participial construction. Thus, in verse 1, "God spekinge" is the literal equivalent of *Deus loquens*, but the familiar wording of the Authorized Version, "God, who ... spake", is much more in keeping with English usage; and in fact, the later Wycliffe version shows an appreciation of this, for in it the Epistle of Hebrews begins with eth words "God, that spak".[57]

The Wycliffe Bible was condemned and burned in 1415 AD. Purvey and Nicholas were jailed and forced to repudiate their teachings. In 1428 AD Pope Martin V ordered that Wycliffe's body be burned and his ashes thrown into River Swift at

---

[56] F. F. Bruce, *History of the Bible in English* (Cambridge: The Lutterworth Press, 2002), 15.
[57] Bruce, *History of the Bible in English*, 16.

Lutterworth.[58] About one hundred and eighty copies of the whole or of parts of the Wycliffe Bible have survived, mostly dating from before 1450 AD. The Wycliffe Bible had a huge influence on the development of the English language.

The fifteenth and sixteenth centuries saw the publication of Scriptures in their original languages. Up till this time, copies of the Bible could only be made by hand. The invention of the printing press in 1443 AD catalyzed the production of vernacular Bibles. In 1458 AD, the University of Paris started teaching Greek; the first Greek Grammar book was published in 1476 AD and the first Greek lexicon in 1492 AD. The first Hebrew Grammar book was published in 1503 AD and the first Hebrew lexicon in 1506 AD. The first printed Hebrew Bible was issued in 1488 AD, and the first printed version of the Greek New Testament, an edition of Desiderius Erasmus, was published in 1516 AD. More than eight Latin versions of the Bible were published in Europe before 1500 AD. Thus, the study of the grammar of the three languages (namely, Greek, Hebrew and Latin) gave birth to printed versions of the Bible in these languages. In addition, Johann Mentelin published a German Bible in 1466 AD based on the Vulgate. A number of European versions printed at that time include: Italian, 1471 AD; Spanish, 1478 AD; and French, 1487 AD. However, a printed English version was yet to appear.

Tyndale's translation became the next important English Bible after Wycliffe's Bible. The Tyndale's Bible refers to the translations of various books of the Bible by William Tyndale (c. 1494–1536 AD) in the 1500s. Tyndale's Bible was the first English translation to work directly from Hebrew and Greek texts. His English New Testament was produced based on the Greek edition of Desiderius Erasmus and published in 1525 AD.

The third phase is the translation of the Bible into dialects of German, Dutch, French, Italian and Spanish. Martin Luther's German version of the Bible (printed in 1534 AD) is one of the significant translations in this era. Like other Reformers, Luther did not rely on the Vulgate, but on the original Hebrew and Greek versions, for his translation. This made his translation different from earlier ones which were based on the Vulgate. Luther used these five principles in his translation: "(1) the priority of meaning; (2) the need to change linguistic form; (3) expression of implicit information; (4) retention of the original unnatural form in places; (5) the importance of discourse analysis to exegetical study." Luther's work differed from Jerome's in that the former was literal while the latter was dynamic (meaning-based). Luther's use of common language made his work accessible to the ordinary German. His translation was for common people and in the language of the people. He believed that a Bible in

---

[58] Metzger, *The Bible in Translation*, 57.

the language of the elite is not "the people's Bible." Therefore, the Bible must be read in German according to the German style and not those of Hebrew and Greek. He prioritized clarity and naturalness and was therefore careful to mediate between the German culture on the one side and biblical culture on the other side in such a way as to maintain a balance between them. Luther's work did not only standardize the German language but also served as a model for translations into several other languages that appeared later (especially in the sixteenth century). Of Luther, Robinson states that:

> Luther's most important contribution to translation theory lies in what might be called his "reader-orientation"... he formulates the standard principle that translations should be made out of good target-language words, idioms, syntactic structure, and the like ... [he] personalizes [the TL], humanizes it, blends it with the vitality of his own sense of self. In so doing ... he socializes it: what he internalizes is no ... fantasy-system but language as social communication, language [of] real-life speech situations.[59]

The sixteenth century also witnessed a number of other European (Protestant and Roman Catholic) versions of the Bible. Translations of the New Testament appeared in Portuguese in 1505 AD, Danish in 1529 AD (and again in 1550 AD), in Swedish in 1530 AD, in Czech between 1579 AD and 1593 AD and in Slavonic in 1581 AD. Translations and revised versions of existing translations continued to appear in English, Dutch, German and French.

Sixteenth-century Bible translations had close ties with the rise and spread of Protestantism in Europe. These translations aimed at: (1) clarifying errors arising from previous versions due to inadequate source language manuscripts or linguistic incompetence; (2) producing an accessible and aesthetically satisfying vernacular style; and (3) clarifying points of dogma and reduce the extent to which the scriptures were interpreted and re-presented to the lay people as a metatext.[60] Luther's extensive use of the verbs *übersetzen* ("to translate") and *verdeutschen* ("to Germanize") in his 1530 AD *Circular Letter on Translation* underscores the importance he attached to (2). He also stressed the importance of the relationship between style and meaning: "Grammar is necessary for declension, conjugation and construction of sentences, but in speech the meaning and subject matter must be considered, not the grammar, for the grammar shall not rule over the meaning." Etienne Dolet's 1540 AD publication entitled *La manière de bien*

---

[59] Robinson, *Western translation theory from Herodotus to Nietzsche*, 84.
[60] Susan Bassnet-McGuire, *History of Translation Theory*, 12.

traduire d'une langue en aultre (How to Translate Well from one Language into Another) established five translation principles (in order of significance): (1) The translator must fully understand the sense and meaning of the original author, although he is at liberty to clarify obscurities; (2) The translator should have a perfect knowledge of both source language and TL; (3) The translator should avoid word-for-word renderings; (4) The translator should use forms of speech in common use, and (5) The translator should choose and order words appropriately to produce the correct tone.[61]

The Authorized King James Version (AKJV) of 1611 AD is also one of the major translations in the history of the Christian Church. Before this version, Miles Coverdale had published an English Bible in 1535 AD. The AKJV became the official English version for the church in England and other English-speaking countries. The project was commissioned by King James and executed using the *Textus Receptus* (Latin for "received text") as the source language. This version has had a great influence on the church and the development of the English Language. Today, most Christians regard it as "the Bible" and perceive it as more sacred than other modern translations. The language used by the AKJV, both in poetry and prose, is so majestic and inspiring that it illustrates the potential of literary translation. The translation style is more literal than dynamic.

Different views on translation continued to emerge in the subsequent centuries. Towards the end of the eighteenth century, in 1791 AD, Alexander Fraser Tytler's *The Principles of Translation*, the first systematic study in English of the translation processes, was published in which he set up three basic principles: (1) The translation should give a complete transcript of the idea of the original work. (2) The style and manner of writing should be of the same character as that of the original. (3) The translation should have all the ease of the original composition. This work and others continued to influence translation theory and practice for so many years.

Bible Translation in the Missionary and Bible Societies Era

After the second epoch in the history of Bible Translation is the missionary and Bible Society era, which I consider in this section. In this period, Bible translation took place in many places within the context of Christian missions. Missionaries pioneered the translation of the Bible into various vernaculars to enhance the propagation of the gospel. The efforts by

---

[61] Etienne Dolet, "The Way to Translate Well from One Language to Another." *Translation Theory and Practice: A Historical Reader.* Eds. Daniel Weissbort and Astradur Eysteinsson (Oxford: Oxford University Press, 2002), 73-77.

missionaries in translating the Bible into other mother-tongues is discussed extensively in the next chapter with a focus on the African continent. Therefore, I will concentrate on the formation of various Bible Societies and how the Societies affected Bible translation.

The formation of Bible Societies in the nineteenth century facilitated Bible translation in many parts of the world. The formation of the Bible Society of England led subsequently to the formation of various Bible societies in other parts of the world: Dublin (1804 AD), East Pakistan (1811 AD), Ceylon (1812 AD), Ethiopia (1812 AD), Mauritius (1812 AD), the United States (the American Bible Society, 1816 AD) and South Africa (1820 AD) was very instrumental in various Bible translation projects. The story of the formation of the Bible Society of England is traced to Mary Jones, who at age fifteen, saved money for six years and walked twenty-five miles to own a Bible in her own language from the Reverend Thomas Charles, the seller of Welsh-language Bibles. Reverend Charles had just sold his last copy when Mary arrived, but he was so impressed with her diligence and determination to own a Bible that he gave it to her, telling her the other buyer would just have to wait. Mary's hunger for the Bible moved Reverend Charles to discuss with the Religious Tract Society in London (in 1802 AD) the need to help in the production of Bibles for the public. The Society had to turn him away because it was not part of their job description to produce Bibles. In the midst of this situation, the Reverend Joseph Hughes, a member of the Society, proposed that another Society be formed for the purpose of publishing Scriptures. Discussions went on from this time, and fifteen months later, the spark of Reverend Hughes' suggestion became a reality when The British and Foreign Bible Society was officially inaugurated on March 7, 1804. Other Bible Societies were formed following this model. The most important event that followed was the formation of the United Bible Societies (UBS) in 1946 to promote unity, co-operation and fellowship among the various Bible Societies. Today, the various Bible Societies in various countries are key to the publication and distribution of Bibles.

The SIL (or Wycliffe Bible Translators) was founded in 1942 by Cameron Townsend to support the work of Bible translation teams around the globe. The SIL has an interest in language learning and analysis to establish orthography of various languages and produce literacy material to enhance translation work. Initially, The SIL had the New Testament as its primary focus, but now their interest has shifted to the entire Bible. Other translation agencies include Pioneer Bible Translators, Lutheran Bible Translators and International Bible Translators.

The production of mother-tongue Scriptures took place at a very high rate after the formation of the various national Bible Societies. Taking English as an example, translations that have emerged include the American Standard

Version (1901), the Revised Standard Version (1952), the Jerusalem Bible (1966), Today's English Version, also known as the Good News Bible (TEV 1966, 1976, 1994; GNB, 1976), the Revised English Bible (1970), the New American Bible (1970), the New Living Bible (1971, 1989, 1996), the New Jerusalem Bible (1985), and the Contemporary English Version (CEV 1995).

Conclusion

Since the beginning of Bible translation, various events have taken place, and each of them has contributed to the development of translation work. Bible translation must certainly not be abandoned but continued because each language group needs to hear God speak to them in their own tongue. In this chapter, I have shown that the availability and quality of original language source texts and the methods and focus have changed over time. The history of Translation Studies should therefore be seen as an essential field of study for the contemporary theorist, but should not be approached from a narrowly fixed position. The historical survey is to equip modern translators to be in a better position to undertake their task by standing on the shoulders of past scholars in Translation Studies. While the present chapter focused mainly on Bible translation outside African (with the exception of the LXX), the next chapter considers the history of Bible Translation in Africa.

Review Exercise

1. Critically examine Bible translation before the Reformation. How relevant is this historical study to modern Bible translation?

2. How does Bible translation enhance literacy development? Use a named community as a case study.

3. Explain the philosophy behind Luther's translation. What contributions has this translation made to global Bible translation?

4. What role does the LXX play in modern Bible translation?

5. How relevant is the UBS in Christian mission?

6. The sixteenth century witnessed a number of Bible translation projects. What factor(s) accounted for this?

7. What should be the methodological framework of Translation Studies in your country?

Chapter 6

History of African Bible Translation

In the previous chapter, I examined the history of Bible translation from the pre-Christian era to the twentieth century. In this chapter, I focus on the history of Bible translation within the African context. According to Paul Bandia, "there is no doubt that translation has played an important role in ensuring communication and exchanges between the numerous linguistic and ethnocultural groups on the African continent" and that "given the continent's vast oral traditions and the many non-alphabetized languages, the writing of these cultures can be viewed in terms of translation."[1] Based on this assertion, the present chapter begins with the linguistic diversity in African, proceeds to examine ancient translations in African and finally gives regional accounts of Bible translation in the continent.

Diversity of African Languages

Statistics show that Africa has about two thousand languages, one-third of the world's six thousand languages. The numerous dialects pose a challenge to Africa in terms of completing a whole Bible in every language or dialect. Africa's languages fall into four main categories. The first category is the Niger-Congo, with about 1436 languages.[2] It is the largest language group in Africa in terms of the number of languages spoken within its geographical extent and the number of speakers. About 85 percent of Africa's population speak a Niger-Congo language. There are nine subdivisions: Mande, Kordofanian, Atlantic, Ijoid, Kru, Gur, Adamawa-Ubangi, Kwa, and Benue-Congo. About 500 languages in this category belong to the Bantu sub-family, which is spoken in most of Africa from southern Cameroon eastward to Kenya and southward to the southernmost tip of the continent. Twelve Bantu languages are spoken by more than five million people, including Rundi, Rwanda, Shona, Xhosa, Zulu, Sotho, Gciriku (Diriku), Yei (Yeye), and Mbukushu. South Africa has nine indigenous official languages distributed among four of the five language

---

[1] Paul Bandia, "Translation Matters: Linguistic and Cultural Representation" InTranslation Studies in Africa, edited by Judith Inggs and Libby Meintjes, 1–20 (London: Continuum, 2009), 2.

[2] Aloo O. Mojola, *Issues in Bible Translation: Navigating Troubling & Tempestuous Waters* (Nairobi: Tafsiri Printing Press, 2019), 126.

clusters, as follows: Nguni comprising isiZulu, isiXhosa, Siswati, isiNdebele; Sotho-Tswana comprising Sesotho, Setswana, Sepedi; Changana-Tsonga made of Xitsonga and Venda which includes Tshivenda. All these nine languages are Bantu languages.

The next is the Afroasiatic (formerly Hamito-Semitic, Semito-Hamitic, or Erythraean languages) which has a North-African origin and about 371 languages.[3] It comprises six main sub-families: Berber, Chadic, Cushitic, Egyptian, Omotic, and Semitic. The Nilo-Sahara language group, with about 196 sub-divisions, is also one of the four language stocks or families on the African continent.[4] Its sub-families include Kanuri (mainly in Nigeria), Nile Nubian, and the Nilotic languages Dinka (South Sudan), Kalenjin (Kenya), Luo (mainly in Kenya and Tanzania), and Teso (Uganda and Kenya). The last category is Khoisan with about 35 languages,[5] including Hadza, Sandawe, Khoe, Tuu, Kx'a.

With such a wide variety of languages in the continent and the high cost of translating the Bible into a language, the question of which language to consider in a translation project and which one to ignore (at least for the time being) is difficult. Another challenge is that of language clusters and political groupings in Africa. Sub-dialectical differences make Bible translation difficult because various sub-dialect speakers would insist that their sub-dialect be used for the translation. In situations where sub-dialects of a particular dialect differ widely, some sub-dialects are inevitably left out in translation. Language clusters are found in many places in Africa. Mojola gives the following clusters from Kenya: *Swahilli* cluster (comprising the Chimiini, Kitikuu (Bajuni), Kipate, Kisiyu, Kiamu, Kimvita, Chifundi, Kivumba, Kishirazi, Kijomvu, Kimtanata, Kipemba, Kitumbatu, Kihadimu, Kiunguja, Kingazija, Kinzwani; Bantu *Mijikenda* cluster comprising Giriama, Duruma, Rabai, Digo, Kauma, Chonyi, Jibana, Ribe and Chwaka; Bantu *Meru* cluster comprising Imentu, Igembe, Tigania and Miutini, Igoji, Tharaka, Nithi, Mwimbi-Muthambi and Chuka; the Nilotic *Kalenjin* cluster comprising Nandi, Kipsigis, Keiyo, Tugen, Markweta (Endo, Borokot, Almo, Kiptari, Sengwer, Cherang'any, Markweta), Sabaot (Sebei) and Pokot; the Nilotic *Maasai* cluster which extends from Southern Kenya into Tanzania including Samburu, Arusha, Kisongo, Parakuyo, Kajiado and Narok

---

[3] Mojola, *Issues in Bible Translation*, 126. See also Zygmunt Frajzyngier and Erin Shay, *The Afroasiatic Languages* (Cambridge: Cambridge University Press, 2020).
[4] Mojola, *Issues in Bible Translation*, 126.
[5] Mojola, *Issues in Bible Translation*, 126.

Maasai; Cushitic *Kenya Oromo* cluster comprising the Borana, Gabra, Sakuye, Garreh, Ajuran, Orma, Waata and Boni.[6]

Bible Translation in Africa before the Nineteenth Century

We have noted earlier that the LXX, the mother of all mother-tongue Bible translations, was translated in Africa, Alexandria (Egypt), which had a famous library serving as the world centre for the translation of every literature.[7] North Africa was the first part of the continent where the gospel message was first heard. As Christians in this area needed to have the Scripture in their own language, the need for translation arose. Before the end of the second century AD, some Christian communities in Alexandria had translated the Bible into Sahidic, an ancient Egyptian language.[8]

Other translations were done in Coptic dialects. The Coptic language is an Afro-Asiatic language spoken in Egypt from about the second century AD and represents the final phase of the ancient Egyptian language. In contrast to earlier stages of Egyptian, hieroglyphic writing, hieratic script, or demotic script were used, but Coptic (the final phase) was written in the Greek alphabet, supplemented by seven Egyptian-demotic letters used to express sounds that are absent in spoken Greek. Coptic is used mainly for religious literature that is translated from Greek. The dialects of the Coptic language in which Scriptures have been preserved to date include: (a) Sahidic dialect used in the area of Thebes (now Luxor); (b) Bohairic dialect, used in Alexandria and the Western Delta of the Nile and Lower or northern Egypt; (c) Achmimic dialect, used in the Panopolis region; (d) Asyuṭic, or Sub-Achmimic dialect[9], which stands between Achmimic and Middle Egyptian; (e) Middle Egyptian (the Oxyrhynchite dialect); and (f) Fayyumic dialect, used in the region of the Fayyum in Middle Egypt.[10] The Bohairic dialect is the most widely used, whereas Sahidic is the oldest. Coptic translations were first made in the third or fourth century AD and later revised. Several manuscripts of different parts of the Gospels exist today, the oldest ones dating from the fourth century.

---

[6] Mojola, *Issues in Bible Translation*, 4.

[7] Mojola, *Issues in Bible Translation*, 48.

[8] Mojola, *Issues in Bible Translation*, 48.

[9] Texts of the Gospel According to John, of the Acts of the Apostles and of Gnostic writings have been preserved in this dialect.

[10] Mojola, *Issues in Bible Translation*, 48; Metzger, *The Bible in Translation*, 36.

In the fifth century, about nine Syrian monks used the Ethiopic script to translate the Bible into Ge'ez, an Ethiopian language.[11] While the time and circumstances of the planting of the Ethiopian Church cannot be known with certainty, one may assume that the Ethiopian who got converted to Christ through Philip (Acts 8:26–39) introduced Christianity to Ethiopia. On the Ge'ez Bible, Elena Di Giovanni and Uoldelul Chelati Dirar assert that,

> Scholars agree that Ge'ez developed as a literary language from between the fifth and seventh centuries AD and connect this with introduction of Christianity into the region, which occurred in the fourth century. Thus, the development of Ge'ez language and literature can also be seen as the result of intense translation processes, mainly effected for religious purposes.[12]

This quote highlights the role of literary translation in the development of Ge'ez as a language from which other languages were derived. In other words, the translation of the Bible into the Ge'ez language ensured the preservation of the Ge'ez as a language or a tool for cultural expression. The translation of the Bible into Ge'ez constitutes the bulk of these activities that facilitated linguistic and theological debates.[13] The fact that the Ge'ez Bible translation brought about epistemological expansion is noted in the following quote: "It is also worth noting that these translation processes involved many books which are not part of the Biblical tradition in Western Christianity and that, to date, the oldest sources for many crucial documents on the history of Western and Eastern Christianity are mainly available in Ge'ez translations."[14] The Ge'ez Bible has 54 books in the Old Testament and has remained so up till now in the Ethiopian Orthodox Church.[15] Form the twelfth century, there was a political turmoil that shifted the center of power from Ge'ez dominated cultures to dominant Amharic areas.[16] By the sixteenth century, a linguistic dualism had emerged whereby Ge'ez remained the language of education, literacy and religion, and Amharic had become the dominant oral language in

---

[11] Mojola, *Issues in Bible Translation*, 49.
[12] Elena Di Giovanni and Uoldelul Chelati Dirar, "Reviewing Directionality in Writing and Translation: Notes for a History of Translation in the Horn of Africa," *Translation Studies: Routledge*, 8 (2) (2015): 175-190, 177.
[13] Di Giovanni and Dirar, "Reviewing Directionality in Writing and Translation," 177.
[14] Di Giovanni and Dirar, "Reviewing Directionality in Writing and Translation," 177.
[15] Mojola, *Issues in Bible Translation*, 49.
[16] Di Giovanni and Dirar, "Reviewing Directionality in Writing and Translation," 177.

the area.[17] The hierarchical relationship among indigenous languages in the region was greatly influenced by translation processes.

The Portuguese came to the African shores of the Reed (Red) Sea in 1541 AD to ally with the Abyssinian Empire in order that they might contain the Ottoman presence in the Red Sea region. Jesuit missionaries followed the Portuguese with a high determination to convert local Orthodox Christians to Catholicism. The proselyting campaign included the translation of Ge'ez literature into Latin. The indigenes reacted to this spiritual invasion by using Amharic to write religious texts for catechetical purposes. Consequently, by the seventeenth century, the Amharic had become a fully-fledged written language, basically as a reaction to Portuguese missionary encroachment.[18]

Nubia is also recorded to have a vernacular Bible. Nubia was the region that lay between Egypt and Ethiopia and consisted of three independent kingdoms. Christianity reached this land and flourished until the Islamic invasion led to the conversion of the people into the Islamic religion. There were also Nubian translations for lectionary purposes. Getting to the end of the twentieth century, fragments of the Nubian text of verses from John's Gospel and Revelation were found.[19] Apart from offering inspiration and examples, these ancient African mother-tongue translations do not have any impact on modern Bible translation in Africa. In the next section, I discuss four major developmental stages associated with modern Bible Translations in Africa. [20]

Modern Bible Translation in Africa

The Missionary Period

Modern African mother-tongue translation began in the context of Christian missionary activities. The first period of modern African Bible translation, the missionary period, can be traced to about 1800 AD, when European Protestant missionaries travelled around the globe to spread the Christian faith. About half a century later, many missionary-translated Bibles were published in African languages. Most of the missionaries who carried out the translation work in this period lacked formal training in exegesis, linguistics, theology and source languages. Missionaries followed the logic of the translatability of the Christian faith and submitted the Christian religion to the terms of indigenous culture.

---

[17] Di Giovanni and Dirar, "Reviewing Directionality in Writing and Translation," 177.
[18] Di Giovanni and Dirar, "Reviewing Directionality in Writing and Translation," 177.
[19] Metzger, *The Bible in Translation*, np.
[20] See Mojola, "Bible Translation in Africa", 206

The linguistic barrier that Christian missionaries faced made them realize the need to develop African vernaculars and subsequently have the Bible translated into the African mother-tongues. In this regard, missionaries were indigenizers rather than cultural imperialists.[21] Translation served as a catalyst for Christian mission, allowing indigenes to have vernacular expressions of the gospel and to assimilate the Christian faith.

The missionaries learnt the African language and, based on their understanding of the language and culture, gave a rendition of the Bible in African mother-tongue, usually based on a literal approach to translation. The model text used in most of these translations was the King James Version because of the belief that this version is more "inspired" than other versions.[22] In this era, the missionaries did virtually everything in the translation process and, if need be, employed the services of informants/assistants/helpers indigenous to the receptor culture. "During the missionary era, the role of mother-tongue speakers was ill-defined, and 'native assistants' often remained unnamed."[23]

> Bible translation in this period encountered some challenges. The first was a linguistic challenge in that African languages had not been developed. The missionaries had to carry out orthographic tasks such as establishing the alphabetical system, forming words, preparing grammar books and carrying out literacy campaigns. The second challenge was the difficulty in getting the needed funds for undertaking the task. Again, Bible translation in the missionary era was met with the challenge of the lack of exegetical, theological and translation expertise and aids. The unstable political situation, as well as health challenges, also hindered Bible translations in the missionary era.

The Missionary Revisions and Corrections Period

The second period of Bible translation in Africa is the missionary revisions and corrections era which covers the period from the publication of the first missionary translations to about the 1960s/1970s and beyond. The main task was to revise the Bibles that were produced under the missionary era with regards to orthographies, grammar, exegetical errors and format. The

---

[21] Lamin Sanneh, *Translating the Message: The Missionary Impact on Culture* (New York: Orbis Books, 2002), 90.

[22] Sidney K. Berman, *Analysing the Frames of a Bible: The Case of the Setswana Translations of the Book of Ruth* (PhD Dissertation: Stellenbosch University, 2014), 80.

[23] Zogbo, "Bible, Jewish and Christian", 23.

revisions were carried out by a team of theologically and linguistically competent people who were assisted by well-educated mother-tongue speakers.[24] The missionary translator served as the principal translator and employed the services of dependent or auxiliary native translators. The auxiliary translator differs from the informant in that the latter was usually illiterate while the former was literate, who could in some cases be asked to prepare the first draft to be checked by the missionary translator (who was to make the final decision on the translation).

This era coincided with the formation of Bible Societies in many parts of Africa. After some time, the Bible Societies assumed oversight responsibility of the various revisions that were going on. New projects were also started to have the Bible translated into other African mother tongues.

The Bible Societies Era

The emergence of various African Bible Societies (under the umbrella of the UBS) goes back to about 1960/70. For example, the Bible Society of South Africa was formed in 1965 to supervise and coordinate translation activities in southern Africa. The Bible Society of Ghana was also established in 1965 to ensure availability, affordability and accessibility to God's word. The main responsibilities of UBS included oversight, coordination, sponsorship and publication of translations. The UBS, through the national Bible Societies, facilitated translators' training programs and the appointment and training of Translation Consultants. Translation teams comprised native speakers, mission-appointed European translators and coordinators, and Consultants appointed by Bible Societies. In other words, native translators worked in their own languages with the help of missionaries who served as advisors/consultants/exegetes. The native translators received training in translation but still needed the help of foreign scholars for the quality control of the translation. The foreign scholar determined the validity of the translation. The translation approach saw a gradual progression from literal to more interpretive translation. This period saw the introduction of Nida's meaning-based dynamic equivalence to translation projects around the world (both within and outside of the UBS).[25] Nida's philosophy reached translators

---

[24] Aloo O. Mojola, "Bible Translation in Africa: What Implication does the New UBS Approach Have for Africa? An Overview in the Light of Emerging New UBS Translation Initiative," *Acta Theologica Supplementum*, 2, (2002): 200-213, at 205.

[25] S. Pattermore, "Framing Nida: The Relevance of Translation Theory in the United Bible Societies," *A History of Bible Translation* edited by P. A. Noss, pp. 217-263 (Rome: Edizioni di Storia e Letteratura, 2007), 219.

mainly through conferences, seminars and workshops. For example, in South Africa he presented papers at a conference for translators in 1967 and had translators' workshops in 1979, 1982 and 1985.

From the 1970s onwards, African Bible translations have been carried out by independent, well-trained translators working in their own languages, and making crucial decisions about the final form of their texts, though they may also receive technical help and advice from consultants and experts in the field of translation.[26] Yet, they are responsible for the final text. This shift addressed the limitations of foreign missionaries who had to learn the African mother tongue before undertaking translation works. The foregoing discussion supports Nida's observation (in 1991) that "when the United Bible Societies began, fully 90% of Bible translations in the Third World were being made by missionaries with the help of informants or translation helpers. Now in 90% of the projects, the translators are nationals, and missionaries have become the resource persons."[27] Smalley makes a similar point in the assertion that "overall, the balance has shifted again in considerable degree back toward people translating into their own language, with or without foreign consultants or assistance."[28] Today, there are various African mother-tongue translation projects going on throughout the continent, with most (human) resources coming from indigenes. The following quote by Zogbo accurately captures this point:

> While in the 1970s translator training was being discussed and encouraged, today, mother-tongue exegetes and translators are being trained at a very high level around the world. Undergraduate and graduate training programs, including studies in linguistics, communication theory, biblical exegesis, Hebrew and Greek, along with translation theory and practice, are producing highly qualified mother-tongue personnel. Whereas in the past most Bible translation consultants were Bible, Jewish and Christian Western expatriates, today's Bible translation consultants come from every continent on the globe.[29]

---

[26] Mojola, "Bible Translation in Africa," 205.
[27] Mojola, "Bible Translation in Africa," 206.
[28] Mojola, "Bible Translation in Africa," 205.
[29] Zogbo, "Bible, Jewish and Christian," 23-24.

Regional Accounts of Modern African Bible Translation

Bible Translation in East Africa

In East and Central Africa, Johann Ludwig Krapf (1810-1881) became the first missionary to translate the Scripture into the Swahili language. Krapf became impressed with the Swahili language when he realized its Arabic root and its wide geographical coverage.[30] He was one of a number of Lutherans trained at the Basel Missionary Institute who worked for the Church Missionary Society (CMS) in the early nineteenth century. Krapf was first posted to Ethiopia, where he worked from 1837 to 1842 before leaving for Cairo in order to fetch his bride.[31] Krapf went to Shoa together with C. W. Isenberg to visit Sahela Selasse of Ethiopia, hoping to evangelize the Oromo people so that he could extend his missionary tentacles to other parts of East Africa. He was allowed to establish a school at Shoa but was forbidden to preach the gospel in the pagan Oromo community.[32] In spite of the opposition, Krapf laid a solid foundation for Oromo missions by translating the Gospels into the Oromo language and, together with Isenberg, publishing an introduction to the Oromo language. In 1842 Krapf was forbidden by Sahela Sellase to return to Shoa, and he had to move to another part of the continent.

Krapf arrived in Zanzibar on the coast of East Africa on 7th January, 1844 in the service of the Anglican Church Missionary Society. As noted earlier, his stay in Ethiopia with the hope of evangelizing Shoa and the rest of Africa had ended in expulsion. He had embarked on translation works in Ethiopia, and in Kenya he continued this enterprise.[33] He joined the Church Missionary Society (CMS) in Kenya to participate in new Protestant mission initiatives in Christian Ethiopia. Krapf later moved to Mombasa, where he stayed for thirty (30) years and embarked on the study and development of local Kenyan dialects for the purpose of embarking on Bible Translation projects. He prepared wordlists for a number of Kenyan coastal dialects (Mijikenda languages such as Nyika and Kamba) and Kikamba language spoken in the

---

[30] Bengt Sundkler and Christopher Steed, *A History of the Church in Africa* (Cambridge: Cambridge University Press, 2000), 518.

[31] John Baur, *2000 years of Christianity in Africa: An African Church history* second edition (Nairobi: Paulines Publications Africa, 2018), 155.

[32] Baur, *2000 years of Christianity in Africa*, 155.

[33] Sundkler and Steed, *A History of the Church in Africa*, 517.

hinterland.[34] Later, Krapf was joined by two German missionaries Johannes Rebmann (1846) and Jacob Erhardt (1849), who assisted him in geographical exploration, contacts with African chiefs, Bible translation and missionary work.[35] Krapf moved from Mombasa to Rabai after Rebmann's arrival to continue his translation work. He prepared the grammar and dictionary of Kimvita Swahili and also drafted Kimvita Swahili New Testament (1846), thereby laying a foundation for the further development of the Kenyan languages and the translation of the Bible into the various Swahili dialects.

After Krapf came Bishop Edward Steere, a great Swahili linguist, who arrived in Zanzibar in 1864 as a missionary. Steere held the view that missionary work is "unsound without a vernacular Bible."[36] Using Krapf's work as a foundation, Steere mastered the Swahili of Zanzibar and then prepared a grammar book which he used as the basis for his Bible translation work. Steere produced the Swahili version of portions of Ruth and Jonah in 1868, Matthew's gospel in 1869 and then the complete New Testament (in 1880), the revised version of which was produced 1882 before his death in 1883.[37] The printing of the Swahili text and the binding of the Bible, including sewing the copies together, were all done by Steere himself.[38] In 1883, 5050 copies of the Swahili New Testament were shipped to Zanzibar. Steere also began the translation of Old Testament books such as Kings and Isaiah, and by the time of his death in 1883, there were the corrected proofs of Isaiah in Swahili. After his death, Steere's colleagues continued with the Swahili Bible translation project and published the entire Bible into the Swahili language (in 1891). Steere's Swahili translation influenced other leading East African vernaculars, such as George Pilkington's Luganda translation in the 1890s. In fact, Steere's translations were reference materials for several translations in East Africa, which took place just before the First World War.

---

[34] Mojola, Issues in Bible Translation, 53; Viera Pawlikova-Vilhanova, "Biblical Translations of Early Missionaries in East and Central Africa. I. Translations into Swahili," *Asian and African Studies*, 15 (2006): 80-89, 83; Sundkler and Steed, *A History of the Church in Africa*, 517.

[35] Sundkler and Steed, *A History of the Church in Africa*, 517

[36] Sundkler and Steed, *A History of the Church in Africa*, 525.

[37] Mojola, *Issues in Bible Translation*, 53; Pawlikova-Vilhanova, "Biblical Translations of Early Missionaries in East and Central Africa. I. Translations into Swahili," 84.

[38] Sundkler and Steed, *A History of the Church in Africa*, 525.

Bible Translation in West Africa

At the same time that Krapf was developing the East African languages, J. F. Schön, another Basel graduate and CMS employee, was also working on Hausa and Igbo, while Samuel Ajayi Crowther, his African counterpart, was working on the Yoruba New Testament, which was finally completed in 1884. Crowther was the leader of the CMS's Christian mission in the Niger Delta from 1857 to 1891. He was among the slaves rescued by British anti-slavery forces and released into the care of the Christian Mission Society in Sierra Leone in 1822. He was nurtured by the missionaries, who facilitated his conversion to Christ and thereafter sent him off to England to train as a missionary. He was ordained in 1843 as a minister of the Gospel. On January 9, 1844, Crowther preached in Yoruba for the first time in Freetown, Sierra Leone. His sermon was based on Luke 1:35, which he had translated into Yoruba as "... *ohun ohworh ti aobih ni inoh reh li aomakpe li omoh olorun*" (literally "... that holy one who is to be born will be called the son of God"). His efforts motivated two European missionaries, Henry Townsend and C. A. Gollmer, to develop a keen interest in the translation of Bible passages into Yoruba. In 1846 he went to Abeokuta as the first missionary to the land. He went with Townsend and Gollmer. He assisted with the codification and standardization of the Yoruba language and translated the Bible, the Book of Common Prayer and other religious texts into Yoruba (and subsequently Igbo), to enhance the dissemination of the Gospel within the Yoruba community and beyond. Crowther translated the New Testament of the Bible into Yoruba from 1850 to 1856. He continued the Yoruba Bible Translation Project and finally published the complete Yoruba Bible (*Bibeli Mimọ tabi Majẹmu lailai àti Tituncame*) in 1900. The Yoruba Bible was published by International Bible Association, Dallas, Texas. The right to publish the Bible was later transferred to the Bible Society of Nigeria, which has been printing it for decades now. In 1993, Kaybal Bible Mission Nig. INC published a new version of the Yoruba Bible (Bibeli Yoruba Atọ́ka) based on the 1974 Yoruba standard orthography. A Catholic version of Yoruba Bible (Bíbélì Mímọ̀ Atọ́ka ati Ìwé Deutero-Kànóníkà [Àpókrífà] appeared in 2002.

In Ghana, the history of mother-tongue Bible translation is traced to the mid-nineteenth century. Like other parts of the continent, this task was pioneered by foreign missionaries who had then realised that their work was negatively affected by language barrier. The missionaries were determined to help indigenes hear the gospel message and read the entire Bible in their own languages. There were indigenous people who also helped in translating the Bible and other Christian literature into Ghanaian languages. For example, Jacobus Elisa Joannes Capitein (1717-1747) was an indigenous minister who translated the Lord's Prayer from Old Dutch to Fante. Capitein (ca. 1717-1747) was a Christian minister of Ghanaian birth who became one of the first known sub-Saharan Africans to study at an European university and one of the first Africans to be ordained as a minister in the Dutch Reformed Church. He translated the Lord's Prayer into Fante, his native language. A careful study of Capitein's work on the Lord's Prayer reveals that he "made good use of his solid academic background and ministerial formation in the Netherlands in order to approach his translation task scientifically, artistically, and under the deep conviction that divine guidance was crucial for an effective mother tongue translation."[39]

Capitein's translation of the Lord's Prayer was informed by his African communal worldview. He translated the first line as *Hɛn nyina hɛn Egya a ntsi ɔwɔ sor* (Matt. 6:9b) "The Father **of us all** who is unquestionably in the exalted place above."[40] Capitein's reference to God as "The Father **of us all**" reflects the worldview of his audience, the Akan in general and Edina in particular, who express this thought in the saying *Nyimpa nyinaa yɛ Nyame nye mba* ("All humans are God's children"). More importantly, Capitein's idea that God is the Father of all humans draws on the doctrine of the *Imago Dei* to underline his opposition to the ruthless exploitation, enslavement and humiliation that characterized the slave trade of his day. He used his translation to make the point that all humans are the children of God and God's image-bearers; therefore, it is both theologically and ethically wrong to maltreat any of God's children based on race, color, gender, and other factors.

The Ga, Akuapem-Twi, Ewe and Fante were the first languages to benefit from the translation enterprise. The missionaries first translated portions of the Gospels and later parts of the rest of the New Testament to help linguistic and literacy development. Johann Gottlieb Christaller translated the four Gospels and the Acts into Akuapem-Twi. He worked hard to produce a comprehensive Twi grammar book in 1875.[41] Johannes Zimmerman translated the four Gospels into Ga in 1855 and published a Grammar book and a Dictionary in Ga in 1857.[42] The Ga New Testament was published in 1859, while the Akuapem-Twi New Testament came out in 1863. The Ewes and Fantes had portions of the Bible published in their

---

[39] John D. K. Ekem, "Jacobus Capitein's Translation of 'The Lord's Prayer' into Mfantse: An Example of Creative Mother Tongue Hermeneutics," *Ghana Bulletin of Theology*, Vol. 2 (2007): 66-79, 75.

[40] Ekem, "Jacobus Capitein's Translation of 'The Lord's Prayer' into Mfantse," 75. The Greek text reads: Πάτερ ἡμῶν ὁ ἐν τοῖς οὐρανοῖς· ("Our Father who art in heaven").

[41] J. Kofi Agbeti, *West African Church History: Christian Missions and Church Foundations 1482-1919* (Leiden: E. J. Brill, 1986), 69.

[42] Agbeti, *Church History*, 69.

languages in 1858 and 1896, respectively. The Ewe New Testament came out in 1877. The complete translations of the whole Bible into Ga, Akuapem-Twi, Ewe and Fante were achieved in 1866, 1871, 1913 and 1948, respectively. Later, various attempts were made to produce a unified Akan orthography to be used for a unified Akan Bible. This attempt however failed. Today, Fante, Asante-Twi, and Akuapem-Twi Bibles exist for the Akan community. Bono-Twi, which is also part of the Akan language, is also being worked on.

Bible Translation in Southern Africa

Robert Moffat (1795-1883), a British missionary, was the first missionary translator in the southern part of Africa. Moffat was sent by the London Missionary Society in 1817 to Southern Africa, and he worked mainly in Botswana. He translated the Lukan gospel into Tswana (Setswana) in 1830, the New Testament in 1840 and the entire Bible in 1857.[43] Moffat's missionary and translation activities took place in the period of colonization when Europe was seeking to expand outside its boundaries for territory. Moffat, like most other early missionaries, learnt indigenous African languages to enhance his work. He learnt the Setswana language on his own, having realized that the indigenes could not teach him due to a lack of literacy materials on the language at that time. He explained as follows:

> The acquisition of the language was an object of the first importance. This was to be done under circumstances the most unfavorable, as there was neither time nor place of retirement for study, and no interpreter worthy the name. A few, and but a few words were collected, and these very incorrect, from the ignorance of the interpreter of the grammatical structure either of his own or the Dutch language, through which medium all our intercourse was carried on. It was something like groping in the dark, and many were the ludicrous blunders I made. The more waggish of those from whom I occasionally obtained sentences and forms of speech, would richly enjoy the fun, if they succeeded in leading me into egregious mistakes and shameful blunders; but though I had to pay dearly for my credulity, I learned something.[44]

---

[43] Mojola, *Issues in Bible Translation*, 51.
[44] Moffat quoted in Itumeleng Daniel Mothoagae and Boshadi Mary Semenya, "The Operation of Memory in Translation: On Moffat's Desecration of the Batswana Linguistic Heritage in The Production of the 1857 English-Setswana Bible," *Studia Historiae Ecclesiasticae* 41 (3), (2015): 44–62, 48-49.

Moffat relied on the language he learnt to translate the 1611 KJV into the Setswana dialect. Like other Bibles produced by missionaries, Moffat's Bible was not without challenges. His rendering of "demons" with the Setswana expression "*Badimo*" ("ancestors") was one of the serious issues. In Setswana traditional worldview, *Badimo* are sacred and friends of the living; in fact, they are the living dead who are capable of blessing their living relatives. Take, for instance, the story of Jesus and the demoniac of Gadarene (Matt. 8:28-34). One finds the *Badimo* trembling and begging Jesus to leave them alone, to spare them or to cast them into pigs that ran away and drowned in the sea (v. 32). Moffat's characterization maintains Jesus as holy but assigns a new role to *Badimo,* which is unacceptable in the Setswana socio-religious worldview. It is noted by the Comaroffs that "Moffat's use of *Badimo* (ancestors) to denote demons ... did violence to both biblical and conventional Tswana [Setswana] usage."[45] Musa Dube remarks:

> It is hard to avoid thinking about the Setswana readers/hearers who first read the Setswana Bible in 1857 and those who continued to read it for the next 150 years that followed: Did these Setswana readers/hearers discover their own *Badimo* as devils and demons? Did the written Setswana Bible prove to them that they were lost and knew no God so much so that they venerated demons and devils as sacred beings?[46]

Christianity came to South Africa in 1652, but serious missionary outreach to the indigenous population only began in the nineteenth century. Bible translation work in South Africa began in the nineteenth century through missionary activities. Early Bible translation projects were undertaken by an individual or a group of missionaries. The Wesleyan Missionary Society were the first to translate the Bible into Xhosa. The missionaries who were involved included William Boyer, William Shaw, W. J. Shrewsburg and Richard Haddy. They completed the Xhosa New Testament in 1846 and the entire Bible in 1859. The Zulu Bible translation project was pioneered by the American Zulu Mission of the American Board of Commissioners of Foreign Missions, who came to Durban in 1835.[47] The missionaries, including George Champion, J.

---

[45] As cited in Musa W. Dube, "Consuming A Cultural Bomb: Translating *Badimo* into 'Demons' in the Setswana Bible" in *Postcoloniality, Translation, and the Bible in Africa* edited by Musa W. Dube and R. S. Wafula, pp. 3-25 (Eugene, OR: Pickwick Publications, 2017), 10.

[46] Dube, "Consuming A Cultural Bomb: Translating *Badimo* into 'Demons' in the Setswana Bible", 10.

[47] Mojola, *Issues in Bible Translation,* 52.

C. Bryant and Lewis Grout, translated portions of Matthew which was published in 1848; the New Testament was published in 1865 and the entire Bible in 1883.[48]

The account of Bible translation into Oshikwanyama dialect (of the Oukwanyama people of Nambia) also highlights the fact that early Christian evangelism went hand in hand with Bible translation. As soon as a Christian community was established in Oukwanyama,[49] the need for translating the Bible into the native language became obvious. Two missionary groups visited the land in the late nineteenth century. The Finnish missionaries from the Finnish Missionary Society (FMS) arrived in 1870 and stayed only for a short period.[50] It is not, however, clear whether the Oshikwanyama Bible translation project was initiated by the missionaries or the indigenes. On the one hand, the missionaries needed the translation to enhance their work, and on the other hand, the indigenous were eager to have the Bible in their language to understand God's word better.[51] In the early 1850s, some Oukwanyama pastors, namely Vilho Kaulinge, Paulus Nailenge, and Simson Shituwa, asked the Finish Missionaries to produce a Bible for them in their own tongue.[52] Initially, the missionaries were reluctant to work on the Oshikwanyama Bible; however, pressure from the native saw the commencement of the Oshikwanyama Bible project. The translation of the Bible into Oshikwanyama went through different stages, namely, the German Missionary era, and the Finnish missionary and Bible Societies era.

The German missionaries from the Rhenish Missionary Society (RMS) arrived on 3rd September, 1891 and stayed for twenty-five years (1891-1916). The first German missionaries to arrive in Oukwanyama were Friedrich Meisenholl, August Wulfhorst, Herman Tonjes, Heinrich Welsch, Albert Hochstrate, Schar, and Paul Schulte. In addition to preaching and building mission stations, the German missionaries studied the Oshikwanyama language and cultural traditions with the aim of preparing literacy material for the people and translating the Bible into their language. They first learnt the Otjiherero dialect, which has similar lexical items as the Oshikwanyama dialect. Farmers and other people who came into contact with the

---

[48] Mojola, *Issues in Bible Translation*, 52.

[49] *Oukwanyama* is the largest sub-group of Oshiwambo-speaking people who migrated from central Africa around the 1600s.

[50] Martin Ngodji, *The Story of the Bible Among Ovakwanyama: The Agency of Indigenous Translators* (Master of Theology Thesis: University of KwaZulu-Natal, 2004), 33.

[51] Ngodji, *The Story of the Bible Among Ovakwanyama*, 48.

[52] Ngodji, *The Story of the Bible Among Ovakwanyama*, 48.

missionaries introduced them to the native dialects, thus giving them the basic knowledge of the local dialect to start the translation project with.

Missionary Peter Heinrich Brincker was instrumental in the translation. He translated the Small Catechisms of Martin Luther into Oshikwanyama, published the first literature book in Oshikwanyama called ABD, which was first used to teach the Ovakwanyama how to read and write and translated The Acts of the Apostles, and the First Epistle of John; all of these were done in a year (1902).[53] By the time that the German missionaries left Oukwanyama in 1916, they had translated the New Testament and Psalms into Oshikwanyama. Paul Schulte was sent to Oukwanyama to complete the translation project. He continued the work with the assistance of teachers Mika Ngiyoonanye and David Nghilokwa until the manuscript was ready in 1940.[54] During the Second World War, part of the manuscript which was kept at Karibib got burnt but was replaced. However, when the time came for printing, the manuscript could not be sent for printing because the print-ready manuscript was stored at Karibib by the Rhenish Missionary Society.[55] The Oshindonga manuscript (Oshindonga is another local Namibian dialect) was available to be sent to London for printing because it was kept by the FMS at Olukonda.[56]

The FMS took over and, with new strategies and principles, worked to have the Bible in three dialects, Oshindonga, Oshikwanyama and Rukwangali (Kavango).[57] There was an initial attempt to produce only one Bible for the people speaking these languages. However, at a translation committee meeting held in 1937, a conclusion was reached that there is no way the three languages (Oshindonga, Oshikwanyama and Rukwangali) could be fused into one because the local people could not be forced to change their native tongue.[58] The Finnish missionaries began the translation of the Bible into Oshikwanyama in 1957 and completed it in 1974.

The translation of the Bible into the Shona language also took place in a missionary context in the 1890s. The Shona language (comprising the Karanga, Zezuru, Korekore, Mayinka and Ndau dialects) is a Bantu language spoken by many people in Zimbabwe and some parts of Mozambique, Botswana and Zambia. Christianity was introduced in Zimbabwe in the context of colonization which began with the arrival of British politician Cecil

---

[53] Ngodji, *The Story of the Bible Among Ovakwanyama*, 51.
[54] Ngodji, *The Story of the Bible Among Ovakwanyama*, 53.
[55] Ngodji, *The Story of the Bible Among Ovakwanyama*, 53.
[56] Ngodji, *The Story of the Bible Among Ovakwanyama*, 53.
[57] Ngodji, *The Story of the Bible Among Ovakwanyama*, 57.
[58] Ngodji, *The Story of the Bible Among Ovakwanyama*, 58.

John Rhodes (5 July 1853–26 March 1902) to the land in 1890. Many earlier attempts to evangelize Zimbabwe had failed.[59] The missionaries who accompanied Rhodes' Pioneer Column, upon arriving in Harare, divided the region around Harare amongst themselves.[60] Soon they realized that the success of their mission was dependent on the translation of the Bible into the vernacular of the people. The Shona Bible translation project took place in various phases. The first stage comprises efforts by different missionary groups to translate different biblical passages and other Christian literature for Christian worship.[61] An example of such efforts was Andrew Louw's translation which he refers to in the following notes which he wrote in his diary in 1891: "Today I found time to review the translation of Psalm 23, John 3:16 and 'Our Father.'"[62] Louw completed the Karanga (Shona dialect spoken in southern Shona) version of the Markan gospel in 1897 and the full Shona New Testament in 1900.[63]

At the same time, there were other translation projects undertaken by other missionaries in other parts of the country. John White, a Methodist missionary, translated the Gospel of Mark into the Shona dialect of Zezuru and published it in 1898, following it with the Zezuru version of John in 1903 and the full Zezuru New Testament in 1907.[64]

The Manyika Bible translation project was pioneered by E.H. Etheridge, who first translated the Gospels and Acts and subsequently completed the full Manyika New Testament in 1908. The Ndau New Testament was also completed before 1910. Therefore, by 1910 there were four versions of the New Testament in Shona in Karanga, Manyika, Zezuru and Ndau, showing remarkable theological and orthographic differences due to differences in theological and linguistic backgrounds of the translators who undertook the projects.[65]

The situation led to the quest for a common and standardized orthography as the basis for a common Bible translation for the Shona people. After many meetings and debates over the subject, a standardized Shona orthography— called "Union Shona" orthography, which unified the five Shona dialects—was

---

[59] Lovemore Togarasei, *The Bible in Context Essay Collection* edited by Joachim Kügler, Lovemore Togarasei and Masiiwa R. Gunda (Bamberg: University of Bamberg Press 2009), 20.

[60] Togarasei, *The Bible in Context Essay Collection*, 21.

[61] Togarasei, *The Bible in Context Essay Collection*, 22.

[62] Togarasei, *The Bible in Context Essay Collection*, 22.

[63] Togarasei, *The Bible in Context Essay Collection*, 22.

[64] Togarasei, *The Bible in Context Essay Collection*, 22-23.

[65] Togarasei, *The Bible in Context Essay Collection*, 23.

prepared and approved by the government in 1931.[66] A Union Shona New Testament was prepared by Louw and published by the British and Foreign Bible Society in 1941. The translation was accepted but criticized as been Karanga biased. Louw continued with the Old Testament and in 1950 the whole Bible in Union Shona was published.[67] Louw resolved the issue of dialectical differences by appending to the Bible a glossary of words in other dialects.

Conclusion

The survey of Bible Translation projects in Africa has shown Africa's impressive contribution to global Bible Translations studies and projects. The cases used in the discussions were picked from various regions of the continent. The issue of how the sub-dialectical differences among the Shona was resolved through the formation of a unified Shona orthography has great lessons for many African societies with sub-dialectical differences. I believe (based on my experience as a translator) that the best way is to find a way of unifying the various sub-dialects so that one Bible version can benefit the various communities who use the language in question. This must, however, be done through consultations and consensus building.

Review Exercise

1. Give a brief account of the pioneering Bible translation projects in your country. What lessons can contemporary African translators learn from it?

2. Discuss the assertion that "Missionary translations in Africa ended up distorting God's word due to the translators' lack of adequate understanding of the African languages into which the translated the Bible."

3. Discuss the role of the translator as a cultural mediator with reference to the translation work pioneering indigenous translators like Ajayi Crowther, Jacobus Capitein or any other from your context.

4. What contributions has Africa made to Bible translation globally?

5. What four major stages has Bible translation in Africa gone through since missionary Christianity? Explain each of them.

---

[66] Togarasei, *The Bible in Context Essay Collection*, 24.
[67] Togarasei, *The Bible in Context Essay Collection*, 25.

Chapter 7

Major Theories of Bible Translation

Translation theories are the methodologies, approaches or strategies used in rendering a text from one language into another. Since the emergence of translation activities, various philosophies and theories of translation have emerged. Different scholars have argued for different theories of translation, including literalist, relevance, interpretive, functionalist, descriptive, text-linguistic, comparative, professional, literary-rhetorical and intercultural approaches. Three key factors account for the diversity in translation theories: "(1) the nature of the message, (2) the purpose or purposes of the author and, by proxy, of the translator, and (3) the type of audience."[1] None of the theories of translation is adequate to translate the entire Bible because of the complex nature of the process of translation. Translation is an interdisciplinary exercise that draws from academic fields such as linguistics, sociolinguistics, psychology, sociology, cultural anthropology, communication theory, literary criticism, aesthetics, and sociosemiotics. In an introductory study like this, one cannot delve into each of these methodologies. What I offer in this chapter is a brief outline of three key theories, namely, linguistic approaches, equivalence theories and functional theories of translation. I have chosen to discuss these not only because they are the most influential but also because they relate with the other theories at one point or the other; therefore, by discussing these three theories, the others are indirectly catered for to some extent.

Linguistic Approach (Formal Equivalence)

The formal equivalence (also called literal equivalence) theory of translation is the best-known representative of linguistic approaches to translation. The word literal derives from the Latin word *littera,* which means "letter." A literal translation is concerned with the very letters (that is, the actual words formed by the letters) and purposes to follow and represent the exact words of the source text in the receptor text. Thus, in this approach, the basic unit of translation is the word. Therefore, a literal translation renders text from one language to another (that is, from the original language into the receptor language) one word at a time with or without conveying the sense of the

---

[1] Nida, "Principles of Correspondence," 126.

original whole. The main objective is to achieve such correspondences as "phrase for phrase, poetry for poetry, sentence for sentence or concept for concept." This type of translation has been described as a "gloss translation" aimed at allowing the reader to understand as much of the source language context as possible. Robert P. Martin gives the following description of the formal equivalence approach to translation:

> With this philosophical orientation, the translator is ... concerned that paragraph corresponds to paragraph, sentence to sentence, clause to clause, phrase to phrase, and word to word. The formal equivalence philosophy or method of translating attempts to say "what" the original text says by retaining "how" it says it (as far as [receptor language] grammar allows). Although clear [receptor language] expression does not always allow the formal equivalence translator to do so, he tries not to adjust the idioms which the original writer used; rather he attempts to render them more or less literally...[2]

The following quote by the English Standard Version (ESV) Committee is significant at this point:

> The ESV is an "essentially literal" translation that seeks as far as possible to capture the precise wording of the original text and the personal style of each Bible writer. As such, its emphasis is on "word-for-word" correspondence, at the same time taking into account differences of grammar, syntax, and idiom between current literary English and the original languages. Thus, it seeks to be transparent to the original text, letting the reader see as directly as possible the structure and meaning of the original.[3]

The accuracy and correctness of a translation based on this theory are determined by comparing the message in the receptor culture with the message in the source culture. This approach seeks to have equivalence between words in the source and target languages. For example, the English word "door" translates as "pono" in Akan (Bono); therefore, one can say, "door" = "pono". Here, what matters is the semantic relationship between these two words, not their context of usage or cultural connotation in their respective languages.

---

[2] Robert P. Martin, *Accuracy of Translation and the New International Version* (Edinburgh: The Banner of Truth Trust, 1989), 8.

[3] *The Holy Bible: English Standard Version* (Peabody, ME: Hendrickson Publishers, 2009), ix.

The formal equivalence theory argues that the best way to help the reader to better understand the Bible world is to be literal. Again, if the Bible is the word of God, then there is no legitimate reason to modify the biblical text unless it becomes inevitable. This theory is based on dogmatic presuppositions, specifically the mechanical theory of inspiration of Scripture. It assumes that translation involves conveying the vocabulary terms and grammatical forms of the source text. It, therefore, emphasizes fidelity to the lexical details and grammatical structure of the original language. All translations involve some form of interpretation. The formal equivalence approach keeps this at the barest minimum because this philosophy holds that interpretation is the work of expositors, commentators and exegetes, not translators. Therefore, the translator should be interested in what the text says, not what it means (which should be left to the expositor, commentator or the exegete). Literal translations are very "useful for theological students who wish to know something about the wording of the original text but do not read Hebrew or Greek."[4]

Nonetheless, the literal approach to translation has been criticized for insensitivity to the linguistic and socio-cultural contexts of the receptor community. It has the tendency of distorting the grammatical and stylistic patterns of the receptor language and hence distorting the message. Words are generally not used in isolation; therefore, by paying no attention to contextual issues, this approach has the tendency of leading to obscure translations. More so, this approach becomes inadequate in cases where there is no literal equivalence of a word in the source language in the receptor language or where one word has different meanings in one or both of the languages. In most African societies, for example, there is no literal equivalence for pomegranates (cf. Exod. 28:34). Translators are, in such circumstances, compelled to look for the closest equivalence in their setting. In practice, it is extremely rare to achieve absolute formal equivalence between two words. Consequently, a literal translation of a word may at times pose hermeneutical and exegetical problems to its readers. The New American Standard Bible (NASB, 1971) and its significant revision, the New American Standard Bible, Updated Edition (NASU, 1995); the King James II (KJ II, 1971); the New King James Version (NKJV, 1982); and the New Revised Standard Version (NRSV, 1989) are examples of translations based on formal equivalence.

---

[4] Ernst R. Wendland, "Theology and ministry in Africa through Bible translation: 'How firm a foundation?'," *The Bible Translator* 57(4), (2006): 206-216, 208.

Equivalence Theory (Dynamic/Functional Equivalence)

Until the middle of the twentieth century, most translations followed the literal approach. In the middle of the twentieth century, Eugene Albert Nida led a campaign towards the establishment of another approach to Bible translation, the "dynamic equivalence" theory. Nida argued that translation falls within the general domain of communication. Based on the code model of communication, he made two fundamental assumptions, namely, any message can be communicated to any addressee in any language if the most effective form of expression is found, and humans share a core of universal experience which makes such communication possible. The dynamic equivalence theory is the "quality of a translation in which the message of the original text has been so transported into the receptor language that the response of the receptor is essentially like that of the original receptors."[5] Nida's aim was to shift attention from word-for-word translation (or strict arrangement of words, grammar or syntax as in source text) to thought-for-thought translation, which seeks to make the receptor the focus of the communication.

For Nida, the goal of translation is to produce the total "dynamic" or "meaning" character of the original text. The translator is not under any obligation to retain the form of the source text. The expression "dynamic equivalence" means "the closest natural equivalent to the source-language message."[6] There are three key terms in this definition. The first term is "equivalent", which relates to the message carried by the source text/language; the second is "natural", which relates to the receptor language; and the third, "closest," combines the two orientations on the basis of the highest degree of approximation.[7] Said differently, a translation must attempt to produce an equivalent response from the new audience as the source text produced from the original audience; it must be natural in that it must fit the receptor language and culture as a whole, the context of the particular message, and the receptor-language audience; and must be closest in that it must bind the two orientations together on the basis of the highest degree of approximation.

In this approach, meaning is of primary importance, and the style of the source language (Aramaic, Hebrew or Greek) is of secondary importance. According to Nida, "Since no two languages are identical, either in the meanings given to corresponding symbols or in the ways in which such

---

[5] Eugene Albert Nida and Charles Russell Taber, *The Theory and Practice of Translation* (Leiden: Brill, 2003), 200.
[6] Nida, "Principles of Correspondence", 136
[7] Nida, "Principles of Correspondence", 136.

symbols are arranged in phrases and sentences, it stands to reason that there can be no absolute correspondence between languages. Hence there can be no fully exact translations."[8] Therefore, there is room for semantic adjustments in dealing with special difficulties associated with idiomatic, pleonastic, formulaic, and figurative expressions. Nida's approach also gives room for various kinds of structural adjustments at the discourse, sentence and word levels. There must be equivalence between the function of the source text in the source culture and the function of the target text (translation) in the target culture. In this sense, "function" can be thought of as a property of the text.

Dynamic equivalence gives the modern reader a text that will produce the same response as the original hearers of the same text.[9] To achieve this, dynamic equivalence translation goes through a three-fold process of analysis, transfer, and restructuring. The translator analyzes (interprets) the original text in terms of grammatical relations to know the meaning of the words and combination of words to the original audience, transfers that meaning to the modern reader in a way that bridges the gap between the language and culture of the biblical world and those of the contemporary world, and restructures the message in a way that sounds natural and acceptable in the receptor language.[10]

The dynamic equivalent theory is useful in making difficult theological concepts clear. For example, a comparison between the RSV's literal rendering of Romans 3: 28 and the dynamic equivalent rendering of TEV and CEV shows that the latter translations make the message clearer to contemporary speakers of English than the former translation.

RSV: For we hold that a man is justified by faith apart from works of law.

TEV: For we conclude that a person is put right with God only through faith, and not by doing what the Law commands.

CEV: We see that people are acceptable to God because they have faith, and not because they obey the Law.

---

[8] Nida, "Principles of Correspondence", 126.

[9] Eugene H. Glassman, *The Translation Debate* (Downers Grove, IL: InterVarsity Press, 1981), 52.

[10] Nida and Taber, *The Theory and Practice of Translation*, 33.

An archaic expression like "girding the loins with truth" can also be dealt with using the dynamic equivalent approach. The translator can "unpack" the phrase to ascertain Paul's message and then render it in the closest natural way in the receptor language. The TEV achieves this by replacing the old-fashioned verb "gird" and the confusing Old English "loins" to obtain "stand ready, with truth as a belt tight around your waist" (TEV). Obscurity in meaning may disappear through grammatical restructuring. For example, "Cup of the Lord" (1 Cor. 10:21) may be rendered "the cup by which the Lord is remembered," "wisdom of words" (1 Cor. 1:17) may become "well-arranged words," and "sons of wrath" (Eph. 2:3), "those with whom God is angry."

The question that comes up is, "How does one go about transferring the message from the source to the receptor language in such a way that it retains the dynamics of the original?" Nida argued that languages consist of surface structures and deep structures (kernels), and that structural differences between languages are more pronounced at the surface structure level than at the deep structure level.[11] Therefore, the best way to translate is to reduce the source text to kernel sentences, transfer these into the receptor language, and then reformulate to form a natural receptor-language. The diagram below depicts the process.[12]

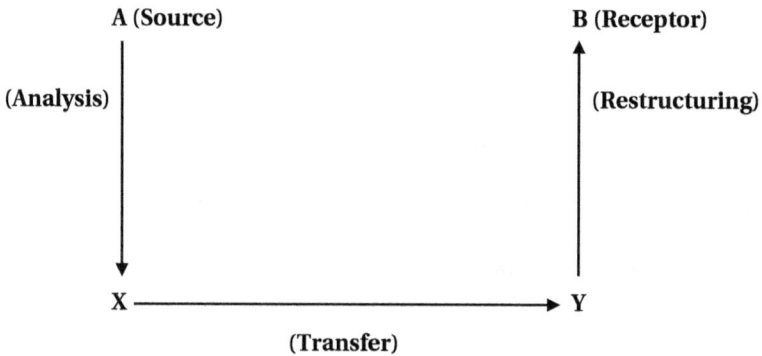

A (Source)   **B (Receptor)**

(Analysis)   **(Restructuring)**

X ————————————————————————————————→ Y

(Transfer)

This three-fold process of analysis, transfer, and restructuring is clearly expressed in the preface of the Today's English Version of the American Bible Society:

---

[11] Nida and Taber, *The Theory and Practice of Translation*, 39.
[12] The diagram was taken from Nida and Taber, *The Theory and Practice of Translation*, 33.

The primary concern of the translators has been to provide a faithful translation of the meaning of the Hebrew, Aramaic, and Greek texts. Their first task was to understand correctly the meaning of the original...After ascertaining as accurately as possible the meaning of the original, the translators' next task was to express that meaning in a manner and form easily understood by the readers...Every effort has been made to use language that is natural, clear, simple, and unambiguous. Consequently, there has been no attempt to reproduce in English the parts of speech, sentence structure, word order, and grammatical devices of the original languages.[13]

A similar statement is made by New Living Translation Committee: "The goal of this translation theory is to produce in the receptor language the closest natural equivalent of the message expressed by the original-language text— both in meaning and in style. Such a translation attempts to have the same impact on modern readers as the original had on its own audience."[14] Burton L. Goddard served on the NIV Committee of Bible Translation and has the following to say about the philosophy of dynamic equivalence as it was set down in the NIV Translators' Manual:

The translators will seek to communicate to their readers what the inspired Word was intended by God to communicate to those who read or heard it as originally given—no more and no less. They will approach a passage with this question: "What was the writer saying in his language to the people of his day?" They will then say, "How do we express the same meaning in our language today?" Sometimes equivalent words and the same sentence structure will suffice; at other times, they will prove inadequate. The translators, then, will not be tied to words but to meaning.[15]

Dynamic equivalence theory has been criticized for making readers lose the form, style and grammar of the source text. It relates (directly or indirectly) to other theories like meaning-based translation, cultural equivalence or transculturation, complete equivalence, optimal equivalence, closest natural equivalence, and functional equivalence. [16] The New English Bible (NEB,

---

[13] *Good News Bible* (Np: American Bible Society, 1976), "Preface."

[14] *Holy Bible: New Living Translation* (Tyndale House: Wheaton, Ill, 1997).

[15] Burton L. Goddard, *The NIV Story* (New York: Vantage Press, 1989), 38-39.

[16] G. J. Kerr, "Dynamic Equivalence and Its Daughters: Placing Bible Translation Theories in Their Historical Context," *Journal of Translation*, 7(1), (2011):1-19, 1.

1961) and its revision, the Revised English Bible (REB, 1989); the New International Version (NIV, 1978); the Good News Bible (GNB, 1976); the Jerusalem Bible (JB, 1966) and its thorough revision, the New Jerusalem Bible (NJB, 1985); and the New Living Translation (NLT, 1996) are examples of dynamic equivalence translations.

Functional Approach (Skopos Theory)

Until the 1970s, the idea of equivalence remained the unquestioned standard for translation. However, the illusion of equivalence continued to stare at the face of scholars so much that at a point, Mary Snell-Hornby had to conclude that "equivalence is unsuitable as a basic concept in translation theory: the term equivalence, apart from being imprecise and ill-defined (even after a heated debate of over twenty years) presents an illusion of symmetry between languages which hardly exists beyond the level of vague approximations and which distorts the basic problems of translation."[17] The quest for a new approach for translation (due to inadequacies associated with the idea of equivalence) led to the emergence of two new theories aimed at shifting attention from the source text to the target text. One was the empirically-based descriptive study of translations in their target culture, and the other one was the Skopos theory, whose later developments and applications are now well-known under the name of "functionalism." My focus in this study is on the latter.

Developed by Katharina Reiss and Hans J. Vermeer and influenced by Justa Holz-Mäntärri and Christiane Nord, Skopos Theory proposes that any translation is a goal-oriented task, and thus any translating action needs to have a skopos (purpose) which is "the most important fact in translation."[18] The functionalist approach was a reaction to the source language emphasis of "equivalence-based linguistic approaches," which viewed translation as a "code-switching operation."[19] This new perspective on Translation Studies was informed by insights from action theory, communication theory and cultural theory, among others. This approach shifts attention from words and meaning to the intended function of translation in its societal context of production. What matters to the translator is the function of the translation in the target culture rather than how it functions in its home culture. Nord quotes Vermeer as saying, "Linguistics alone won't help us; first, because translating is not merely

---

[17] Snell-Hornby, *Translation Studies*, 21.
[18] Mary Snell-Hornby, *The Turns of Translation Studies: New Paradigms or Shifting Viewpoints?* (Philadelphia: John Benjamins Publishing Company, 2006), 54.
[19] Nord, *Translating as a Purposeful Activity*, 7.

and not even primarily a linguistic process. Secondly, because linguistics has not yet formulated the right questions to tackle our problems. So let's look somewhere else."[20] Vermeer contended that "a translation is not the transcoding of words or sentences from one language into another, but a complex form of action in which someone gives information about a text (source language material) under new functional, cultural and linguistic conditions and in a new situation, while preserving formal aspects as far as possible."[21] The theory contends that equivalence-based linguistic approaches to translation cannot yield the desired results because of differences between the original and the receptor cultures. Therefore, there is the need to move away from those approaches to a functionally and socio-culturally oriented framework that focuses on the receptor community. The target-side purpose has priority in the translator's decisions. To translate means to produce a target text in a target setting for a target purpose and target addressees in target circumstances. One of the main advantages of the approach is that it moves translation theory beyond lower linguistic levels toward a consideration of the communicative purpose of translation.

The skopos refers to the function/purpose of a given text in a particular cultural setting, so in Bible translation, a target text might have a missionary purpose, catechetical purpose or liturgical purpose. The translation is determined by its purpose, and this varies according to the target culture's needs. Here, the purpose of a translation is informed by the target culture expectations, norms, conventions, requirements, and this varies from society to society. In other words, the decision over whether to translate dynamically, literally or anywhere along the free/faithful spectrum depends on the needs of the receptor community. Since the factors that determine the style of target text depend on the context of the receptor community, skopos theory does not have a specified form and style at the outset of a translation activity as other theories (like dynamic equivalence) have.

Every text has a skopos, which may be explicitly stated or implied. The skopos theory depends on the needs of the audience, and this makes any translation type—be it foreignizing or domesticating, idiomatic or literal, gender-neutral or otherwise—potentially viable. It is a purpose-driven translation that says: give the customers what they want. Therefore, skopos theory can be "applied" to an already completed translation: every production of a text can at least retrospectively be assigned a purpose (skopos). Assigning skopos to a text retrospectively requires one to assume the purpose and the

---

[20] Snell-Hornby, *The Turns of Translation Studies*, 53.
[21] Snell-Hornby, *The Turns of Translation Studies*, 53.

needs/expectations of the target audience. For Bible translations, such information can be obtained in the preface or the introduction. For example, though the CEV was not explicitly produced using the functional approach, the American Bible Society reveals their emphasis as being placed on hearing [not reading] the Bible, calling their translation "an ear-oriented text."[22] As a translation for the ear, the CEV avoided "a series of unaccented syllables, as well as potential tongue twisters,"[23] as both features can make reading difficult and hinder understanding for listeners.

In this sense, a text may be described as something that offers information rather than a transfer of meaning. A source text offers information from the original author to the original addressees, while a target text is a secondary offer of information in another language for another culture. The information the target text offers is relative to the needs of the receptor culture. As Nord explains:

> The translator offers this new audience a target text whose composition is, of course, guided by the translator's assumptions about their needs, expectations, previous knowledge, and so on. These assumptions will obviously be different from those made by the original author because source-text addressees and target-text addressees belong to different cultures and language communication. This means the translator cannot offer the same amount and kind of information as the source-text producer. What the translator does is offer another kind of information in another form.[24]

Skopos theory differs from dynamic equivalence in that the former "underlines the importance of the translation's function within the *target-language* setting for determining the manner and style of translation."[25] Nida's approach emphasizes the functions of the source language text, while Skopos theory emphasizes the function of the translation for the target audience. The following are key functional rules for the skopos theory arranged hierarchically: (a) translating text must be determined by its skopos (purpose); (b) a translating text gives information in a target language and culture concerning certain information in a source language and culture; (c) a translating text does to offer information in a reversible manner; (d) a

---

[22] *Contemporary English Version* (CEV) (np: American Bible Society: 1995), "Introduction".

[23] Contemporary English Version, "Introduction"

[24] Nord, *Translating as a Purposeful Activity*, 35.

[25] Aloo O. Mojola and Ernst R Wendland, "Scripture Translation in the Era of Translation Studies," In *Bible Translation: Frames of Reference* edited by T. Wilt, p. 1-25 (Manchester: St. Jerome, 2003), 14.

translating text must be internally coherent; (e) a translating text must be coherent with the source text. This requires the translator to distinguish between the intention on the sender's intention and the function on the receiver's side. Though the sender's intention is expected to be a congruity of intention and function, this is not the case in real situations due mainly to the large cultural gap separating the source text and the recipients of the translation. To achieve this, the translator needs to know what the receptor text intends to achieve. The aim of translation is not to have functional equivalence as that of the source text but to achieve the purpose stipulated in the translation brief.[26] The translation brief must define the skopos of the translation, and this skopos must then guide the translator in deciding what method or strategy he/she should implement during the translation process of a text in order to achieve the intended skopos.[27]

As hinted earlier, the skopos theory is function-oriented; thus, it requires the translator to first determine the function of the source text and communicate the same function accordingly in the target text. Concerning what text-function is and how it can be figured out, Nord writes, "text function is not something inherent in a text, but a pragmatic quality assigned to a text by the recipient in a particular situation after intuitively or cognitively analyzing both the function signals offered by the situational factors (participants, medium, time and place, occasion) and the linguistic, stylistic, semantic or non-verbal textual markers indicating the sender's intention(s)" that is, "after the situational markers have produced a particular expectation in the recipient with regard to the function or functions the text is probably intended for, and the recipient then looks for confirmation (or correction) in the text itself."[28] The variety of functions a text can have can be categorized into four, namely, referential function, expressive function, appellative function, and phatic function. Except for phatic function, texts are usually multifunctional; yet one function may stand out among others.

The referential function corresponds to the factor of context and describes a situation, phenomena of the world, object or mental state. It depends on the comprehensibility of the text by the reader, and as such, it may pose

---

[26] Benjamin Stephen Green, *A Skopos-Based Analysis of Breytenbach's Titus Andronicus* (MPhil Thesis: University of Stellenbosch, 2012), 109

[27] Nord, "Functional Translation Units" *Translation - Acquisition - Use: AFinLA yearbook* (1997): 41-50, 43.

[28] Christiane Nord, "Functional Translation Units" *Mauranen, A. & T. Puurtinen 1997. Translation - Acquisition - Use. AFinLA Yearbook 1997. Publications de l'Association Finlandaise de Linguistique Appliquée 55. Jyväskylä. pp.* 41-50, 43.

translation problems if source and target readers do not share the same previous knowledge about the objects and phenomena referred to. It is associated with an element whose true value is under questioning, especially when the truth value is identical in both the real and assumptive universe. The referential function of a text answers a question like: which object is being talked about? It "relies on an appropriate balance between the information mentioned explicitly in the text and the information that is not mentioned because the addressee is supposed to be familiar with it."[29] Any good writer will not give too much explicit information already known to his/her reader as this will make the text boring and uninteresting. On the other hand, if readers cannot connect the text to what they know already, the text becomes hard to comprehend. This fact underscores the need for the balance Nord speaks about in the above quote. An example of referential text is Paul's reference to himself as a servant and an apostle of Christ in Romans 1:1. The readers are expected to know who Paul is according to their context.

The expressive function of communication refers to the means by which the speaker/writer expresses his/her emotional state and his subjective attitude toward designated objects and phenomena of reality. An expression can be conveyed through the use of various linguistic elements such as interjections, such as "ah!" (conveying surprise, delight, or fright) and "oh!" (conveying dismay, sadness, or pain), and so on. The expressive function is sender-oriented and may pose translation problems if it is merely implied in the text or if the source and the target culture are based on different value systems. For example, Paul uses the statement "You foolish Galatians!" (Gal. 3:1) to express his emotions to the Galatians.

The appellative function is used to appeal to the experience, feelings, knowledge, and sensitivity of the readers so as to prompt a response from them. It includes words used for illustration so that the readers will recognize something known, for persuasion so that a certain viewpoint will be adopted, for commanding so that something would or would not be done, for exhorting so that someone may be comforted/encourages, for advertising so that something would be bought and others. It depends almost exclusively on the receiver of the message. An example is seen in Matthew 5:14-15, where Jesus appeals to the disciples' experience in order to illustrate his point that their Christian way of living must set a "shining" example to unbelievers. In this example, the referential function can be achieved only if the reader knows the reality used as a reference (that is, the city on the hill).

---

[29] Christiane Nord, "Function + Loyalty: Theology Meets Skopos," *Open Theology* 2, (2016): 566–580, 574.

Phatic function is that which keeps the channels of communication open. According to Jacobson, this function "primarily serves to establish, to prolong, or to discontinue communication to check whether the channel works (Hello do you hear me?), to attract the attention of the interlocutor or to confirm his continued attention ('Are you listening?)."[30] The main dimensions of the phatic function include: "a) making contact (e.g., by means of a small-talk about the weather, a greeting, introducing oneself, a title or heading); b) maintaining the channel open (e.g., by means of meta-discourse, topic-comment progression or connectives); c) closing the communicative interaction (e.g., summing up what has been said, saying good-bye); and d) defining and developing the social role relationship (e.g., by using certain forms of address or choosing an appropriate register)."[31] In short, the phatic function establishes, maintains and finishes social contact. Here are few examples from Paul: From Paul, an apostle (not from men, nor by human agency, but by Jesus Christ and God the Father who raised him from the dead) and all the brothers with me, to the churches of Galatia (Gal. 1:1-2); From Paul and Silvanus and Timothy, to the church of the Thessalonians in God the Father and the Lord Jesus Christ (1 Thess. 1:1); From Paul and Silvanus and Timothy, to the church of the Thessalonians in God our Father and the Lord Jesus Christ. (2 Thess. 1:1; for other examples, see 1 Cor. 1:1-2; 2 Cor. 1:1; Phil. 1:1; Rom. 1:1, 7; Col. 1:1-2). The translation must be done in such a way that the phatic function of the text is achieved in the receptor language.

The skopos theory has been criticized for its tendency of making the translator miss the intention of the original authors as it lays strong emphasis on the receptor community rather than the original audience. It has been argued that the skopos theory is not suitable for literary texts because texts involve highly stylistic and expressive language for which equivalence may not be achieved. Another criticism is that this theory does not give a clear guideline to be followed in the translation process. It has also been criticized for promoting cultural relativism, which could distort the biblical message from one culture to another. Another argument against the skopos theory is that not all actions have a purpose, so it is not applicable to certain texts.

Which Translation Approach is Applicable?

The question of which translation approach to use for a translation project is very important and must be given attention at this point before concluding

---

[30] Roman Jakobson, *Selected Writings: Poetry of Grammar and Grammar of Poetry* edited by Stephen Rudy (New York: Mouton Publishers, 1981), 24.
[31] Nord, "Function + Loyalty," 572.

this chapter. No theory of translation is completely adequate for translating the whole Bible. The translator should try as much as possible to provide a clear and natural translation. Naturalness takes precedence over literalness. As a rule, the translator must translate literally to the extent that it is clear and natural in the receptor language. The choice of the approach also must be governed by the following prioritized areas: (1) contextual consistency has priority over word-for-word correspondence (verbal consistency), (2) dynamic equivalence has priority over formal correspondence, (3) orality of language has priority over the written form, (4) forms that are used by and acceptable to the receptor community have priority over forms that may be traditionally more prestigious. A literal translation may be suitable for most passages, especially for poetry that emphasizes form a lot. Even though some English versions (e.g., RSV) render *doulous* as "servant," I believe strongly that Paul intended *doulos* to be understood as "slave" in the Greco-Roman world where slavery was a common practice. The Swahili word *mtumishi* (servant) or the Akan word *paani* (paid worker) may be inappropriate in this context. If, however, such an approach does not allow the translator to convey the meaning of the text in the receptor language as it is in the source language, then a dynamic equivalent translation (or perhaps an interpretation) should be preferred.

A literal translation is not appropriate for nonsensical phrases, that is, phrases which, when translated literally, do not make sense in their contexts. The word Eglath-shelishiyah (Isa. 15:5), which literally means "a three-year-old calf," for example, falls in this category. The challenge this expression poses comes from the fact that it has no linking adverb, preposition, conjunction or anything to assist translators decipher how to render it. What we have in the Hebrew text is "My heart cries out for Moab; his fugitives flee to Zoar, … Eglath-shelishiyah." The possibilities are "**to** Eglath-shelishiyah", "**like** Eglath-shelishiyah", "**and** Eglath-shelishiyah" and so on. If one chooses to insert "to", then a literal translation like "**to** a three-year-old calf" is inappropriate within the context, "**to** Eglath-shelishiyah" is (for instance, RSV and NRSV). The NASV inserts the conjunction "and" to create the allusion of a second town called Eglath-shelishiyah. The NKJV inserts "like", making it inappropriate to consider Eglath-shelishiyah as a town but as "a three-year-old calf." In this case, the text describes how the Moabite refugees running to Zoar were running.

The expression Adam "knew Eve his wife" (Gen. 4:1) is the literal Hebrew in which the verb "knew" has been used figuratively to mean "had sex with." Translators are expected to select a term or an expression for sexual intercourse between spouses that can be read in public and in a mixed group without feelings of embarrassment, shock, or amusement. The Asante-Twi

Bible (1964; 2012), by translating it literally as *Adam hunuu ne yere Hawa* ("Adam saw his wife Eve"), fails to convey the message in Hebrew into Twi. In the revised version (Asante Twi Bible 2017), it has been replaced by the expression: *Adam ne yere Hawa hyiaeε* "Adam met his wife Eve" (Gen. 4:1), which is more natural in the Akan cultural context. This is a natural way of expressing sexual intercourse in Akan society.

In Luke 24:25, Jesus rebukes the disciples for their unbelief: "Then Jesus said to them, 'How foolish you are, how slow you are to believe everything the prophets said!'" (TEV). It seems to me that the main point of this passage is that the disciples do not believe. If it is translated with this word order, the text would imply that the disciples believe everything the prophets said, but they do so slowly. This, however, is not the case. One may have to translate the text as, "And Jesus said to them: 'You are foolish! And your hearts are dulled! Everything which was said by the prophets, you do not believe it.'"

The expression "greeting with a holy" (Rom. 16:16; cf. 1 Cor. 16.20; 2 Cor. 13.12; 1 Thess. 5.26) reflects the manner of sacred greeting among the early Christians, which later became a part of the church liturgy. In some cultures (including most African societies), however, one cannot employ a specific equivalent of a kiss, which would be too closely associated with sexual interest. The literal translation of this expression as *mfeano kronkron* (holy kiss) in Akuapem and Asante may have to be given a second look. In most African societies, one may have to say "greet one another affectionately", "give one another a warm handshake," or "give one another a hearty handshake all round," thus employing a general term for the more specific expression of "kiss" in Greek. In societies in which two different terms for "kiss" are used, one which identifies kissing on the mouth (which may have sexual connotations) and the other which specifies kissing on the cheek (which denotes greeting), the latter form of kissing should be used in this context.

One challenge in translation is the lack of vocabulary in the receptor language for different words in the source language. Of interest at this point are the four Greek words for love, namely, *stergein* (love rooted in obligatory affection for objects of nature), *eran* (love of passion and sex), *phelein* (love based on a pleasurable response to something; it is not for pleasure but comes due to pleasurable memories) and *agapan* (love that is evoked from a sense of worth found in an object which causes one to value that object highly). Many languages, including English and Akan, do not have words to reproduce these shades of meanings. Therefore, with reference to the concept of love, a literal (word-for-word) translation may not be possible or appropriate. There are even cases where the receptor language has no word at all for a given word in the source text, so translators have to speculate.

Translators may as well use interpretation rather than follow pure literal translation principles. A classic example can be found in John 8:25, where Jesus answers the question "Who are you?" with the words, "The beginning that which I also assert to you." The RSV translates it literally as "Even what I have told you from the beginning." Contextual analysis of the text reveals that Jesus was telling them that he is the same person he has been saying he is from the beginning of his ministry. The literal approach does not help because it does not make Jesus' response clear. The NRSV improves this translation by rendering it as "Why do I speak to you at all?" In this case, the translators shift from the literal approach and interpret the statement as a question which means "I have told you severally and so there is no need to repeat myself." The Bono-Twi version reads, "*Mene nipa korɔ a maka sɛ meyɛ ofiri me dwumadie ase he*" (I am precisely that person that from the beginning of my ministry I told you I am." Cleary, a non-literal translation (such as Bono-Twi or NRSV) is preferred in this case. The above examples underscore the fact that translation involves far more than the replacement of lexical and grammatical items between languages, as literal theorists would like us to believe.

This does not, however, mean dynamic equivalence or skopos theory is a better option. The use of a meaning-based approach gives the translator the freedom to use a modern, understandable expression instead of being compelled to reproduce original idioms. Yet, it may affect the precision of the translation. This approach may omit subtle clues to understanding the text, which only a literal approach can preserve. The tendency of introducing doctrinal biases into the translation is also high. The modifications that come with this approach may create additional commentaries which readers may assume to be original. Translating poetry using dynamic equivalence may lead to some challenges. To illustrate this point, let us consider Psalm 19:1-3, which literally says, "The heavens declare the glory of God, and the expanse inscribes his handiwork." ESV: "The heavens declare the glory of God, and the sky above proclaims his handiwork." TEV: "How clearly the sky reveals God's glory! How plainly it shows what he has done. Clearly, the dynamic equivalent rendering of the TEV misses the "speaking" linkage intended by the writer. The ESV seems more appropriate with its relatively literal rendering of the text.

Considering the way vernacular language groups have shown open-mindedness to learning theological terms such as "Amen", "Abaddon", "Halleluiah", "Alpha and Omega" and "Hosanna" that are used extensively, untranslated in vernacular liturgy and current translations, it will be out of place for translators using the dynamic equivalence approach to translate these terms (e.g., Amen= "Let is be so") in the name of making their text translation comprehensible. The literal approach is preferred in translating such terms.

The foregoing clearly bears witness to the inadequacy of using one translation theory for translating the entire Bible. In my candid opinion, the translator has to decide which philosophy to use on a case-by-case basis. I believe that the skopos of the translation should serve as a guide in terms of choice of word or expressions (when there are alternatives). For example, if the skopos of a project is to get a youth Bible, then the translators would have to use words and expressions that the youth is familiar with. If the project has all ages as targets, then the choice of words and expressions should suit all the age groups. The skopos, should, however, not make one alter the original meaning of the text. In other words, the purpose for which a project is undertaken should not be the controlling factor in determining what message the translation should convey to the recipients. The meaning of the text must be maintained regardless of the method used. The same divine message must be received in all communities; the application may, however, differ from context to context.

Conclusion

I have argued strongly that no one translation approach can be used to translate the entire Bible. There are texts which may require dynamic equivalence; there are others for which literal translation may be most appropriate. The level of resemblance required between the original and the translation is one of the factors that inform the choice of the approach. For example, a literal translation will yield complete resemblance; other methods may not give this result. The literal approach has been noted for presupposing verbal, plenary inspiration, for placing importance upon knowing the Scripture as it was originally stated, for giving mother-tongue readers access to the form and meaning of the Scripture in the original languages. It has been praised for proclaiming a single intended meaning, for being more objective, and for helping readers do a better inductive study for themselves. The lack of an exact equivalent for each and every word and the production of awkward statements in receptor language due to strict adherence to the form of the source language have been identified as major flaws of this method. Overliteralness is a hazard for any translator.

The meaning-based approach distinguishes the meaning of a text from its form and then translates the meaning so that it makes the same impact on modern readers that the ancient texts made on its original readers. Its advantages include a high degree of clarity and readability and its appeal to a wider range of audiences. However, it has been criticized for not being transparently dependent on original language, for having the tendency to promote multiple meanings, for being less objective and more interpretative, thereby making translations not faithful to the original language. The skopos theory also has its pluses and minuses, as outlined in the discussions above. Whatever the case may be, it is the translator's task to determine which method is most appropriate for a given text, making sure meaning is not compromised.

Review Exercise

1. What is a translation philosophy? How can one determine which translation philosophy is appropriate for a given text?

2. What is meant by dynamic equivalence? Give adequate examples to explain the challenges associated with the use of this approach for Bible translation.

3. What is meant by the skopos theory? What are its strengths and weaknesses?

4. To what extent do you agree that the formal equivalent approach to translation is inadequate for Bible translation?

5. With adequate examples, explain how the choice of an appropriate translation approach is affected by the genre of the source text.

6. Discuss the translation theories used in translating your mother-tongue Bible.

Chapter 8

Textual Criticism and Bible Translation

How would a translator feel if he/she realizes after his/her work that what he/she has done was based on the wrong source text? Certainly, a translation based on the wrong text is useless. This underscores the fact that the reliability of the manuscript used in Bible translation is crucial to the success of the project. It is therefore very important that the translator establishes the originality of the source text before the actual translation begins. The process involved in this exercise is referred to as **Textual Criticism**, the subject of discussion in the present chapter.

What is Textual Criticism?

Textual criticism deals with the process by which the original biblical text is determined. The foremost task the translator needs to undertake is to establish which biblical manuscript is original and can be used as an authentic source text. This task has a three-fold aim, namely, to determine the transmission process of a text and the factors that have led to its variant forms, to determine, as close as possible, the original wording and structure of the text, and to produce a reliable (Hebrew or Greek) biblical manuscript. Textual criticism is both an art and a science at the same time. As an art, it involves the collection and comparison of data, and as a science, it makes use of specified rules in determining what the original wording of a text is. The process involved entails the comparison of the various readings in order to decide which one is the **preferred reading**.

The first notable attempt at textual criticism could be traced to Origen's work, the Hexapla. In this work, he sought to establish the original text by the widest possible collation and comparison. This monumental work set forth six transcriptions of the entire Old Testament in parallel columns, namely (1) the Hebrew text, (2) its transliteration into Greek letters, (3) the extremely literalistic Greek translation made in the first half of the second century AD by Aquila, a Jewish proselyte; (4) the freer Greek translation made in the latter part of the second century AD by Symmachus, an Ebionite Christian; (5) the LXX translation made in the third and second centuries BC; and (6) the free revision of the Septuagint made in the second century AD by Theodotion, variously described as a Jewish proselyte (so Irenaeus), an Ebionite Christian (so Jerome), or a follower of Mardon (so Epiphanius).

Other forms of biblical criticism exist, including form criticism, which focuses on the period of oral transmission and on the form a text took before being put into a written document; source criticism, which deals with how the different literary units were compiled; literary criticism which focuses on the analysis of the literary features of a given document to determine its literary character, origins and states of written composition; rhetorical criticism which is the study of a biblical text to determine the structural patterns and literary devices used by the author in order to communicate his intended meaning; and redaction criticism, which highlights ways in which compilers and authors edited their source text to compose their documents.

The Need for Textual Criticism

Several factors make textual criticism a key task within the discipline of biblical studies. In the first place, none of the original autographs of the biblical texts has survived up till now; all of them have perished.[1] The loss of autographs is attributable to the perishable nature of the materials (including papyrus, vellum and parchment) which were used to preserve texts, and frequent use and circulation of materials (making them prone to loss and destruction), the constant persecution of the Jews, and the destruction of their Temple and synagogues. The biblical text has been transmitted in many ancient and medieval sources and what we have today are just fragments of leather and papyrus scrolls. They are not originals but copies of copies, the earliest of the Hebrew manuscript dating from the seventh century BCE and for the Greek New Testament, the earliest dates from the second century AD.[2] These sources shed light on and bear witness to the biblical text; therefore, they are referred to as "textual witnesses." Since the available manuscripts are copies of the original texts and a time gap exists between the original texts and the hand-written copies, we cannot assume that the copies are exactly the same as the original autographs. Therefore, the original wording of the text has to be determined by a critical examination of the surviving ancient manuscripts.

Secondly, the textual witnesses differ from one another to some extent due to scribal errors that were introduced during copying and re-copying. Therefore, no two manuscripts containing a major portion of the Bible are exactly the same. All extant (existing) copies and translations of the Hebrew Old Testament and the Greek New Testament have transcriptional variations.

---

[1] W. Randolph Tate, *Handbook for Biblical Interpretation: An Essential Guide to Methods, Terms, and Concepts* (Grand Rapids, MI: Baker Academic, 2012), 441.
[2] Tate, *Handbook for Biblical Interpretation*, 441.

The ancient world was not like the modern world in which exact copies of a document can be produced in no time. Ancient people relied on scribes who made copies of the original text for the public. Since the available copies differ from one another, it is necessary to determine what the original author wrote. The difference between the wording of two or more manuscripts due to (but not limited to) "changes in a letter, a word, a phrase or even additions and omissions of whole sentences or paragraphs"[3] leads to different readings of the same passage which scholars refer to as **textual variants** or **variant readings**. Textual variants tend to group themselves into four. They include the difference in reading "(1) between manuscripts in the original languages; (2) between manuscripts in early translations; (3) between ancient manuscripts in the original languages and early translations and (4) between quotations in early Jewish and Christian writings."[4] Textual critics consider the longer ending of Mark's Gospel (16:9-20) and the account of the woman caught in adultery (John 7:53-8:11) as constituting textual variants (up to a paragraph or more).

Thirdly, most of the available manuscripts contain incomplete sections of the original, making it very difficult but necessary to put the pieces together to reconstruct the biblical text. Since no textual witness contains what could be regarded as the biblical text, there is the need to study all sources and then reconstruct the biblical texts based usually on incomplete sections available today. This means that in the process of textual analysis, one section may complement another section and so on.

Fourthly, so many extant manuscripts of varying textual content exist such that there is the need to find out what the original manuscripts looked like. These manuscripts date from the third century to the sixteenth century. There are over five thousand (5000) copies of the New Testament that have survived to date. The manuscripts of the New Testament are subdivided into four categories: (1) the papyri are very old, written on an ancient paper made from the pith of the papyrus plant, usually grown in Egyptian marches; (2) there are about 300 uncial manuscripts (also known as majuscules and composed during the fourth through the tenth centuries) which were written in a formal style, using large letters similar in size to capital letters; (3) there are about 2700 *minuscule* manuscripts written in smaller letters in a cursive or free-flowing hand and date in the late ninth through the sixteenth centuries (4) there are about 2000 lectionaries prepared for church service containing

---

[3] Craig L. Bloomberg and Jennifer Foutz Markley, *A Handbook of New Testament Exegesis* (Grand Rapids, MI: Baker Academic, 2010), 5.
[4] Tate, *Handbook for Biblical Interpretation*, 442.

selected readings from the Gospels, the Acts and the Epistles. The availability of these numerous gives the indication that we can certainly trace the original. Yet, the same situation makes the work of textual critics very difficult as they have so many manuscripts to study.

Fifthly, manuscript evidence suggests different textual traditions that developed geographically over time, which can only be handled effectively through textual criticism. That is to say, although it is true that no two manuscripts are identical, it is also equally true that many are so much alike that they tend to group themselves into major families of texts. Each group or family, exhibiting certain distinguishing features, is called **a text type**. Copies belonging to the same text type usually emerge from a particular geographical area and are based on a parent copy that originated from that area. New Testament text types emerged in the early centuries of the church from three major regions, namely, the West, Alexandria and Byzantine.

Common Manuscript Errors

Materials that were used in writing biblical texts included clay tablets, stone, bone, wood, leather, various metals, potsherds (ostraca), papyrus and parchment (vellum). Papyrus was produced from the papyrus plant by dividing it with a needle into thin strips. It was invented in about 3000 BCE in Egypt to record Pyramid Texts and the Prisse manuscripts.[5] Papyrus sheets came in all sizes, depending on the size of the usable strips cut from the plant. Scrolls of papyrus were rolled out horizontally rather than vertically. Papyrus spanned 3500 years.

Parchment replaced papyrus around the twelfth century AD. It was more durable, and both sides could be used, corrections and erasures could easily be made, and it could be reused by scraping off. It was made from the skin of goats, sheep and calves. Vellum was also prepared from animal skins and came from calves, while parchment refers to all other animal skin used in papermaking, such as bulls and goats, and was inferior in quality to vellum. Vellum was more durable and could preserve the text for a relatively long time. Since scribes either copied manuscripts or wrote from dictation, manuscript variants could be of several types: copying, hearing, accidental, or intentional. In what follows, we examine major manuscripts errors evident in the biblical text.

First of all, let us consider haplography and dittography. Haplography occurs when a letter, syllable, or word which is supposed to be written more

---

[5] Bediako, *History of the Bible,* 36.

than once is written only once.[6] Consider the sentence: I have given them your word, and the world has hated them because they **do not belong to the world**, just as **I do not belong to the world** (John 17:14). This can easily be copied as "I have given them your word, and the world has hated them because they **do not belong to the world**." This is obviously a reading that omitted the words between two identical ends of lines ("just as").

Dittography ("writing twice"), on the other hand, refers to the error that occurs when a letter, syllable, or word which is supposed to be repeated is written just once. In many cases, it is difficult to know whether a particular situation is a case of haplography or dittography (see below) since only by means of an examination of the context can one determine the nature of the phenomenon. A case of either haplography or dittography can be found in 1 Thessalonians 2:7, depending on how one examines the text. Some manuscripts read *nēpioi* (babies/infants) but most translations read *ēpioi* (gentle). The two words are similar in spelling and can easily be confused, especially since the previous word (*egenēthēmen*) ends in "n". Two possibilities exist in this case. First, it is possible that the original word is *nēpioi* (babies/infants), but copyists' eyes accidentally jumped over the letter "n" since the previous word also ends with "n". In other words, after writing the last "n" of the previous word, the copyist looked at the text, saw *nēpioi* but thought he had written the first letter "n" and so went on to write the other letter, eventually writing *ēpioi* instead on *nēpioi*. If this is the case, then it is a situation of haplography. The second possibility is that the original word is *ēpioi*, but the copyists accidentally copied it twice (a case of dittography). Either interpretation is possible.

Another manuscript error is metathesis which refers to the error that occurs when the proper position of letters or words is reversed. That is, metathesis is the transposition of two adjacent letters or words. In Mark 14:65, some manuscripts have *elabon* ("received") and some others *ebalon* ("struck"). Also, in Deuteronomy 31:1, the Masoretic Text reads "Moses went", Qumran reads, "Moses finished".

Fusion and fission are also among the errors associated with biblical manuscripts. The combination of two separate words into one leads to an error called fusion; for example, writing "no where" as "nowhere." Fission, on the other hand, occurs when a single word is mistakenly divided up into two words. An example in English would be the erroneous writing of "hardship" as "hard ship." Some manuscripts of Mark 10:40 read *all' ois* ("but for whom"),

---

[6] Emmanuel Tov, *Textual Criticism of the Hebrew Bible* (Minneapolis: Fortress Press, 2001), 279. Pdf

others *allois* ("for others"). This could be a case of fission or fusion, depending on which one is correct.

More so, manuscript errors include homoioarcton and homoioteleuton. Homoioarcton ("similar beginning") occurs due to similarity in letters occurring at the beginning of adjacent or close words. During the process of copying, "if two lines which [were] close together began or ended with the same group of letters or if two similar words stood near each other in the same line, it was easy for the eyes of the copyist to jump from the first group of letters to the second, and so for a portion of the text to be omitted."[7] That is to say, the copyist's eye jumped from the first appearance of a letter (or letters) to its (their) second appearance so that in the copied text, the intervening section was omitted together with one of the repeated elements. An example of this occurs in 2 Peter 2:6, where external evidence is equally divided between the plural dative case, *asebesin* "to ungodly persons" and the infinitive *asebein* "to act impiously." Oman opines that "since the verb *mellein* ('to be about to') is always followed by an infinitive, it is more likely that copyists changed the noun to the infinitive than vice versa."[8] However, both possibilities can fit the context.

Homoioarcton (similar ending), on the other hand, occurs due to the similarity of letters occurring at the end of adjacent or close words. In other words, it is the omission of an intervening letter because the copyist's eye had skipped from one ending to a second similar ending.[9] Both homoioarcton and homoioteleuton are put together and referred to as both phenomena are sometimes jointly called *parablepsis* (scribal oversight).

The next kind of error is itacism. Errors of hearing are particularly common when words have the same pronunciation as others but differ in spelling (as in English: "fate, faith"; "meet, meat"). This happened because, at times, many scribes were copying at the same time, and so they did their work as one dictated to them. In Greek, vowels like $\bar{e}$, *i*, and *u* and diphthongs such as *ei*, *oi*, and *ui* all sounded alike. Mistranslations can occur as, for example, in 1 Corinthians, chapter 15, verse 54: "Death is swallowed up in victory" (*nekos*) becomes by itacism (pronunciation of the Greek letter $\bar{e}$) "Death is swallowed up in conflict" (*neikos*). Another problem of itacism in Greek is the distinction between declensions of the first and second persons in the plural, which can sound the same (*hemeis*, "us"; *humeis*, "you") because the initial vowels are

---

[7] Korger L. Omanson, *A Textual Guide to the Greek New Testament* (Stuttgart: German Bible Society, 2006), 16.

[8] Omanson, *A Textual Guide to the Greek New Testament*, 496.

[9] Omanson, *A Textual Guide to the Greek New Testament*, 487.

not clearly differentiated. Also, the difference between "your" (*hemon*) and "our" (*humon*) in Greek is very slight and could easily be confused.

Errors of memory also occurred when a copyist reads a manuscript and then writes, depending upon his short recall of memory. This is common in our days, too, when people memorize phone numbers and write them wrongly. In spite of these errors, the Bible is still a reliable document because the comparative analyses by textual critics help in knowing (as close as possible) what the original text is. In the end, the overall message of the Bible is not compromised in any way.

> a careful study of the variants of the various earliest manuscripts reveals that none of them affects a single doctrine of Scripture. The system of spiritual truth contained in the standard Hebrew text of the Old Testament is not in the slightest altered or compromised by any of the variant readings found in Hebrew manuscripts of earlier date found in the Dead Sea caves or anywhere else. It is very evident that the vast majority of them are so inconsequential as to leave the meaning of each clause doctrinally unaffected.

> ... Even though the two copies of Isaiah discovered in Qumran Cave 1 near the Dead Sea in 1947 were a thousand years earlier than the oldest dated manuscript previously known (AD 980), they proved to be **word for word identical with our standard Hebrew Bible in more than 95 percent of the text.** The 5 percent of variation consisted chiefly of obvious slips of the pen and variations in spelling.[10]

Procedure for Textual Criticism

The task of textual critics is divided into two stages. The first step is to collect data for the reconstruction of Hebrew variants, while the second step is the evaluation of variants to determine which one is "original".[11] Textual critics rely on ancient and Middle Age translations of the Bible into different languages, like Greek, Aramaic, Syriac, Latin, and Arabic. Data is collected from these and other documents based on the assumption that the biblical text as found in Hebrew manuscripts is reflected in the ancient translations. Old Testament textual critics must necessarily examine biblical texts in Hebrew. For this reason, they use existing ancient translations to attempt a

---

[10] Gleason L. Archer Jr., *A Survey of Old Testament Introduction* (Chicago, IL: Moody Press, 1974), 56-57. (my emphasis)
[11] Tov, *Textual Criticism*, 120.

reconstruction of the Hebrew texts underlying them (that is, the Hebrew text from which these translations were made).[12] The reconstructed text from which a translation was made is referred to as the **Vorlage** of a translation, that is, the text that lay before the translator. Before the discovery of the Qumran scrolls (Dead Sea Scrolls) in 1947, manuscripts of the ancient translations were the earliest sources for our knowledge of the biblical text.[13] The Dead Sea Scrolls have given us earlier Hebrew manuscripts and thus have seemingly decreased the value of the ancient translations because every scholar would prefer Hebrew texts to ancient translations (of unknown Hebrew source).

In terms of manuscript reliability, Old Testament scholars agree that the Masoretic Text (MT) is the most reliable witness to the original text because it is based on direct transmission in the original language and has been transmitted through the various epochs with great care. The accuracy of the textual work by the Masoretes can be verified in several ways, including archaeological discoveries, the similarity of duplicating passages found in different books, and the substantial agreement with the textual readings of the Samaritan Pentateuch, the Dead Sea Scrolls, and the Septuagint. The Dead Sea Scroll of Isaiah was 95 percent identical, word-for-word, with the standard MT. Yet, one cannot also say that the MT is entirely free from textual problems. The order of decreasing relative reliability and importance of various Old Testament sources is as follows: MT, Dead Sea Scroll, Samaritan Pentateuch, Septuagint (Greek), Aquila, Symmachus, Theodotion, Peshitta (Syriac), and Targums (Aramaic). For the New Testament, textual critics rely basically on three main sources, namely, Greek manuscripts such as papyri, majuscules (or uncials), and minuscules; ancient translations such as Latin (esp. the Vulgate), Syriac, Coptic, Ethiopic, Georgian, Slavonic, Armenian, etc.); and patristic citations (such as from the works of Church Fathers like Justin Martyr, Irenaeus, Clement of Alexandria, Origen, Athanasius, Eusebius, Cyril of Alexandria).[14]

Textual criticism requires sifting through all available materials, carefully collating and comparing each manuscript with all others in order to detect errors and changes in the text, and thus decide which variant reading is more likely to be original. Old Testament textual criticism involves all Hebrew and reconstructed texts that differ from an accepted form of MT (usually the text referred to as Leningrad codex B19A). Differences to be noted include pluses,

---

[12] Tov, *Textual Criticism*, 121.
[13] Tov, *Textual Criticism*, 121.
[14] Bloomberg and Markley, *A Handbook of New Testament Exegesis*, 2-4.

minuses, differences in letters, words, and the sequence of words, as well as differences in vocalization, word division, and sense divisions. This MT is used as the basis for describing textual variations because it has become the *Textus Receptus* of Hebrew Scripture. The aim of the comparison is to select the one reading that was presumably contained in the original form of the text.

Through the comparison of manuscripts, textual critics establish the degree of certainty of each text or passage. Decisions as to whether a particular verse(s) should be included in the main text or footnote (with some comments clarifying the decision taken) or be omitted altogether are informed by the degree of certainty established for that text. The comparative evaluation of variants is necessarily subjective because it is limited to readings that emerged during the textual transmission, excluding those created during the literary growth of the book, even though they are included in textual witnesses. However, there are certain rules which help the critic to decide which text is original. I proceed to outline these rules below.[15]

External Evidence

There are two basic criteria for the evaluation of variant readings: (1) Common sense, which requires the critic to choose the reading which best explains the origin of the others, and (2) the reconstruction of the history of a variant reading is a prerequisite to forming a judgment against it. Two kinds of evidence are taken into consideration: external evidence and internal evidence. External evidence is evidence derived outside the text, and they include: (a) The date and character of the textual witness. Greater importance is attached to the date of the text type than the age of the document; (b) The geographical distribution of the witnesses that agrees with a variant; (c) The genealogical relationship of texts and families of witnesses. Manuscript evidence is weighted, not counted. I proceed to explain further.

The older reading is to be preferred. While an older reading is not necessarily the most carefully copied manuscript, textual critics tend to give preference to older readings where they are at least as reliable as later ones and equally free of oddities or peculiarities. Generally speaking, earlier manuscripts are more likely to be free from or to have suffered the least transmission error. This means that if manuscripts X and Y of the same text

---

[15] I have gleaned most of the ideas from Gleason Archer Jr., *A Survey Of Old Testament Introduction* (Chicago: Moody Press, 1994), 11ff; see also Blomberg and Markley, *New Testament Exegesis*, 19-24.

date 100 AD and 321 AD respectively, X must be given priority over Y because it (X) is closer to the date the original was written than Y.

The reading with the widest geographical acceptance is to be preferred. For example, a reading that favored the LXX, the Itala, and the Coptic is not to be selected against another reading favored by both the *Peshitta* and the Samaritan because the LXX, the Itala, and the Coptic belong to the Alexandrian tradition, whereas the *Peshitta* and the Samaritan represent somewhat different textual traditions. Similarly, a text that is attested by different text-types from Rome, Spain, and North Africa is more likely to be original than one that is found only in Rome. Geographically remote textual witnesses are actually independent of one another.

The reading with the highest relative weight is to be preferred. By textual weight is meant the number of manuscripts from a different ancestor containing a particular reading; that is, the genealogical relationship a text has with families of witnesses. If reading A is found in fifty manuscripts and reading B is found only in one manuscript, the relative numerical support for A is clearly higher than that of B. This does not, however, necessarily mean that A is to be taken as the original. What has to be done at this point is to determine the number of ancestor manuscripts (that is, manuscripts from which others are copied) that can be identified within the fifty supporting manuscripts. Let us assume that it is discovered that all the fifty manuscripts are copies made from a single manuscript C, no longer extant, whose scribe first introduced that particular variant reading. The relative textual weight of A then becomes just one (that is, the number of ancestor manuscripts connected to A). In this case, the comparison is to be made between the one manuscript containing reading B and the single ancestor of the fifty manuscripts containing reading A. If, on the other hand, A is found to have more textual weight than B, then it will be given preference and then taken as the original. The above illustration underscores the fact that mere numbers of witnesses supporting a given variant reading do not necessarily make that reading superior. Therefore, textual witnesses are to be weighed rather than counted.

Internal Evidence

Critics are familiar with the process of the composition of texts, their copying, preservation and transmission. This makes it possible to identify textual variants and assign reasons for their existence. What textual critics do with the available manuscript is to work backward from the variants towards the original text. Internal evidence refers to evidence gathered from within the text itself. It is divided into two kinds of probabilities: Transcriptional probabilities basically related to the difficulty in reading and the length of the text, and intrinsic probabilities related to contextual issues, style and vocabulary of text, doctrinal biases, harmony or disharmony with other related passages and so on. I now proceed to outline each of these factors.

The more difficult (*lectio difficilior*) and obscure reading is to be preferred. The reason for this rule is that during copying, a scribe was more likely to simplify, smoothen or clarify the wording of an original text (by changing words, inserting some words for explanation or doing other things) than he was to make it harder. Scribes wanted to make the text easily understood than to make it hard for their reader to read or understand.

The shorter reading is to be preferred. The reason is that while scribes found it difficult to leave out God's word during copying, they were ready to insert new materials for the sake of clarity. The following situations are, however, exceptions to this rule. These are cases where an omission of material has occurred, and this omission is judged to superfluous, harsh, contrary to pious belief, liturgical usage or ascetic practice; where the passage (in a parallel reading) that stands in verbal dissidence with the other is to be preferred as similarity may indicate harmonization by the scribe and where the shorter reading was an attempt by a scribe to smoothen the text by replacing words with synonyms, altering a less refined grammatical form, and pronouns, conjunctions and expletives to make the reading of a text smooth.

The reading that most closely conforms to the style, diction and theological framework of the author is to be preferred. The context in which the variant occurs must play a major role in deciding which variant is original. If, however, contextual analysis favors any reading, then the one that conforms to the author's theology and his usual way of expressing that type of thought is preferred.

For parallel passages, the variant that is less harmonious is to be preferred. Studies have shown that the scribes were more interested in harmonizing seeming contradictions in parallel passages than introducing new problems into the texts. The translator's job is not to resolve the tension but to carry the same meaning from the source text to the receptor text in as natural and meaningful way as possible.

The reading which reflects no doctrinal bias is to be preferred. Sometimes copyists write in a way to support their doctrinal biases. For example, the Targums and the LXX make us know that later Jewish thought did not favor humanlike representations of God or "anthropomorphism" (use of human parts to describe God). For example, in Isaiah 1:12, one finds the variant readings "to see", "to be seen," and "to appear". The MT which supports the latter is to be rejected because it was pointed deliberately to avoid saying that God can see.

Conclusion

Textual criticism is an indispensable step in Bible translation. In this chapter, I have examined the tools and procedures used in establishing what could be regarded as the original biblical text. Those without workable knowledge of biblical languages may have to rely on various (English) translations to reconstruct the source text. To end this chapter, it must be noted that the various copying errors in no way make the biblical text unreliable. God has faithfully preserved the truth in his word all these years in spite of his use of (imperfect) human beings as agents in the preservation.

Review Exercise

1. What is textual criticism? Why is textual criticism necessary in Bible translation?

2. What two steps are involved in textual criticism? Explain each of them.

3. What is the correct ending for Mark's gospel?

4. Can we be certain that the biblical text has been transmitted faithfully? Can we be certain that our mother-tongue translations reflect what the authors originally wrote in Hebrew and Greek?

5. What principles are used to determine the originality of a manuscript during textual criticism?

Chapter 9

Exegetical and Intertextual
Considerations in Bible Translation

The focus of this chapter is to highlight the place of exegesis and intertextuality in Bible translation. There are people who argue that exegesis is not required in translation. It is argued that by introducing exegesis into Bible translation, one risks adding to or subtracting from God's word. It is also argued that most translators lack exegetical training, and so if exegesis is a part of translation, then Bible translation will be practically impossible. As a translator, I am fully aware of the significance of exegesis in the translation process. Without interpreting the text to know what it means, one will definitely produce wrong translations full of misunderstandings, ambiguity and obscurity. A key argument in this chapter is that while a good exegete does not automatically make a good translator, a good hermeneutical/exegetical skill is an indispensable tool for producing a high-quality translation. A good translation "requires skillful exegesis of the source text, taking into account its 'discourse features, rhetorical devices, and social Conventions.'"[1]

The relation between biblical texts is very crucial in Bible translation. Knowing how one text relates to the other helps the translator to have a better understanding of the various components and dimensions of culture, religion, and language and keep them together. A special relationship that is very important in this regard is what is referred to as **intertextuality**, which I discuss in the second part of this chapter.

Hermeneutics

From the verb *hermeneuo* (meaning "to interpret or explain"), the word "hermeneutics" refers to the art and science of Biblical interpretation. Hermeneutics differs from exegesis in that the latter refers to the task of determining the meaning of a text for its original audience, while the former deals with the task of explaining the meaning of scripture and drawing out implications

---

[1] Smith, *Bible Translation and Relevance Theory*, 228.

for modern-day audiences.[2] That is, hermeneutics refers to principles of interpretation, whereas exegesis has to do with the practice of explaining texts.[3] Hermeneutics can therefore be considered as a cookbook, exegesis as the preparing and baking of the cake, and exposition as serving the cake.[4]

Translation is not just about replacing words with words; it is about carrying meaning from one language to another. As such, the translator cannot carry out his/her task without interpretation. He/she needs to interpret the text within its context before determining exactly what it means in the original context and then what it means in his/her context too. Unfortunately, most people believe that translation can be done without interpretation. That is not true. As a matter of fact, each translation is a product of interpretation. Translation implies interpretation, and interpretation presupposes exegesis. As Gordon Fee and Douglas Stuart assert, "translation is in itself a (necessary) form of interpretation. Your Bible, whatever translation you use, which is your beginning point, is, in fact, the end result of much scholarly work. Translators are regularly called upon to make choices regarding meanings, and their choices are going to affect how you understand."[5] While a critical examination of the hermeneutical principle goes beyond the scope of the present book, I find the following premises vital for the translator.[6]

1. Literal affirms that the meanings to be interpreted are textually based. This premise sets the framework for the system. All the other premises are derived from and developed within the scope of what literal affirms.

2. Grammatical affirms that these textually based meanings are expressed within the limits of common language usage. Language is polysemic, which means that any word or phrase or even any sentence is capable of multiple senses. These limits may be difficult to discern, but they still exist in theory and remain a legitimate aspect of hermeneutical study and interpretive goals.

---

[2] Tate, *Handbook for Biblical Interpretation*, 194.
[3] Walter C. Kaiser and Moises Silva, *An Introduction to Biblical Hermeneutics* (Grand Rapids: Zondervan, 1994), 285.
[4] Zuck, *Basic Bible Interpretation*, 22.
[5] Gordon D. Fee, Douglas K. Stuart, *How to Read the Bible for All Its Worth: A Guide to Understanding the Bible* (Grand Rapids, MI: Zondervan, 1982), 17.
[6] Adapted from Elliott Johnson, *Expository Hermeneutics: An Introduction* (Grand Rapids, MI: Zondervan, 1990), 21-22.

3. Historical affirms that these textually based meanings refer, depending on their textual usage, to either historical or heavenly realities, to either natural or spiritual subjects. Moreover, we can look for allusions and references to situational meanings of the time when the piece was written.

4. Literary affirms that these textually based meanings are in part determined within the context of textual design considered in the composition as a whole. The textual composition incorporates such literary characteristics as coherent unity and prominence. In addition, the textual design incorporates the conventional norms of the literary genre.

5. Theological affirms that the textually based meanings are ultimately expressed by God through human agency. As such, the historical realm is not the source nor even the primary influence of the human author's knowledge and textual message. Therefore, textually expressed meanings that have their source in God are necessarily true and must be understood in a sense consistent with the theological context and the theological meanings. In addition, the message must be understood as progressively revealed in the historical progress of the canon.

Exegetical Considerations in Bible Translation

Earlier, I defined exegesis as the means by which the meaning of a text in its original context can be determined. My focus here is to examine some forms of exegetical analyses that must be considered in the translation process.

Linguistic Exegesis

Linguistics is the study of language. Therefore, linguistic exegesis has to do with the language aspect of the translation. First, we have linguistic identification, which involves the identification of all forms (such as morphemes of the nouns and verbs) in the source language, as well as the relationship between the words (syntax). More often than not, the specific intended meaning of a word is informed by the grammatical constructions in which it occurs (that is, syntactic marking). For example, in the sentences (1) "Christian is a man," and (2) "Benedict will man the company for the next ten years," the meaning of the word "man" is dependent on the syntactic constructions in which it occurs. In this case, the grammar itself indicates the meaning (it is a noun in sentence 1 but a verb in 2). In other cases, the specific intended meaning of a word could be from the interaction of that word with the meanings of other terms in its context. This conditioning by the meanings of surrounding terms is referred to as **semotactic marking**. Consider the three sentences below: (1) Kofi, the shepherd, is looking after his sheep, (2) The Lord is my shepherd, (3) He will shepherd me. In sentence 1, the fact that Kofi is looking after his sheep indicates that the word "shepherd" is used to mean sheep-watcher. In 2, since I am not a sheep for the Lord to watcher after me, the word "shepherd" must be taken metaphorically as meaning "The Lord cares for and watches over me the same way as the "shepherd" does to his flock." The last sentence uses shepherd as a verb connecting the subject (He) and object (me) to mean "provide for." This is a crucial step as one cannot translate a text without knowing the words and the relationship between them.

The second aspect of linguistic identification is semantic exegesis which has to do with the meaning of all the words in the source language. The translator needs to know what the text means in the source language in order to determine what it means in the translating language. One can only translate if he/she is able to go behind the words to the meaning of the words. The following guidelines are very helpful in conducting an effective word study.[7]

  i.   Most words have a range of meaning so that one word does double duty with regard to the concept of symbols. Word meanings can overlap with the meanings of other words.

 ii.   Word meanings change over time; therefore, it is the context rather than the original meaning of the term that must determine how the exegete will appropriately define and understand any given word.

iii.   In addition to having denotative meaning (the literal meaning of a word), words also have connotative value (that is, special meaning for a particular person or group, perhaps only in certain contexts), which is why it is important to survey the literary and historical backgrounds of a passage before studying the words in that passage.

iv.   Individual words function with the rest of the words in the context to express larger sets of concepts; they can rarely accomplish the feat of expressing a complete concept themselves.

---

[7] These guidelines have been adapted from Blomberg and Markley, *New Testament Exegesis*, 119.

v.   The priority in determining word meaning should almost always go to the findings of synchronic (that is, "with time") analysis of the word under study rather than those of diachronic (that is, "through time") analysis.

After the semantic exegesis, the translator has to determine the equivalence of each source-language word in the target language based on his/her knowledge and sensitivity of the receptor language. The use of fixed equivalents makes translation literal, while the use of less fixed equivalents makes it free. Experience has shown that it is virtually impossible to obtain linguistic equivalence between different languages. Generally speaking, any person who does not have adequate knowledge of the translating language cannot be a good translator for a project in that language. This does not mean, however, that the translator must know endless and infinite sets of sentences; what is important is the linguistic knowledge required for effective and faithful translation work. This step is taken to bridge the linguistic gap between ancient and modern languages. There are other non-linguistic exegeses, and to those we now turn.

Contextual Exegesis

The idea behind contextual exegesis is that the meaning of words needs to be derived based on the context in which they appear. The following quote by Tov is insightful, "The linguistic exegesis mentioned in paragraph ay describes the determining of equivalents on the basis of linguistic-semantic identification alone. Like linguistic exegesis, contextual exegesis also has linguistic aspects, but often the overall meaning of the context is more influential for determining equivalents."[8] A word may have many basic meanings. However, in most cases, the context points out quite clearly which of the basic meanings of a word is intended.

Three contexts may be studied in this regard. The first is the historical context, which deals with the general history behind a given text in terms of its authorship, date of composition, audience (recipients), occasion and purpose, the socio-economic, political and religious contexts of the book. Other aspects of historical context that the translator may study include where the book falls in the life of the author, the circumstances of the author at the time of writing, and the relationship between the author and the recipients.

---

[8] Tov, *Textual Criticism*, 126.

Social context deals with the world that existed at the same time as the text, that is, "the world of the text." There are different aspects of social context. We have the cultural context, which refers to the ways of understanding and living of a particular society, including the society's political, social and religious beliefs and practices, economics, music, art, values, military/war customs, material customs and others. The data collected for this level are usually unfamiliar to the modern translator. The audience context is also another aspect of social context. It deals with the experiences and specific knowledge common to the biblical audience. Information about the Roman rule at the time of Jesus falls under this category.

The literary context of the text must also be considered as it also informs the meaning of words and expressions. Every word is part of a sentence; every sentence is part of a paragraph; every paragraph is part of a book; and every book is part of the whole of Scripture. Meaning must therefore be informed by the context in which the word finds itself. Literary context may be immediate context (immediate surrounding text), book context (the book in which text is found) or canonical context (the text located in the entire canon of Scripture). Of these, the immediate context is most influential in exegetical considerations.

An example is the translation of the word *pleroo* (Matt. 5:17). This word literally means "fill up something," as in "fill a cup with water." However, the word also has a figurative sense of "fulfil" (make something come true or come to pass) the actions and events required by the Law (see TEV, GNTD, NIV, NAB) or foretold by the Prophets or fill up in the sense of making complete that which was not yet complete or give a complete understanding of what was said in the Law and the Prophets (that is to make the Law and the Prophets have their true meaning).[9] The first translation agrees with Mathew's use of the same term in his Gospel (cf. 1:22; 2:15, 17, 23; 3:15). The second meaning links verse 17 with 21-48, where Jesus gives a fuller understanding of certain Old Testament commands. I agree with Barclay M. Newman and Philip C. Stine that a better understanding of *pleroo* in the present context is "fulfil," that is, make something come true.[10] It is important to note that though there is no scholarly consensus as to what the verb *pleroo* means in this context, one thing that is clear is that it does not mean that Jesus came to "make the Law and the Prophets stronger" as in the literal sense of fill up. Granted that this analysis is right, then one

---

[9] Barclay M. Newman and Philip C. Stine, *A Handbook on The Gospel of Matthew* (New York: UBS Handbook Series, 1988), electronic edition.
[10] Newman and Stine, *A Handbook on The Gospel of Matthew*, np.

can conclude that some Akan translations of *pleroo* as *ma* (fill up) needs a relook because it makes the reader think that the reason why Jesus came was to make the Law and the Prophets stand firmly rather than to come true or to have complete meaning. This shortfall has been addressed by the Bono version of the New Testament by rendering *pleroo* as *"aba mu"* (to come true). The full verse reads: *Honnwene sɛ mebaa sɛ meebeyi mmara anaa adiyifoɔ he hɔ; mamma sɛ meebeyi no hɔ, na mmom maaba sɛ meebɛma no aba mu* ("Do not think that I have come to abolish the law or the prophets; I have come not to abolish but to fulfill").

In Colossians 2:17, Paul gives the reason for which he says in verse 16 that the Colossians should not let anyone condemn them in matters of food and drink or of observing festivals, new moons, or Sabbaths. The first part of the verse (v. 17) says those things are "a shadow of the things that were to come" (NIV). This means that those things served as a mirror reflection of what was to happen in the future. Paul was referring to how those things were observed in the Old Testament. He then moves on to the second part, where he says that, in contrast to those things which were shadowed, the *soma* is found in Christ. My interest lies in the translation of the word *soma* in some Akan dialects. *Soma* has different meanings, two of which we consider below. First of all, it could refer literally to the living or dead body of a human being or animal (see Matt. 6.25; Mark 15:43; Heb. 13:11; James 3.3). It may, however, be used figuratively to refer to as substance or reality in contrast to shadow. It appears in Colossians 2:17 in the sense of "actual substance or reality" (what is true) as opposed to shadow, delusion or illusion (see NIV [reality], NRSV [substance]). While the majority support this interpretation, a few also argue that soma should be understood as "the body of Christ," the Church. The NAB seems to follow this thought when it writes, "the reality is the body of Christ." Whichever way one takes it, it is clear that the text intends to show a contrast between what is real and what is a mere shadow. There is, therefore, the need to have words such as reality, substance, what is true, what is real in the second part of the text. In Akan, *soma* is translated as *"nipadua"* (Asante/Akuapem) and *"frɔdɔɔ"* (Fante). By rendering it literally, the Asante/Akuapem translation gives the human body as Christ's and hence misses the contrast intended by Paul. The Asante Diglot (2018) renders it *"deɛ ɛdi mu"* ("what is important" or "the substance"). This is an improvement over the old Asante translation (which says literally, "the human body belongs to Christ"). A study of the context points to the fact that Paul used the word *soma* in the figurative sense to mean reality. Akan words like *"kann"* (what is real or reality), *"pɔtee"* (the actual thing) and the like would better translate soma in Colossians 2:17. The reader should consider which term will be more appropriate in his/her context and then apply it.

Theological Exegesis

According to Tov, theological exegesis has to do with "the description of God and his acts, the Messiah, Zion, the exile, as well as various ideas, such as that of repentance."[11] The role of theological exegesis in translation is not that the translation of the Bible should be controlled by the theological position of a particular church. A translation done under the influence of any church tradition is prone to saying what the text does not say. Theological exegesis helps the translator to conduct his/her task within the context of divine revelation. We have noted earlier that words may have different meanings. Theological exegesis helps the translator to choose options that are theologically suitable for the context in question. Tov makes this point when he says, theological exegesis "may be expressed through theologically motivated choices of translation equivalents, in changes in words and verses (either slight or great) or in expansions or omissions of ideas considered offensive."[12] The translation of the term *prototokos* in Colossians 1:15 is our first example. This term has shades of meanings such as firstborn, preeminence, and source, among others. The choice of the equivalent term should be informed by what theology such choice will teach. The Akan translation (Asante and Akuapem) chose firstborn (*abakan*) and say Christ is *adebɔ nyinaa abakan* (Christ is the firstborn of all creation). In the Akan language such a rendering implies Christ is the first to be created. This, however, contradicts the theology of the immediate context (v. 16-17) as well as the canonical context (e.g., John 1:1). The translator needs to decide which term will teach the true theology as revealed in Scripture. In the present discussion, *prototokos* should best be rendered "source" (Akan: *farebae* and therefore yield, *adebɔ nyinaa farebae*, see Asante Diglot, 2018 version). This is how theological exegesis/hermeneutics comes to play in the translation process.

   With this brief discussion on exegetical considerations in Bible translation, I now consider intertextuality in the next section.

What is Intertextuality?

According to Gérard Genette, intertextuality refers to "all that sets the text in a relationship, whether obvious or concealed, with other texts."[13] Intertextuality presupposes that a text does not come into existence in isolation; it must

---

[11] Tov, *Criticism*, 127.
[12] Tov, *Criticism*, 127.
[13] Gérard Genette, *Palimpsests: Literature in the Second Degree* Translated by Channa Newman and Claude Doubinsky (London: University of Nebraska Press, 1997), 1.

relate to other texts. Thus, Michael Foucault argues that "there can be no statement that in one way or another does not re-actualize others."[14] Therefore, intertextuality shows the influence or presence of one text in another text. It differs from intratextuality which is the interconnection between texts of the same literary work. It implies interaction between culture, an author, a text, and a reader in which the writer includes echoes from other texts and leaves the reader to decode the pattern.

When applied to biblical texts, intertextuality means the interconnection between two biblical texts from two different books. It may be inter-canonical (between two canons). For example, the use of an Old Testament text by a New Testament writer. New Testament writers provide their readers with clues that they are drawing another text into the present discourse by using quotation formulas such as "it is written", "for the Scripture says." Such a use involves moving between the Covenants. The language of 2 Timothy 4:6(-8) echoes Philippians 2:12-18 in terms of the theme of Paul's suffering as a sacrifice. Quotations may be a chain of passages (Rom. 15:9-12); a commentary pattern (Rom. 9-11) and merged citations (Rom. 3:10b-18), paraphrase or allusions (cf. Luke 4:18ff with Isa. 61:1ff; and Luke 3:4ff and Mark 1:3 with Isa. 40:3, and others). New Testament writers may have used Old Testament sources to authenticate their writings. More than that, the New Testament writer expects his readers to place the quoted text within its original context in order to discern its sense and function in the present discourse. Thus the meaning of a story retold in Scriptures cannot be divorced from the original narrative structure and sequences in and by which that story was originally told. Intertextuality may be intra-canonical (within the same canon). For example, Old Testament writers alluded to Israel's Exodus and Wilderness experience in several texts in connection with Israel's current disobedience and reminded them of God's covenant faithfulness.

The term intertextuality was introduced by Julia Kristeva in 1969, who argued that a biblical text makes meaning only when it is interconnected with earlier uses and understanding. She argued that the contexts of a text in its former and contemporary usage are usually fluid; the meaning of a text should be considered provisional rather than definitive.

---

[14] Michel Foucault, *The Archaeology of Knowledge* translated from the French by A.M. Sheridan Smith (London: Tavistock Publications, 1972), 98.

Techniques in Intertextuality

An intertextual connection may be in the sense of "echo," which serves as a pointer, pointing to the original source. The writer assumes that his readers are very familiar with the prior source and expects them to bring the echoed source into play when interpreting his source. For example, the expression עָזִּי וְזִמְרָת יָהּ וַיְהִי־לִי לִישׁוּעָה (Exod. 15:2) is echoed in Psalm 118:14 and Isaiah 12:2. Also, the title "lion of Judah" (Rev. 5:5) echoes the language of the blessing of Judah in Genesis 49:9-12.

Another technique in intertextuality is the appeal to other traditions in other sources. In doing so, the new author may infuse new nuances into the tradition. For example, Paul appeals to rabbinic tradition in Romans. Intertextuality can also be expressed in terms of linkages to Old Testament genres with the expectation that the New Testament reader is conversant with that genre and reads the genre in the New Testament in a similar fashion. An example is the use of *Makarios* the New Testament (e.g., Matt. 5:3-12), which really belong to the אַשְׁרֵי texts (translated Μακάριος by the LXX, e.g., Psa. 1:1) that denote a state rather than received a blessing. Another example is the poetic literature in the New Testament, such as the genre of Wisdom literature (e.g., James). Compare James 4:6 with 1 Peter 5:5, "God opposes the proud but gives grace to the humble," and compare them with Proverbs 3:34.

A Study of Intertextuality in the Epistle of James

I have chosen to concentrate on the epistle of James to have a more focused discussion on intertextuality. A careful reader of James 1 cannot miss the point that James' focus on wisdom (1:5) for the believer is borrowed from the wisdom books in the Old Testament. He borrows an analogy for the shortness of life from Proverbs 27:1; Ecclesiastes 12:6; and Job 15:31, comparing the length of our lives to that of a fading flower (1:17). In 2:8, James employs Rabbinic tradition that regarded love-your-neighbor rhetoric (Leviticus 19:18) as the basic principle of the entire Torah. James also shows an intertextual connection with the Ten Commandments (Exod. 20:1ff) when he prohibits his reader from committing murder, adultery and becoming a law breaker (James 2:10-13). Additionally, James echoes Second Temple and early rabbinic sources that show how Abraham fulfilled the Torah perfectly. For example, Ben Sirach 44:19-21 notes that Abraham kept the law, and he was found faithful too (cf. Gen 26:5). He was found faithful when he was tested (see Jubilees 17:15-18; 1 Macc. 2: 52).

As James addresses the use of the tongue in chapter three, he gives echoes of passages like Proverb 10:19; 17:27 and 21:23, all of which talk about the need to control the tongue. James 4:6b is a striking parallel to 1 Peter 5. Both quote

Proverbs 3:34 "God opposes the proud, but gives grace to the humble" (James 4:6b; 1 Pet 5:5). Interestingly, both texts have the same deviation from the LXX text. There is also a clear textual connection between James 4:8 and Ben Sirach 38:10 (both talk about coming near to God for purification) and between James 4:9 and Ben Sirach 21:20 (both deal with sorrow). More so, James' discussions about disdainful speech and judgment in 4:11-12 are connected to texts such as 1 Clement 30:1ff; 2 Corinthians 12,10; 1 Peter 2,1; The Shepherd of Hermas 2,3. Early Christian tradition is also reflected loosely in the phrases "there is one who can save and destroy" (James 4:12 cf. Matt. 10,28; The Shepherd of Hermas 12,6,3; Sim 9,23,4) as well as "judging someone else" (James 4:11 cf. Matt. 7:1-5; Rom. 2:1ff.; 14,4).

In James 5 are echoes of themes that are found in some Old Testament prophetic books. For example, James 5:1-6 has a strong connection with the book of Amos. In this text, James rips into the rich, who are most likely corrupt landowners, causing injustice. He predicts their coming destruction for their worship of material wealth. This echoes Amos' condemnation of the rich for their injustice towards the poor and the prediction of the impending destruction of their riches (Amos 1:12, 14; 5:6; 7:4; 8:4-6).

Intertextuality and Bible Translation

Intertextual relationship between texts implies that texts develop meaning in a collective manner. Therefore, intertextuality helps the translator to at least partly determine the meaning of a text by the meaning of other texts. In other words, intertextual study enhances the translator's exegetical considerations. In translation, the production of the translated text depends to a larger extent on the translator's knowledge of other pertinent or related texts and contexts. The translator's ability to connect the expressions, themes and stylistic devices used in the text under consideration with those of another text (if any) enhances the translation process. If the connection between these two passages is intentional, then translations of each text must be such that they grant access to the intertextual connection. Recognition that this New Testament material ought to be read like its Old Testament counterparts both liberates meaning conveyance and makes it possible for translation consistency between the Testaments.

Conclusion

No translation is free from interpretation. This chapter has shown that exegetical analysis is indispensable in the translation process. This means that the translator must have some basic exegetical training. However, since not all translators have this skill, we can help the situation by referring to exegetical comments provided by scholarly commentaries. Fortunately for us, ParaText has such resources to be used by the translator. The translator must avoid being too close to the original text that he/she appears too far from the receptor language and produce translations which cannot easily be understood. Such a situation creates "a gap between what the translator-exegete understands, and what is or is not understood by his intended readers." While I agree that a translator's work necessarily requires some interpretation, care must be taken not to introduce doctrinal biases in the translation. Finally, the translator needs to establish any intertextual relationship the text may have with other text and translate in a way to reflect this relationship.

Review Exercise

1. What is exegesis? How important is it in the process of Bible translation?

2. What is meant by the term hermeneutics? How different is it from exegesis?

3. Explain the three kinds of exegesis with examples.

4. What is intertextuality? How relevant is intertextuality in Bible translation?

5. With reference to Matthew 5 (RSV), show how syntactic marking determines the meaning of the words: meek (v. 5), salt (v. 13), and prophets (v. 17).

6. Outline the five hermeneutical premises given in this chapter.

7. How would you translate the Greek word *talanton* (Matt. 25:14-15) into your dialect? Give support for your answer from the context.

8. Conduct an intertextual study of Matthew 1:1-18.

Chapter 10

Linguistic Aspects of Bible Translation

I have noted earlier that translation goes beyond changing words from the original language to another. It also involves decoding and deciphering all the aspects and functions of the original language into the new language. A task of this nature requires knowledge about language studies, linguistics. It is in this light that I examine some basic aspects of linguistics necessary for the work of Bible translators.

What is Linguistics?

Linguistics refers to the science and study of language. Language may be defined as "a collection of symbols, letters or words with arbitrary meanings that are governed by rules and conventions that help people to communicate effectively."[1] Language may be used to give information; to obtain information (by asking questions); to stimulate actions (by giving instructions); to express desire, feeling or emotions (by exclamations or by poetry) and to indicate an attitude. Human language uses vocal sounds (that is, sounds made with the mouth and other speech organs) or written forms which represent verbal sound. It is a complex system that involves the interaction of signals. Also, language allows for the expression of new ideas through creativity. "Language, any language, has a dual character: it is both a means of communication and a carrier of culture."[2] As a carrier of culture, language gives people their identity. A person who speaks Igbo will easily be identified as a Nigerian of Igbo origin. Language identifies the culture and language of a people as well as their history and identity.

As a communication tool, language has three elements. The first element is what Karl Marx once referred to as the language of real-life which has to do with the origin and development of a language— that is, "the relations people enter into with one: another in the labor process, the links they necessarily establish among themselves in the act of a people, a community of human

---

[1] Kofi Agyekum, *Linguistics: Ethnography of Speaking* (University of Ghana, Accra: Institute of Continuing and Distance Education, 2010), 18.
[2] Ngugi wa Thiong'o, *Decolonising the Mind: The Politics of Language in African Literature* (Nairobi: East African Educational Publishers, 2004), 13

beings, producing wealth or means of life like food, clothing, houses."[3] This element is built on the fact that historical developments of human societies begin with interaction and cooperation in production through the division of labor. Here, the basic community is the household, made up of husband, wife and children. A more complex community is, say, a factory where many minds and hands come together for the production of an item. Thus, "production is co-operation, is communication, is language, is expression of a relation between human beings and it is specifically human."[4]

The second aspect of language is speech which imitates the language of real life, that is, "communication in production"[5] Language functions as a verbal signpost to make communication possible. The spoken word serves as a mediator between two parties just as hand mediates between two humans. The verbal signposts both reflect and aid communication or the relations established between human beings in the production of their means of life.

The third aspect of language as communication is the written signs which imitate the spoken word.[6] The first two aspects of language through the hand and the spoken word historically evolved more or less concurrently, but the written aspect emerges after the first two have evolved. The written language develops gradually from the use of visual symbols to signify sounds to the use of the most complicated and different letter and picture-writing systems of the modern world.

Beyond the communicative function, language also plays socio-cultural functions in that people can be identified by the languages they speak. In other words, language makes people groups different from others. Language expresses the culture of the speaker and transmits this culture from one generation to another. It binds people together by forming a network of communication and providing each language group with a common history and identity. The language that people share serves as the medium by which they share memories of their joint history and tradition. The identity language gives to people can be considered at three levels, namely, national identity, ethnic identity and social identity.[7] Ghanaians, Nigerians, and Gambians speak English as their official language. English, therefore, gives these countries a national identity, the identity that they were all colonized by Anglophone nation(s). The Akan group of Ghana speak the Akan language.

---

[3] Thiong'o, *Decolonising the Mind,* 13

[4] Thiong'o, *Decolonising the Mind,* 13

[5] Thiong'o, *Decolonising the Mind,* 13

[6] Thiong'o, *Decolonising the Mind,* 14.

[7] Agyekum, Linguistics, 27.

The Bono speak Bono dialect to identify themselves as Bono. The language of a people has their art, religion, music, tradition, politics, history, philosophy and other cultural values in it.

Every language has its own distinctive systems for linking sounds with meanings. The first feature is vocabulary which refers to the list of meaningful words which have been (unconsciously) agreed and accepted by speakers of a language. The inventory of words for a language is referred to as **lexicon**. The second feature is grammar referring to the agreed set of patterns for making meaningful utterances. The third feature is phonology, which we considered shortly.

Various levels of language analysis (or linguistics) can be noted and outlined.[8] Language can be analyzed at the phonetic or phonological level, that is, the sound system, their combination and contrast. The phonological study of a language includes such issues as a fixed number of phonetic sounds, sound distribution as well as prosodic features such as pitch, intonation, stress, tone, loudness, duration and rhythm. Another way of analyzing language is morphology which deals with word formation and component parts of words. Lexicology, that is, the form, meaning, classification and behavior of words, is another level of language study. One can also conduct a syntactical analysis of a language; this deals with the rules governing how words are ordered to form phrases, clauses and sentences. There is also semantic analysis which focuses on the meaning of words and the relationship between meaning and form. Further still, language may be analyzed at the symbolic level by focusing on the manner in which speakers express cultural attitudes in their choice of words. It deals with both what a word stands for and what it connotes. Other sub-divisions of language are historical linguistics (the study of language evolution over time), socio-linguistics (the study of how language is used in society), psycholinguistics (the study of how language is processed within the mind), neurolinguistics (the study of the actual encoding of language in the brain), and computational linguistic (the study of natural linguistics using the techniques of computer science).

It is crucial to acknowledge that each language is unique, having certain distinctive characteristics which give it a special character (such as word-building capacities, unique patterns of phrase order, techniques for linking clauses into sentences, markers of discourse, and special discourse types of poetry, proverbs, and song). Often, languages tend to be rich in vocabulary in

---

[8] The following discussions have been gleaned from Agyekum, *Linguistics*, 23.

areas of cultural interest, that is, the areas of specialization the people. A farming community has more vocabulary about farming than a fishing community. The frequency of use of figurative language also differs from one language to another. Some languages use passive voice; others do not. To be an effective translator, one has to respect all these unique features as related to the receptor language.

The Role of Linguistics in Bible Translation

Bible translation involves linguistics. First, before a translation project begins, the translation agency conducts a socio-linguistic survey to know how the language is used in the community. In this survey, attention is given to the various subdialects and how they differ from one another. The population that speaks the language as well as the need for the translation may also be considered in the survey. The survey becomes a tool for determining which subdialects may be considered for the translation project. For example, the socio-linguistic survey that was conducted by the Bible Society of Ghana on the Bono dialect was the basis for the selection of subdialects of the Bono dialect of six communities, namely, Dormaa, Berekum, Sunyani, Techiman, Nkoranza and Wenchi to be considered for the Bono Bible Translation Project. Other communities such as Japekrom, Drobo, Atebubu and others were found to have subdialects that differ from those spoken by the six communities mentioned earlier in such a way these subdialects could not be considered fully in the project. These discoveries were made before the team of translators was formed for the Bono Bible Translation Project.

Secondly, it is the tools provided by linguistics that will enable the translation team to prepare an orthography, the rule governing the writing of a particular language. Orthography is a very important tool without which no translation can be done. Translators need to use their linguistic skills to determine the alphabetic system of their language, how letters combine to form words, and how words combine to form phrases, clauses and sentences. These rules must be documented and agreed upon at the initial stage of the translation project. However, since no one is perfect, it may be revised as time goes on.

Thirdly, the translator needs to know, for example, the grammar, the meaning of the words, as well as the phrases and sentences in both the source and receptor languages. Each language differs in its linguistic functions, yet there are commonalities among languages as well. The translator needs to determine areas of similarities and differences between the source and receptor languages. More so, the translator must note that since languages are different, he/she will often have to use grammatical forms and words that are different from those found in the source language. That should not be a problem at all; what is important is that the meaning of the source text should be maintained in the receptor text.

Bible translation is not just about translating meaning. It also involves the translation of culture. There are texts in which the translator maintains the source culture; in others, he/she has to substitute the source culture with the culture of the receptor community. Since the culture of a people group is usually stored in their language, linguistic analysis (especially the choice of words) serves as a tool for the translator to translate cultural values accurately. This also means that the translator should be well-versed in the culture and worldview of the community for which the translation is done.

Those working on a language that has not been documented before would normally find linguistics a necessity in composing a word. People have been speaking with words, but it is the translation project that is putting them in written form. Without linguistic competence, one would be frustrated in the process and give up.

With this background, I continue to consider translation challenges arising from linguistic differences between source and receptor languages.

Some Linguistic Challenges facing Mother-Tongue Translators

Translation work involving two languages belonging to a relatively unified culture has fewer linguistic challenges. Even in that case, there are challenges because no two languages have the same linguistic structure. No two languages have vocabularies which coincide so that every time a word in one language appears in a text, it can be translated by the same word in the other language. Every language has its own peculiar characteristics. Linguistic problems are those which arise from differences in lexical elements, syntactic form, grammatical structure, morphology, discourse features, and others between the source and the receptor languages.

First of all, many words in the source language (Hebrew or Greek) have more than one meaning from which the translator is to choose the best for the context. Some of the meanings are so divergent that, at times, they show contrasting meanings. The Hebrew word *barak*, for example, basically means "to bless"; yet it has been translated "to curse" four times in Job (1:5, 11; 2:5, 9) and twice as "to blaspheme" (1 Kings 21:10, 13; see also Psa. 10:3). The word *logos* (John 1:1) also has many meanings, including "the word by which one expresses inward thought" or "the inward thought and reason itself." Other meanings of *logos* include "saying" (John 21:23), "treatise" (Acts 1:1), "speech" (1 Cor. 2:1), "utterance" (1 Cor. 1:5). The translator has to decide the original author's intended meaning out of the possible meanings of the word. Since different translators see things differently (probably due to personal prejudices, preferences, educational level, and so on), there is sometimes no agreement in the selection of definitions for words. These differences exist among individual translators and among translation teams such that one may find different meanings of the same source language text in different versions of the Bible.

Another linguistic problem translators face has to do with words that have no adequate modern-language equivalence. Since no single word is adequate for conveying the meaning of such words, the translator finds it difficult to translate them. The Greek word *parakletos* translated "comforter" in John 14:16, 26; 15:26; 16:7, and "advocate" in 1 John 2:1 falls in this category. From *para* (beside) and *kletos* (to call), *parakletos* actually means either in the generic sense of "one called alongside to help" or in the technical sense of "defense attorney." The help offered by *parakletos* can be comforting or advocating. Other helps the Spirit renders, which are evident from John's Gospel, include teaching believers, witnessing to Christ, and prosecuting the world. All these elements cannot be fully satisfied by the use of a particular English term. It seems best (in my view) to use the generic term "Helper," though one admits it does not convey the full meaning of *parakletos*. I prefer "Helper" because virtually all the services rendered by the *parakletos* tend to help the believer in one way or the other.

Further still, the English word "power" is used to translate two Greek words, (1) *exousia*, which means power in the sense of authority, privilege, or right, and (2) *dunamis*, which means power in the sense of the ability to do work. While these two expressions are clearly different in Greek, they are usually taken as "power" in English. The Akan of Ghana have rendered *exousia* (John 1:12) as *tumi* (authority) and *dunamis* (Acts 1:8) as *ahɔɔden* (strength [for work]). The Akan gets *dunamis* correct but seems to translate *exousia* wrongly in John 1:12 since, in this text, the idea is not authority (in the sense of power) to become God's children but authority in the sense of right or privilege.[9] That right or privilege of sonship that comes to one who believes may be expressed as "he made it possible for them to become God's children" or "he gave them the place of being God's children."[10] The Swahili New Testament translates *exousia* as *uwezo* (power, capacity) rather than privilege (*upendeleo*) (John 1:12). In Acts 1:8, *dunamis* is translated *nguvu* (power). The terms *uwezo* and *nguvu* are synonymous. The use of *upendeleo* for *exousia* in John 1:12 may be considered in future Swahili projects. Additionally, the Greek word *spoudazo* (cf. 2 Tim. 2:15) has been rendered in English as "study" so that the text reads

---

[9] Newman and Nida, *A Handbook on The Gospel of John*, np.
[10] Newman and Nida, *A Handbook on The Gospel of John*, np.

"Study to show thyself approved unto God." However, a critical study of the word shows that *spoudazo* refers to the act of putting the utmost effort in some activity, that is, "make every effort," or "try as hard as you can," rather than the acquisition of knowledge.

Another key linguistic problem has to do with syntax. There are instances where the receptor language is not able to express the tense of a verb in the source language due to the difference in the verbal system between the source and receptor languages. In most African languages, tenses are used primarily to signify the time of the action of the verb. The biblical languages, however, differ from such languages in this regard. In Hebrew, for instance, a verb is used to show whether an action is complete, incomplete or continuous. Completed action is expressed by the perfect form of the verb, incomplete by the imperfect form, and continuous by the participle (which functions as a verb). An action may be past, present, or future, whether it is complete, incomplete or continuous. The time of the action must be determined by the context. Taking English for instance, translators usually use the general rule that a Hebrew perfect corresponds to the English past or perfect, the Hebrew imperfect to the future, and the Hebrew participle (when used as a verb) to the present. This approach is deficient in that it fails to present the full force of the Hebrew state of completeness or incompleteness, or continual or continuous action (as I demonstrate below). For example, in Isaiah 66:24, the statement "their worm shall not die" suggests that the worms will never die or are undying. However, what the Hebrew text says is that at the time of the observation, the worm was not yet dead. If the writer wanted to convey the idea that that worm will never die, an adverbial modifier would have been added. A similar verb form is found in Genesis 2:25 in the expression "and were not ashamed," meaning at the time of observation they were not yet ashamed, not that they will never be ashamed.

Greek also differs from English in verbal usage. Greek verbs are used to stress the kind of action, differentiating between durative action or continuous action, action conceived of as a whole, completed action in a particular moment of time, or action completed with significant results remaining. It is not easy to carry these ideas into English. This fact can be illustrated with the KJV translation of 1 John 3:9 as "Whosoever is born of God doth not commit sin; for his seed remaineth in him: and he cannot sin, because he is born of God." With this kind of translation, the reader is made to believe that the believer is a sinless person and, therefore, anyone who sins is an unbeliever. However, a critical study of the Greek text shows that the Greek tense of the verb here translated "commit sin" is the present which shows continuous, habitual action. What John is saying is that the believer does not sin habitually; that is, the believer does not "continue to sin" (NIV) or does not remain in sin because he/she does not take delight in sin. One reasons this way because the same author says in the same letter that one (including the writer himself) is a liar if one says he/she has not sinned and went on to encourage his audience to confess their sins (1 John 1:8-10).

The final example is taken from Matthew 16:19, which has been rendered by the NRSV as "I will give you the keys of the kingdom of heaven, and whatever you bind on earth **will be bound** in heaven, and whatever you loose on earth **will be loosed** in heaven" (my emphasis). The implication of this rendition is that God (represented by "heaven") will be obliged to approve or prohibit whatever Peter (and the apostles) approve or prohibits on earth. A close examination of the verbs translated "will be bound" and "will be loosed" shows that they are future perfect, constructed by combining the future of the verb "to be" with the perfect passive participle. The verbs may properly be translated as "would have been bound" and "would have been loosed" so that the text becomes, "I will give you the keys of the kingdom of heaven, and whatever you bind on earth **would have been bound in heaven**, and whatever you loose on earth **would have been loosed in heaven**" (my emphasis). This means that the lower court does not compel the superior court to make any decision. Rather, decisions made by the superior court are manifested in the decisions taken by the lower court. This kind of divine-human collaboration is evident in Acts 1:24, where the disciples (in the process of replacing Judas) prayed that God would show them which of the men he had chosen to replace Judas.

Conclusion

The main point in this chapter is that a linguistically handicapped person cannot be an effective translator. The translator is more than an ordinary language user. The translator's choice of words has a huge influence on people's theology; hence, it is always the best option that must be chosen. The linguistic aspect of a translation project needs to be taken seriously. Therefore, translators who lack such competence must be given adequate linguistic training. It helps if the translators are native speakers of the receptor language because native speakers have much vocabulary of the translating language and would rarely have to rely on others for their choice of words.

Review Exercise

1. Explain the term socio-linguistic survey? How relevant is this research to the translation process?

2. In what ways is human language different from other systems of communication?

3. Critically explain why a Bible translator should be given linguistic training.

4. Explain some of the purposes for which language is used in everyday life.

5. What is meant by the "form" and "meaning" of language?

6. Is meaning universal or perspectival? Explain your answer.

7. In your own words, attempt to make a definition of what language is.

8. Identify some linguistic challenges associated with Bible translation in your community. How can these challenges be resolved?

Chapter 11

Explicitation and Structural Adjustments
in Bible Translation

The previous chapter ended with discussions on linguistic challenges in translation. In this chapter, I consider another crucial challenge, ambiguity. Biblical writers shared certain information with their audience, and so they did not state such data in their texts. The absence of these data did not make the message unclear to the original audience. To the modern reader, however, the absence of such information is a challenge to understanding the message. The translator, acting as the original author, should be able to make what is implicit in the source text explicit in the translating text if, without doing so, there will be difficulty in understanding the message. My focus has to do with the approaches used in dealing with ambiguity and the extent to which the translator can adjust the translating text.

What is Explicitation?

Explicitation is a translation technique used to make explicit in the target text what remains implicit in the source text, relying on the context or the situation for conveying the meaning.[1] J. Vinay and Jean Darbelnet, who first introduced the term, defined it as "a stylistic translation technique which consists of making explicit in the target language what remains implicit in the source language because it is apparent from either the context or the situation."[2] The reverse process which consists of making what is explicit in the source text implicit in the target text based on the context or the situation for conveying the meaning is referred to as **Implicitation**. Explicitation must be regarded as a feature of translation rather than the result of the linguistic and/or cultural differences between the source and the receptor languages. A number of procedures can be used to achieve explicitation, including the (1)

---

[1] Kinga Klaudy, "Explicitation" in *Routledge Encyclopedia on Translation Studies* second edition edited by Mona Baker and Gabriela Saldanha (London: Routledge, 2011), 104.
[2] J. Vinay and Jean Darbelnet, *Comparative Stylistics of French and English: A Methodology for Translation* translated by J.C. Sager and M. J. Hamel (Philadelphia: John Benjamins, 1995), 342.

use of interjections to express more clearly the progression of the characters' thoughts or to accentuate a given interpretation; (2) expansion of condensed passages; (3) addition of modifiers, qualifiers and conjunctions to achieve greater transparency; (4) addition of extra information; (5) insertion of explanations; (6) repetition of previous details for the purpose of clarity; (7) precise renderings of implicit or vague data; (8) more accurate descriptions; (9) naming of geographical locations and disambiguation of pronouns with precise forms of identification.[3] These methods will become clear in the discussions below. Two kinds of implicit information may be identified, namely, linguistically and contextually implicit information.

Linguistic Explicitation

Linguistically implicit information refers to information that is absent in the source language but is required to ensure grammatical correctness and completeness. In other words, linguistic explicitation becomes necessary if, without it, no linguistically correct or clear target text can be produced. For example, 1 Timothy 1:3 starts with *kathos* ("just as"), which need to be completed with "so now." The expression "so now" is absent in the Greek text but needs to be supplied in the receptor language if the passage is to be grammatical correct and complete. Similarly, in 1 Kings 19:20, where Elijah replies to Elisha "what have I done you?" (NIV), one has to add "to stop" and have "what have I done **to stop** you?" in order to make it clear and meaningful.

Another situation that requires explicitation is the translation of unknown ideas (concepts) using a "foreign" word. Since a "foreign" word is not well-known by the receptor community, it is important to make it more meaningful by introducing a generic term before it. That is done by adding a classifier. For example, in translating cumin (Matt. 23:23b) into a culture where it has to be used as a foreign word, it would be helpful to say "… the spice called cumin." Similarly, if camel (Mark 1:6) is to be translated into a culture that is not familiar with it, one may say "… an **animal** called 'camel.'" Other examples are "**precious stone** ruby," "**city** Jerusalem," and "**rite of** baptism."

Another example that shows the need for linguistic explicitation is the statement, "For to those who have, more will be given, and they will have an abundance" (Matt. 13:12). The problem with this passage is the exact thing that people have or do not have. One may be tempted to think of material

---

[3] R. Vanderauwera, Dutch *Novels Translated into English: The Transformation of a "Minority" Literature* (Amsterdam: Rodopi, 1985)

possession, and the meaning will be that to the man who has, more will be given until he grows rich. However, a close examination of the context of the passage shows that the implied object is "understanding," in relation to God's activities in establishing his Kingdom in the world (see Matt. 13:13, 14, 15, 19, 23). The Bono Bible translators have dealt with this issue by rendering it as "*Na bɛ a bɛwɔ ahennie he ho nteaseɛ he Nyankopɔn de nteaseɛ bebree bɛka bɛ ho ama banya no mmorosoɔ*" ("For to those who have **understanding of the kingdom, God will add more understanding** to them to have it in abundance" (Matt. 13:12a, emphasis mine).

Consider the NRSV translation of Ephesians 4:13: "until all of us come to the unity of the faith and of the knowledge of the Son of God, to maturity, to the measure of the full stature of Christ." The expression "to maturity" translates the Greek expression "*eis andra teleion,*" literally meaning "to become a mature person." A literal rendering as we have in Akan "*bɛyɛ onipa a wawie nyini*" (to become people who are fully grown or to mature bodily) may lead to the erroneous impression that the Christian life makes one mature bodily. The NRSV deals with this situation by using the term "maturity" rather than saying "mature people." However, it still leaves room for understating maturity as bodily maturity, which is not the focus in the text. The context of the text shows that Paul is speaking of spiritual maturity, precisely, maturity in faith. Making this implied fact explicit may give something like Ephesians 4:13: "until all of us come to the unity of the faith and of the knowledge of the Son of God, to maturity **in faith**, to the measure of the full stature of Christ." This rendering is recommended for languages in which the text can be misread if the kind of maturity is not made explicit. Also, the statement "They have taken the Lord out of the tomb, and we do not know where they have laid him" (John 28:2, NRSV) may require the translator to state explicitly that it was the Lord's body which was taken, rather than the Lord himself. Otherwise, the implication would be that Jesus was not dead. The adjustment yields the statement, "They have taken the **body of the** Lord out of the tomb, and we do not know where they have laid him."

Contextual Explicitation

Contextually implicit information, on the other hand, refers to information derived solely from the external context of a text. It is sometimes necessary to supply some of these data in order to help the reader understand the text from the perspective of the original audience and hence be in a better position to apply it to his/her context. That is to say, contextual explicitation is necessitated by the differences between the background knowledge of the source and the target reader. This may involve inserting pragmatic particles, explicating inferred meanings, explicit marking of illocution, adding background assumptions needed for the interpretation of the text. For example, the description of the Laodicean church as "neither cold nor hot" (Rev. 3:15, NIV) can better be understood if one gets information about the original context, particular the fact that Laodicea, which had no water source of its own, received lukewarm water from nearby water sources.

The translation of culturally-bound customs may necessitate the supply of sufficient information to make the general meaning clear. For example, "you gave me no water for my feet" (Luke 7:44) may be difficult to understand since the expression "water for my feet" tells the reader nothing about what the water would be used for. The Bono-Twi version of the Bible deals with the difficulty posed by this text by rendering the sentence as "*woamma me nsuo anhohoro me nane ho*" ("You gave me no water **to wash** my feet"). By stating what the water is meant for (that is, "to wash"), one is saved from the tendency of thinking that the water is meant for other things. In the following examples, the expression that needs to be supplied to make an implied idea explicitly known have been emphasized: "the tax collector beat his breast" becomes "the tax collector beat his breast **in sorrow**" (Luke 18:13); "circumcised on the eighth day" becomes "circumcised on the eighth day **from birth**" (Phil. 3:5) and "the walls of Jericho fell down" becomes "the walls **which surrounded** Jericho fell down" (Heb. 11:30). The insertions are necessary because the facts that the beating of the chest implies sorrow, that circumcision is done on the eighth day after childbirth and that "the walls of Jericho" refers to the walls around the city of Jericho are not known in all societies. The translator needs to know which customs the receptor culture shares with the source culture and which ones need to be clarified.

Contextual explicitation may be the supply of additional information about a historical reference to make it clearer. The resulting translation becomes very useful for those who lack knowledge about the Bible world. The following translations of 1 Corinthians 10:1 from the NRSV and the GNB are used to illustrate this point. "I do not want you to be unaware, brothers and sisters, that our ancestors were all under the cloud, and all passed through the sea" (NRSV) and "I want you to remember, my brothers, what happened to our ancestors who followed Moses. They were all under the protection of the cloud, and all passed safely through the Red Sea" (GNB). By including the expression "who followed Moses" and qualifying sea with "Red," the GNB helps the reader to connect the present text with the Exodus of the Israelites through the Red Sea. Explicitation is a necessary tool for the translator in dealing with texts that would otherwise create ambiguity.

The foregoing discussion is suggestive that translation adjustments may be in the form of additions, subtractions and alterations. These adjustments are only permitted when they make the translating text clearer or more explicit without changing the semantic content of the source text. Nida divides additions into the following types:

    a.   filling out elliptical expressions

    b.   obligatory specification

    c.   additions required because of grammatical restructuring

    d.   amplification from implicit to explicit status

    e.   answers to rhetorical questions

    f.   classifiers

    g.   connectives

    h.   categories of the receptor language which do not exist in the source language

    i.   doublets.[4]

An addition that leads to amplification from implicit to explicit status is applicable to Luke 11:31, for example, when the expression "... queen of the South" (Luke 11: 31) is translated into cultures where the ideas of "queen" nor "South" are unfamiliar. In such cultures, the translator may have to say "woman who was ruling in the south country."

"Subtractions" refers to the technique of omitting texts that are not necessary for translation or texts that may adversely affect the language habit of the receptor language. Subtractions are meant to make explicit information implicit without altering the semantic content of the original text.[5] Alterations are basically adjustments (shifts) made in translations. The next section takes care of these adjustments.

Structural Adjustments

In the process of Bible translation, the translator tries to keep the structural form of the source text if possible. In most cases, however, this is not possible to achieve as attempting to preserve the structural form may lead to unintelligible or awkward translation. Translators need to know that linguistic features like sentence structure, sentence length, phrase structure patterns

---

[4] Eugene A. Nida, *Towards a Science of Translating* (Leiden: Brill, 1964), 227.

[5] L. Cyrus, "Old Concepts, New Ideas: Approaches to Translation Shifts," *MonTI*, 87-106, 94. Retrieved from http://hdl.handle.net/10234/11973 on 10th January, 2021.

and other similar features are not untouchable. They can be adjusted for the purpose of achieving clarity, accuracy, acceptability and naturalness. This section discusses how major structural features can be adjusted to enhance the success of translation.

Discourse structure

Direct and indirect discourse is problematic to many translators because different languages accommodate these features differently.[6] Some languages show a decided preference for direct discourse; others show a preference for indirect discourse. In a language where one has to avoid indirect discourse, a statement like "They praised him" may be rendered "They said, 'Praise be unto you'." The challenges associated with discourse structure involve the distinctive use of pronominal forms. For example, the statement "James...to the twelve tribes in the Dispersion" will be rendered "I, James, ...write to the twelve tribes in the Dispersion" (James 1:1). Similarly, a phrase like "an apostle of Christ Jesus" in Pauline discourses may be adjusted to read "I who am an apostle of Christ Jesus."

Another problematic area relates to the manner in which "the receptor language handles the identification of participants, whether by nouns, pronouns, and/or substitute reference."[7] Languages differ as to how a character in a narrative has to be referred to after he/she has been introduced. Many languages use the third person pronoun (he/she) to refer to any person introduced in indirect discourse; others have a fourth person, that is, the second third person introduced into a narrative. One has to know what is suitable in the receptor language and make any necessary adjustments.

The issue of gender-inclusive translations is pertinent to the current discussion.[8] We consider how the generic "he" is to be translated using Matthew 16:24-26: Then Jesus told his disciples, "If any man would come after me, let him deny himself and take up his cross and follow me. For whoever would save his life will lose it, and whoever loses his life for my sake will find it. For what will it profit a man, if he gains the whole world and forfeits his life? Or what shall a man give in return for his life?" (RSV, 1946) The expression "Any man" in verse 24 translates the Greek word *tis*, which also means "someone, anyone." The 1978 NIV renders the verse as, "If anyone would

---

[6] Nida and Taber, *The Theory and Practice of Translation,* 112.

[7] Nida and Taber, *The Theory and Practice of Translation,* 113.

[8] I have gleaned what follows from Vern Sheridan Poythress, "Gender in Bible Translation: Exploring a Connection with Male Representatives" In *Westminster Theological Journal* 60(2), (1998):225-253.

come after me, he must deny himself and take up his cross and follow me."
The NIV's approach ensures that both men and women are included. There
still remains the challenge posed by the generic "he," in the form of "he" and
"his," referring back to "anyone" in the verse cited above from the NIV. The
1996 NIV attempted to deal with this challenge by rendering the verses 24 to
26 as "Those who would come after me must deny themselves and take up
their cross and follow me. For those who want to save their lives will lose
them, but those who lose their lives for me will find them. What good will it be
for you to gain the whole world, yet forfeit your soul? Or what can you give in
exchange for your soul?" The elimination of the generic "he" was achieved by
converting all the singulars, "he/his/him/himself," (in verses 24-25) to plurals.
The NIV then adopts a different approach in verse 26 where it replaces the
third person singular "he/his" with the second person "you." The New NRSV,
(1989) uses "they/them/their" in all three verses, while the NLT (1996) uses
"you" in all three verses. Another example is Deuteronomy 8:3 (quoted in
Matt. 4:4 and Luke 4:4), which the NRSV renders "One does not live by bread
alone" instead of "Man shall not live by bread alone." While such adjustments
may not be out of place, translators should be careful not to alter the meaning
of the text by such changes.

More so, discourse structural adjustment deals with the sequence of tenses.
Nida and Taber have observed that "in some languages only the initial verb of
a paragraph indicates the temporal setting, and all the dependent verbs use a
'neutral tense.' In other languages, one can begin with a historical tense, but
then in narration one regularly shifts to the present in order to present the
story in a [livelier] manner."[9] No hard and fast rules are to be set here. One
simply has to study the pattern of the receptor language and make the
necessary adjustments.

Sentence Structure

The transfer of meaning from one language to another requires the
adjustment of features of the sentence structure, such as word and phrase
order, double negatives, singular and plural agreement, active and passive
structures, coordination and subordination, apposition, ellipsis, and
specification of relationship. I proceed to outline each of these features briefly.
The order of words and phrases varies from language to language. For
example, while a sentence in Hebrew has the order Verb-Subject-Object,
English has Subject-Verb-Object. One has to know the natural structure of the

---

[9] Nida and Taber, *The Theory and Practice of Translation,* 113.

receptor language and adjust accordingly. Another feature has to do with double negatives, an area that may be confusing. In some languages, two negatives add up to a positive, whereas in others they represent an emphatic negative expression. The translator needs to be conversant with these forms in both his/her language and the source language.

Active and passive constructions may also be adjusted in translation. Some languages (such as English) can express both passive and active; others may have no passive at all or may have a decided preference for the active. If the receptor language has no passive, then passive statements in the source language have to be changed to active ones. For example, the statement "Jesus was tempted by the devil" becomes "The devil tempted Jesus." The problem becomes complicated when the agent is not mentioned in the source text; the translator has to supply such an agent from the context. This may be easy in some circumstances. There are, however, other situations in which the agent is only implied, such as the cases of the so-called "passives of divine avoidance," a Semitic way of avoiding the mention of the divine name.[10] Passive of divine avoidance refers to the use of passives in which God is the agent of the action, but he is not mentioned by the writer or the speaker. A classic example of such a sentence is "Judge not that you be not judged," (Matt. 7:1) in which the implied agent of the second event is God. The statement may be rendered "Judge not so that God will not judge you." The Beatitudes have examples of passive statements in which the implied agent is God. These include "be comforted," "be called the sons of God," and "be filled" (Matt. 5:1-12).

The next structural feature for consideration is apposition. An apposition such as "Jesus Christ, the Son of God" can be changed into a dependent expression like "Jesus Christ who is the Son of God." While this kind of apposition is easy to deal with, there is a more difficult type which is formally disguised. For example, the land of Canaan is a form of apposition which may be rendered "the land called Canaan." Another feature is ellipsis. All languages use ellipsis, but the patterns of ellipsis vary from language to language. Ellipsis involves constructions in which a grammatically required element is omitted by the speaker or writer to create a structural hole or gap. At the surface structure, ellipses are grammatically incomplete. An ellipsis such as "Julia is greater than I" may have to be rendered "Julia is greater than I am great" or in another language, "Julia is great, I am not."

Another area that needs a mention is punctuation. The original manuscripts of both the Old Testament and New Testament had no divisions into verses or chapters. Neither did they have marks of punctuation. The beginning of a

---

[10] Nida and Taber, *The Theory and Practice of Translation,* 114.

sentence was not identified by a capital letter. Chapters and verses were added in order to make referencing easier. The division of the Bible into chapters, which, with a small modification, is still in use today, was introduced into the Latin Bible by Stephen Langton at the beginning of the thirteenth century. The issue of punctuation may pose a challenge to the translator. Translators are not bound by any strict rules in punctuating their texts. Punctuation must be done in a way to provide the fullest and most appropriate sense in the context. A direct quotation can usually be determined when it is indicated by a verb such as "said," "asked," "replied," and others. One may, however, have challenges in determining the end of a quotation. For example, the end of Jesus' last statement to Nicodemus is judged by the RSV translators to end at John 3:15 and by the NIV and NRSV translators to end at 3:21. The third petition in the Lord's Prayer has been punctuated in the KJV as "Thy will be done in earth, as it is in heaven" (Matt. 6:10), whereas most modern versions punctuate it as "Thy will be done, on earth as in heaven." The second punctuation seems better because it allows the phrase "on earth as in heaven" to be read together with all three preceding petitions, thereby enlarging the scope and meaning of the Prayer. Punctuation may inform the theology of the text. As noted earlier (for example), Jesus' response to the dying thief in Luke 23:43 has been punctuated traditionally as "Truly I say to you, today you will be with me in Paradise." The Jehovah Witnesses, in their quest to support the doctrine of "soul sleep," have moved the comma so that the verse reads (in the New World Translation), "Truly I tell you today, you will be with me in Paradise."

Translation is not just about the choice of words, but also about the order in which they are arranged. Word order informs the meaning of a sentence. The KJV translation of Jesus' words in Matthew 26:27 as "Drink ye all of it" creates uncertainty as to whether he meant all who drink or all of the contents of the cup. The NRSV deals with this challenge by translating it as "Drink from it, all of you". In view of such difficulties, the NRSV corrects several misleading RSV renderings. Instead of Moses leaving "Pharaoh in hot anger" (Exod. 11:8), the NRSV reads "in hot anger he left Pharaoh," and instead of "Joshua was standing before the angel, clothed in filthy garments" (Zech. 3:3), the NRSV reads, "Joshua was dressed with filthy clothes as he stood before the angel."

Kinga Klaudy has outlined the linguistic changes ("transfer operations") that occur during translation. She divides these "transfer operations" into lexical and grammatical operations. Lexical transfer operations are used in dealing with words, and they include the following categories.[11]

---

[11] Kinga Klaudy, *Languages in Translation: Lectures on the Theory, Teaching and Practice of Translation* (Budapest: Scholastica, 2003), 153–182, 473.

i. Narrowing of meaning (differentiation and specification): This operation is carried out to differentiate between the different shades of meanings that a source text lexical item caries and choose only one.

ii. Broadening of meaning (generalization): This operation is undertaken to replace a term in the source text that expresses a specific meaning with a word that expresses a general meaning in the translating text.

iii. Contraction of meanings: This is when two or more source text items can be expressed by only one item in the translating text.

iv. Distribution of meaning: This is when a linguistic item in the source text has more than one meaning, and so more than one lexical item is used in the translating text to convey the full meaning of that lexical item in the source text.

v. Omission of meaning: This operation is done to omit lexical items of the source text that may confuse the target audience of the translating text. There are also cases where a word in the source text has to be omitted in the translating text because the syntactical tradition of the receptor language does not have it. For example, the Swahili language has no articles, and so definiteness may be expressed by means of demonstratives (*huyu* "this", *yule* "that"), possessives (as in *gari la* Tengan, that is, Tengan's car), and personal pronouns. Consequently, all the definite articles in John 1:1 have been left untranslated in all Swahili versions. The Greek Ἐν ἀρχή (in + anarthrous "beginning"), ὁ λόγος (definite article "the" + the noun "word") as well as the anarthrous θεὸς (god) have been translated respectively as "*katika mwanzo*" (in beginning) or "*hapo mwanzo*" (there in beginning), ὁ λόγος "*neno*" (word) and "*mungu*" (god) [or *Mungu* (God)]. The definiteness required by the verse is then achieved by adding demonstratives to render the entire verse as *Hapo Mwanzo, Neno alikuwako; naye alikuwa na Mungu, naye alikuwa Mungu.*

vi. Addition of meaning: This is when new items are added to the translated text for the purpose of a correct transfer of the exact meaning of the source text.

vii. Exchange of meaning: This happens when a phrase in the source text is replaced by a different phrase in the translated text to express the same meaning.

viii.   Antonymous translation: This operation is performed when a linguistic item (like proverbs and idioms) in the source text is translated into a linguistic item that expresses an opposite meaning in the translated text in order to achieve naturalness in translation.

ix.   Total transformation: This is when the source text and translating text phrasings are different and express different meanings.

x.   Compensation: This occurs when those meanings of the source text, which are lost during translation, are rendered in the translated text in different places or by some other means.

Grammatical operations are used to address issues related to grammar. They are classified as follows.[12]

i.   Specification and generalization: This is when a grammatical unit in the source text is translated into a more specific or general unit in the translating text.

ii.   Division: This is when the translator divided a sentence in the source text into two or more sentences in the translating text to achieve clarity and naturalness. Ephesians 1:1ff

iii.   Contraction: This occurs when two or more sentences in the source text are combined to form one sentence in the translating text.

iv.   Omission: This is when the translator decides to omit grammatical units of the source text that may confuse the readers of the translating text.

v.   Addition: This occurs when a grammatical unit in the source language does not exist in the translating language, and so the adds a grammatical unit in the translating text that cannot be found in the source language text to compensate for this loss.

vi.   Transposition: This operation occurs when the translator uses a word order that is different from what is found in the source text.

---

[12] Klaudy, *Languages in Translation*, 166.

vii.   Replacement: This is when the change occurs within the same
        grammatical category, when, for example, a passive voice is
        changed to active voice.

Conclusion

Not all information in a text may be explicit—biblical writers often depended
on the readers' background knowledge to fill in the links between
propositions. Consequently, there are gaps in the logical progression of a text,
which may need to be made explicit in the receptor text because readers of
this text do not have a common mindset with the original source language
readers. The discussions in this chapter are not a license for indiscriminate
alteration of the text. Adjustments and explicitations are unnecessary unless
without them the text is likely to be misunderstood by the receptors, the text
is likely to be meaningless to the receptors, or the resulting translation is so
"heavy" or "overloaded" that it will constitute too much of a problem for the
average reader to figure it out. In case it becomes necessary to make some
adjustments, the translator may make explicit in the text only what is
linguistically implicit in the immediate context of the problematic passage or
what is known to be part of the source culture but not explicit in the text, and
without it, there is bound to be some shortcoming in the translation.

Review Exercise

1.   What is explicitation?

2.   Explain the term structural adjustment.

3.   Explain, with examples, the two kinds of explicitation.

4.   What conditions make structural adjustment and explicitation
      necessary?

5.   With adequate examples, explain what is meant by linguistic
      explicitation.

6.   Translate John 1:1-18 into you mother tongue using NRSV as a
      model text. Comment on all adjustments made and explain
      the reason for such adjustments.

Chapter 12

Foreignization, Domestication, and Cultural Adaptation in Bible Translation

By the very fact that its primary audience were Jews, the Bible contains many texts that are foreign to many cultures. The Bible contains much material that carries a sense of "otherness" because it was "written by, for, and about people in the ancient Mediterranean world whose culture, worldview, social patterns, and daily expectations differed sharply from those of" many modern societies.[1] The long period of time over which the Bible was written (from the Patriarchal period Genesis to John's visions in Revelation) provides numerous glimpses of societies, cultures and practices that were unfamiliar even to original biblical audiences. This chapter deals with the principles of foreignization, domestication and cultural adaptation as a means of dealing with biblical ideas that may not be familiar in the receptor culture.

Foreignization and Domestication in Bible Translation

As we read the Bible, we sometimes come across practices that are alien to our culture. Some of those practices were even unfamiliar to the original readers of biblical texts. This explains why the writer of the book of Ruth considered it necessary to explain to the then-contemporary readers that in former times in Israel, there existed a practice of exchanging sandals as part of legalizing the redemption and transfer of property (Ruth 4:7). New Testament writers had to explain Aramaic terms to their original audience as evident in John 20:16 (*rabbuni*, teacher); Acts 9:36 (*Tabitha*, Dorcas); Romans 8:15 (*Abba*, father), among others. About foreignness in the New Testament, Dennis L. Stamps writes:

> On every page a reader encounters the distant past – a different thought-world, a different culture, a different way of daily life. In these writings the author, Paul, recounts visions and revelations. There are discussions about meat offered to idols, runaway slaves and slave-owners. The world centres around Rome and Jerusalem and is divided

---

[1] R. L. Rohrbaugh, *The New Testament in Cross-Cultural Perspective* (Eugene: Cascade, 2007), ix.

between Jews and Gentiles. Any translation, any interpretation, any reading of these texts must deal with the historical distance that exists between the world and life referred to in these writings and the world and life of modern interpreter.[2]

Modern readers and translators will definitely find many difficult and foreign concepts and expressions in the Bible. The question that comes to mind is whether a text should be rendered in a way that retains its foreignness or in a way that domesticates the text by removing its foreignness. In the quest to answer this question, two concepts—namely foreignization and domestication—have emerged. Friedrich Schleiermacher (1768-1834) popularized the dualistic translation concept of foreignization (moving the reader toward the author) and domestication (moving the translation toward the target reader). It is Venuti who, in recent times, has coined the terms foreignization and domestication, favoring the foreignizing approach as the more appropriate one for Bible translation.

Foreignization in translation refers to the situation whereby the foreign origins of the source text are made conspicuous in the translation.[3] That is to say, foreignization occurs when the translating text "breaks the conventions of the target language by retaining something of the foreignness of the original text."[4] On the other hand, domestication aims to produce texts that are easy to read, easy to understand, and typical of everyday language in the target audience's culture.[5] Foreignization is somewhat similar to the concept of formal equivalence, whereas domestication is somewhat similar to the concept of dynamic or functional equivalence, though it does not carry a literal mandate. Both strategies have their own merits depending on the situation at hand. Domestication occurs when the translator adheres to the values of the target society or community.

Domestication may be a better option for dealing with texts that might be offensive to the target culture. For example, a foreignizing translation of Ἀσπάσασθε ἀλλήλους ἐν φιλήματι ἁγίῳ in Romans 16:16 as "greet one another

---

[2] Dennis L. Stamps, "Interpreting the Language of St Paul," *Translating Religious Texts Translation, Transgression and Interpretation Edited by David Jasper* (London: The Macmillan Press Ltd, 1993), 26.
[3] Lawrence Venuti, *The Translator's Invisibility: A History of Translation* (New York: Routledge, 2008).
[4] Mark *Shuttleworth, Dictionary of translation studies* (Manchester: St Jerome, 1997), 59.
[5] Andy Cheung, "Foreignising Bible Translation: Retaining Foreign Origins When Rendering Scripture" in *Tyndale Bulletin* 63(2), (2012): 257-273, 257.

with a holy kiss" though helps readers to appreciate the source language culture would be improper in cultures where such a rendering might be seen as profane, "silly and never something for adults to do."[6] Foreignization might be equally good if the resulting translation is acceptable in the receptor culture. This is like saying the expectations and needs of the translating readership must be taken into consideration in deciding which concept to use.

The concepts of foreignization and domestication are also related to the issue of anachronism in translation. Anachronism is a chronological inconsistency in events, objects, language terms and customs from different time periods. Anachronism in translation may "interfere with the historical recreation of the source text world; in the mind of the reader, the scene of a target text may be misplaced or misunderstood with the result that its remoteness is blurred."[7] The Living Bible's account of Og's bedstead being displayed in a "museum" (Deut. 3:11), of Psalm 119:105 as saying God's words as a "flashlight", or its rendering of Assyria as "Iraq" (Isa. 19:23) are all anachronistic. Other examples include the NASB's description of an army's chariots as built with "steel" (Nah. 3:2), the AV's translation of the Greek πάσχα (*pascha*) as "Easter" (Acts 12:4). The following translations of Matthew 1:19 can be noted for further discussions on anachronism.

> NLT: Joseph, her **fiancé**, was a good man and did not want to disgrace her publicly, so he decided to break the **engagement** quietly. (Emphasis mine)

> ESV: And her **husband** Joseph, being a just man and unwilling to put her to shame, resolved to **divorce** her quietly. (Emphasis mine)

The NLT anachronistically portrays Joseph's relationship with Mary using modern Western terms with the notion of a **fiancé** and an **engagement**. This choice helps the NLT to maintain that Joseph and Mary were not yet husband and wife, which is consistent with verses 18 and 20. The ESV's choice of Joseph as Mary's husband makes it strange to read from verse 20 that the angel advised Joseph to "take Mary as your wife." Again, having said in verse 18 that she was betrothed to Joseph, to put "husband" here would be confusing. Both choices lead to the loss of a foreign effect (that is, the hiding of the betrothal

---

[6] Barclay N. Newman and Eugene A. Nida, *A Translator's Handbook on Paul's Letter to the Romans* (New York: United Bible Societies, 1973), 295.
[7] Cheung, "Foreignising Bible Translation," 261.

custom) in the translating text, thus denying the reader the opportunity to see the custom as it stands, even if it might look strange.[8]

Domesticating enhances readability and, at the same time, may hinder readability. In the process of domestication, the GNB has "boat" instead of "Noah's Ark" (Gen. 6:14); "covenant box" instead of "Ark of the Covenant" (Exod. 24:10); "lid" instead of "mercy seat" (Exod. 25:17); "repayment offering" instead of "guilt offering" (Lev. 5:15); or "enemy of Christ" instead of "Antichrist" (1 John 2:18). Similarly, the NCV uses "Holy Tent" rather than "Tabernacle" (Exod. 26:1) and "agreement" instead of "covenant", and so there is "the Ark of the Agreement", and "new agreement" ratified by Jesus' blood (Matt. 26:28). Compare the CEV and ESV in the description of the earthly sanctuary in Hebrews 9:4-5, which also shows domestication and foreignization techniques.

> CEV: The gold altar that was used for burning incense was in this holy place. The **gold-covered sacred chest** was also there, and inside it were three things. First, there was a **gold jar** filled with manna. Then there was **Aaron's walking stick** that sprouted. Finally, there were the **flat stones with the Ten Commandments** written on them. [5]On top of the chest were the *glorious creatures with wings* opened out above the **place of mercy**.

> ESV: having the golden altar of incense and the **Ark of the Covenant** covered on all sides with gold, in which was a **golden urn holding the manna**, and **Aaron's staff** that budded, and the **tablets of the covenant**. Above it were the **cherubim of glory** overshadowing the **mercy seat.**

While this choice may improve readability and understanding, in contexts with established and well-known Christian vocabulary already, the domestication of such terms (that is, the replacement of conventional, well-used terms with new variants) will not only remove the sense of otherness, but will also impede comprehension among readers who are accustomed to established recognized terms.[9] On the other hand, if there are no well-known Christian terminologies, domestication will be appropriate because the use of new variants will enhance readability and comprehension without creating any confusion.

---

[8] Cheung, "Foreignising Bible Translation," 262.
[9] Cheung, "Foreignising Bible Translation," 264.

From the foregoing discourse, I cannot advocate just one approach (foreignization or domestication) because each concept has merits and demerits. The translator must decide what to do depending on the purpose and context of the translation. If one's goal is to retain the source culture and make clear the remote roots of the biblical text, then foreignization is preferable. But if one's goal is to produce a text that can be understood easily through the use of expressions and terms common in the receptor culture, then domestication is preferable.

Cultural Adaptation

With different cultural settings in which different translations take place, each translator adopts their own means of negotiating cultural concepts across to make their translation meaningful and relevant to the peculiar situation of their target readership. Cultural adaptation is a form of communicative translation aimed at using culturally relevant expressions so as to enhance the comprehensibility of the target audience. This requires interpretation of the source text. In this sense, translation may be considered as interpretation, with the translator serving as a mediator between two texts. The cultural adaptation of shepherds in Bible translations is a case in point.

The Akan of Ghana translates the word "shepherd" as *hwɛfo* ("the one who takes care of"). This version avoids the use of the word for "shepherd" ("*dwanhwɛfoɔ*") in other to help the readers to appreciate the fact that God is not a shepherd in the literal sense of the word. The *hwɛfo* (literally "the one who watches over") underscores the fact that God watches over his people just as the shepherd watches over his flock. In the Swahili Bible, "shepherd" is translated "*mchungaji*" ("shepherd", "pastors", "herdsman", among others). The various nuances of *mchngaji* make it possible for the Swahili translators to both offer their readers insight into the biblical idea of shepherding and at the same time avoid considering God as a shepherd in the literal sense of the word. The Igbo Catholic Bible (*Baịbụl Nsọ: Nhazi Katọlik*, 2000) has *onye nche* ("protector"), an expression the makes no connection with herding sheep. The Igbo translation, rather than adapting the concept of "shepherd" for the Nigerian audience, chooses a neutral term that highlights the protective role of the shepherd. These are but a few examples to illustrate cultural adaptations of the Bible to suit different environments.

Conclusion

There is a need to address issues of cultural unfamiliarity in the translating text. The approach to this task depends on the situation at hand; therefore, translators must handle each situation on its own merit. The principles of foreignization may be appropriate for one situation but not the other. Even for the same situation, foreignization may be appropriate for one dialect, while domestication may also work for another. Whatever choice one makes must help render the text in a way that makes the translating text have the same meaning as the source text.

Review Exercise

1. Explain how mother-tongue translators may adapt biblical concepts for their contexts. Use examples to illustrate your answer.

2. What is domestication in translation studies?

3. Explain the term foreignization. Under what circumstance should one prefer foreignization to domestication in Bible translation? Illustrate your answer with example(s).

4. Considering the concept of cultural adaption, do you think Bible translators should apply literal principles at all times? Explain your answer with relevant example(s).

Part II:
Practical Issues in Bible Translation

Chapter 13

Translating Cultural Idioms

The previous chapters gave the theoretical background for translation studies. Practical issues are discussed in the present and subsequent chapters. My aim is to introduce the reader to the principles and procedures involved in Bible translation. These chapters are more practical than theoretical and have adequate examples to illustrate the various principles discussed. I begin with idioms and end with sign language Bible translation.

Everyday communication in most dialects is full of idioms. Yet, idioms pose a challenge to Bible translators and readers. The difficulty lies in recognizing an idiom, understanding it and distinguishing idiomatic from non-idiomatic usage because biblical idioms are not usually natural and meaningful in our context. The present challenge is that most of the existing translations have not dealt well with cultural idioms in a way that removes their alienness to African mother-tongue readers.

What is an Idiom?

An idiom is a group of words established by usage as having a meaning not deducible from those of the individual words.[1] The group of words making up an idiom always functions as a single unit. Examples of idioms in everyday English are to rain cats and dogs, to break the silence, to make ends meet, and so on. The *Encyclopaedic Dictionary of Language and Languages* gives the following characteristics of idioms:

i.   The complete meaning cannot be derived from the meaning of the individual elements, e.g., to have a crush on someone ('to be in love with someone')

ii. The substitution of single elements does not bring about a systematic change of meaning (which is not true of non-idiomatic syntagms), e.g., "to have a smash on someone."

iii. Idioms are multi-word expressions, therefore excluding the possibility of idioms consisting of a single word.

---

[1] Barnwell, *Bible Translation*, 19.

Principles for Translating Cultural Idioms

The first crucial step in the translation of idioms is to be absolutely certain of the meaning of the source language idiom. The translator needs to know the appropriate cultural equivalents of a given idiom in the target language. This requires the ability to distinguish the difference between the literal meaning and the real meaning of the expression.

Once an idiom has been recognized and interpreted correctly in the source language, the translator must then look out for ways of expressing it naturally, clearly and accurately in the receptor language. Some idioms have no equivalence in the receptor language because different languages have different ways of expressing ideas. Therefore, the translator must bear in mind that some culture-specific idioms may not have their equivalence in the target language. Some idioms may have their equivalence in the target language but in a different context of usage. For example, the expression "to sing a different tune" when used by English speakers means to say something that contradicts what has been said earlier. However, the Chinese expression *chang-dui-tai-xi*, which also means to sing a different tune, may connote saying something complementary to what has been said earlier.[2] There are idioms which have both literal and figurative senses in the source language at the same time. In this case, "unless the target-language idiom corresponds to the source-language idiom both in form and in meaning, the play on idiom cannot be successfully reproduced in the target text."[3] Another feature of idiom to consider is that the convention of using idioms in written documents, the context of their use and the frequency of use may vary from the source language to the target language. For example, while in English one can use idioms in both written and oral documents, Chinese and Arabic languages restrict idioms to oral communication.[4]

Depending on the results of the above analysis, the translator may decide to use one of the following strategies.[5] First, the translator may translate an idiom of similar meaning and form. In this case, the idiom in the source language is translated into the target language using another idiom of similar meaning and lexical items. For example, an eye for an eye. The Swahili translation of the Greek ποιήσατε οὖν καρπὸν (make therefore fruit) in Matthew 3:8 is illustrative of

---

[2] Mona Baker, *In Other Words: A Coursebook on Translation* Third Edition, (London and New York: Routledge, 2018), 74.

[3] Baker, *In Other Words*, 75

[4] Baker, *In Other Words*, 77.

[5] Baker, *In Other Words*, 77ff.

this point. Both the *Swahili Union Version Revised* (SUVR) and *Greek-Swahili New Testament Interlinear* (GSNTI) render ποιήσατε οὖν καρπὸν as "*zaeni basi matunda*" (produce then fruits) instead of "*fanyeni basi tunda*" (make then fruit). The Swahili version not only renders ποιήσατε idiomatically by "*zaeni,*" it also changes the Greek accusative singular καρπὸν (fruit) to plural "*matunda*" (fruits), the reason being that naturalness in Swahili cannot allow the literal "*fanyeni tunda*" (make fruit). The two Swahili versions agree that the literal rendering of the Greek idiom into Swahili is not helpful, and so they find another idiom to convey the same meaning.

Secondly, an idiom may be translated using another idiom of similar meaning but dissimilar form from the idiom in the source language. The case of the translation of some idioms involves the determining of stylistic equivalence, which results in the substitution of the Source Language idiom by an idiom with an equivalent function in the TL.

The third strategy is to translate an idiom by paraphrase. This strategy is useful when the translator cannot find a suitable corresponding idiom in the receptor language due to stylistic differences in the target and source languages.

Finally, an idiom may be shifted to a non-idiom in the receptor language (or by explaining it). The idioms "children of the bridechamber" (Mark 2:19) and "heap coals of fire on his head" (Rom. 12:20; cf. Prov 25:22) may be translated using this approach. These are Semitic idioms that cannot easily be understood by the ordinary reader. The expression "children of the bridechamber" refers to "wedding guests" while "heap coals of fire on his head" means "to make a person ashamed." By avoiding the idiom in the translating text, the translator enhances the understanding of the audience. However, it must be noted that such an approach will hide Paul from making a connection with the Jewish scriptures which influenced his text. Another example is that "to gird up the loins ..." (1 Pet I: 13) may be transferred as "to get ready ..." The rendering of ποιήσατε οὖν καρπὸν ("make therefore fruit") in Matthew 3:8 by Biblia Habari Njema (BHN), as "*Onesheni kwa vitendo*" ("show by actions") also gives an example of a translation which avoids a cultural idiom in the source language culture.

Conclusion

The use of idioms in translation may enrich the language and bring about some beauty that otherwise would not be achieved. However, the translator would do well to adopt a strategy that will not make the use of idioms a hindrance to understanding the message of the source text.

Review Exercise

1.   Identify a few idioms or proverbs in your mother tongue and try to translate them into another language. What are the difficulties you face? How would you surmount them?

2.   Give the meaning of the following idioms in a non-idiomatic form in your language:

   a)   they lifted up their voices (Luke 17:13);

   b)   flesh and blood has not revealed this (Matt. 16:17);

   c)   the heaven was shut up (Luke 4:25);

   d)   men's love will grow cold (Matt. 24:12);

   e)   fill up ... the measure of your fathers (Matt. 23:32).

What strategies will you use in translating each of them into your mother tongue?

3.   In each of the following phrases/sentences, replace the word(s) which used figuratively with equivalent literal expressions in English:

   a)   bear fruit that befits repentance (Matt. 3:8);

   b)   the lost sheep of the house of Israel (Matt. 15:24);

   c)   who devour widows' houses (Mark 12:40).

Chapter 14

Translating Metaphors and Similes

Metaphorical language is common in biblical texts. One fact that must be noted is that metaphors from one culture often do not work in a translation for another. The use of metaphors and similes helps writers to turn difficult ideas into simple concepts. Their use produces vivid descriptions that make the text more vibrant and enjoyable to read. Metaphors and similes are among the commonest figures in the Bible. The challenge they pose to translators makes it necessary to devote this chapter to discuss ways they can be handled.

Metaphors

From the Greek word *metapherein,* meaning "to transfer" or "to carry over," a metaphor refers to the use of figurative or descriptive language to compare two or more things. A full metaphor has three parts: the object compared, the image to which an object is compared, and the grounds of the comparison (or point of the similarity, that is, the particular aspect of the image it shares with the object). A metaphor that lacks any of these parts is incomplete. In the metaphor, "Issachar is a strong ass" (Gen. 49:14), Issachar is the object, ass is the image and "strong" is the basis of comparison. In an incomplete metaphor, the speaker expects the audience to deduce (or infer) the missing part from the statement. For example, in the statement "Wasn't our heart burning within us as he spoke to us?" the object is "heart", the image is "was burning," and the basis of comparison is understood as "like fire burns."

Metaphors and similes may be classified as live and dead. A dead metaphor or simile is a fixed idiom, that is, one that has become so much a part of the language that the original reason for its usage may even be forgotten. An example of such expressions is "wind up an argument." A live metaphor or simile, on the other hand, is a new comparison made for an occasion and could easily and immediately be understood by the original audience without any background information. Jesus' statement that "I am the vine, you are the branches" is an example of a live metaphor which could easily be understood by his audience. Other examples are "you are the salt of the earth" (Matt. 5:13) and "you are the light of the World" (Matt. 5:14).

Larson outlines some reasons why it is difficult to translate metaphor and why it cannot be translated literally.[1] Those are:

i. The image used in the metaphor is not recognized in the target language.

ii. The topic of the metaphor is not clearly explained.

iii. The point of similarity is implicit and difficult to be recognized.

iv. The point of similarity can be interpreted differently depending on the culture.

v. There is no comparison for the metaphor in the target language as their existences in the source language.

vi. Every language has differences in the frequency of using metaphors as well as differences in the way they are created.

A key technique in translating metaphor is to determine the point of similarity between the items compared. For example, the metaphor "Oluftu is a fox" may mean that Oluftu is cunning in one culture, while it may mean Oluftu harasses people sexually. The meaning depends on what the fox is noted for in a given cultural context. Also, the statement "Peter is a sheep" may have different meanings in different cultures since the sheep is perceived differently in a different context.

Similes

A simile compares two or more items by the use of words such as "like", similar to" and "as." A simile has four parts, each of which must be considered in the translation process, though sometimes one or even two of these parts is only implied and not stated: (a) The object of comparison, that is the person or thing to which another person or thing is compared; (b) The marker of comparison, that is, the word used to show comparison which in the case of simile may be "as", "similar to" or "like"; (c) The image of comparison, that is, the person or thing which is being compared to another; (d) The basis of comparison.[2] Two types of simile can be identified, namely, complete and incomplete similes. A complete simile is one that has all the four parts of a simile present. The

---

[1] Mildred L. Larson, *Meaning-Based Translation: A Guide to Cross-Language Equivalence* (New York: University Press of America, 1984), 17.
[2] Jacob A. Loewen, *The Practice of Translating: Drills for Training Translators* (New York: United Bible Societies, 1981), 192.

statement, "All we like sheep have gone astray" (Isa. 53:6) is a complete simile. The object of the simile is "All we," the marker is "like," the image is "sheep," and the basis of comparison is "have gone astray." In "We are considered as sheep ready to be slaughtered" (Rom. 8:26), "We" is the object, "sheep" is the image, "as" is the marker of comparison, and "ready for slaughter" is the basis of comparison or the point of similarity. A simile that lacks one or more of the main components of a simile (usually the basis of comparison) is classified as an incomplete one. An example of an incomplete simile is "faith as a grain of a mustard seed" (Matt. 17:20) which has "faith" as its object, "as" as the marker, mustard seed as the image but has no basis of comparison.

The translation of simile comes with two major challenges. First, translation difficulty arises when the image of the simile involves a thing or a person unknown in the receptor language. For example, translators in Africa and other tropical areas will find it difficult to appreciate Jesus' message in the statement, "… his clothes were white as snow" (Matt. 28:3) because in these hot areas, people do not often see snow. The second situation that poses a challenge is where the image in the receptor language means something different and/or carries a different essence from what the original author intended.

Principles for Translating Metaphors and Similes

A survey of literature on metaphor reveals the following approaches for dealing with metaphors and simile.[3] The first option is to maintain the metaphor or simile and translate it word-for-word in the receptor language, provided it has an idiomatic formal equivalent in the receptor language. If such formal equivalent metaphor or simile does not exist, then the translator should convert the metaphor into an idiomatic simile while retaining the image, or in the case of a simile, change one or two parts of it, or state implied parts of a metaphor or simile. The metaphor will be maintained by explaining the meaning or adding the topic of the talk or the point of similarity. Or translate metaphor or simile with simile by adding the meaning or sometimes translate metaphor with metaphor plus the meaning. The statement "and the moon [will be turned into] blood" (Acts 2:20) is a metaphor that may be changed into the simile "and the moon will turn as red as blood" for clarity. Similarly, Jesus' statements "This is my body" and "This is my blood" may be rendered "This represents [is like] my body" and "This represents [is like] my blood" because at the time of making these statements it was not his actual

---

[3] I have gleaned what I present here from Larson, *Meaning-Based Translation* 276 and Peter Newmark, *Approaches to Translation* (Oxford: Pegamon Press, 1981), 88-91.

body he gave to the disciples but bread and wine which he compares metaphorically with his body and blood respectively.

If this is impossible, then one may have to substitute a metaphor in the source language with another metaphor in the receptor language with the same meaning. The statement "Blessed is the man who does not ... stand in the way of sinners" (Psa. 1:1) does not convey the same meaning in English as its Hebrew equivalent. In English, "to stand in the way of" means to obstruct, to hinder, and so the "blessed" man is here one who does not hinder sinners. It is better to say "Blessed is the man who does not ...**follow the example of sinners**". This strategy is suitable when there is a problem of image transfer into the receptor language. Another example is the statement "Wasn't our heart burning within us as he spoke to us?" (Luke 24:32 KJV). Here, one may misconstrue "heart burning" as the burning sensation in the esophagus and stomach due to excess stomach acidity. Therefore, it would be better to use another idiom which has the same meaning but different form, for example, "Didn't it almost take our breath away?" or "Didn't our heart almost stop?" (in which case the image is retained, but not the basis of comparison).

Metaphorical statements may also be translated using a non-figurative language. An example can be found with the old and new man in Romans 6:6. The KJV retains the expression "our old man," but CEV has "the persons we used to be." In their guidance for translators, Newman and Nida write, "In some languages 'our old being' [i.e. old man] may be rendered as 'what we used to be,' 'the way in which we used to live,' or 'as far as our being what we used to be.'"[4] The same scholars later urge the preservation of the imagery of "killing sin" in Romans 8:13:

> The metaphor "kill your sinful actions" is a very forceful one and should be retained if at all possible. In some languages one may retain something of this figure, but in an altered form – for example, "cease your sinful actions as though you were killing them." In other languages one may have to eliminate the metaphor and employ a non-metaphorical equivalent – for example, "stop completely your sinful deeds."[5]

In addition, a metaphor or simile may require a combination of two or more of these strategies to translate. Each statement has to be treated on its own

---

[4] B. M. Newman, and Eugene A. Nida, *Translator's Handbook on Paul's Letter to the Romans* (New York: United Bible Societies, 1973), 115.
[5] Newman and Nida, *Translator's Handbook on Paul's Letter to the Romans,* 153.

merit, and other techniques may evolve for particular situations. The fox metaphor (in the statement: He said to them, "Go and tell that fox for me (Luke 13:32), for example, has been rendered in Bono as: "*Honkɔka nkyerɛ saa dadaafoɔ he mma me*" (literally "Go and tell that deceiver for me"). Here, we have a fox replaced by a deceiver; the metaphor is maintained, but the image is given its actual meaning. In the Bono context, the fox is not associated with deception. The spider is more often than not a deceiver in Akan (Bono) folktales and may be used to replace "the fox" if deemed fit.

Conclusion

Some languages have a fixed number of metaphors and similes. In other words, there are no more metaphors and similes being formed. In a situation where no more metaphors are being formed in the language, translators must use only metaphors and similes native to the language. All others must be explained. I now proceed to consider how to deal with unknown ideas in the source text.

Review Exercise

1. Classify the simile(s) in each of the following passages and attempt a translation of the whole passage into your mother-tongue, using NRSV as your base text: Judges 6:5; 1 Thessalonians 5:2; Matthew 13:44; 10:16; 13: 52; 23:27; Proverbs 10:26; 25:11; Revelation 1:14; Song of Solomon 2:3; Psalm 102:6; 1 Peter 1:2; Psalm 131:2; Isaiah 1:9.

2. Each of the following texts contains a metaphor. Attempt a translation into your mother tongue.

  i. The teaching of the wise **is a fountain of life**. (Prov. 13:14)

  ii. **We are the clay, and You our potter.** (Isa. 64:8)

  iii. The Lord **is my shepherd**, I shall not want. (Psa. 23:1)

  iv. Jesus said to them, '**I am the bread of life** (John 6:35)

  v. **I am the Light of the world**; he who follows me will not walk in the darkness (John 8:12)

  vi. For **the marriage of the lamb has come and His bride has made herself ready**. (Rev. 19:7)

  vii. **He is the rock**! His work is perfect. (Deut. 32:4)

viii.   **The Lord is my rock, my fortress and my deliverer;** my **God is my rock**, in whom I take refuge, **my shield** and **the horn of my salvation, my stronghold.** (Psa. 18:2)

ix.   **I am Alpha and Omega, the beginning and the end.** I will give unto him that is athirst of the fountain of the water of life freely. (Rev. 21:6)

x.   **I am the vine; you are the branches.** If you remain in me and I in you, **you will bear much fruit**; apart from me you can do nothing. (John 15:5)

xi.   Therefore, if anyone is in Christ, **he is a new creation**; the old has gone, the new has come! (2 Cor. 5:17)

xii.   **You are the salt of the earth.** (Matt. 5:13)

xiii.   **For the Lord God is a sun and shield.** (Psa. 84:11)

xiv.   He said: "**The Lord is my rock, my fortress**, and my deliverer (2 Sam. 22:2)

xv.   And one of the elders saith unto me, Weep not: **behold, the Lion of the tribe of Judah**, the Root of David, hath prevailed to open the book, and to loose the seven seals thereof. (Rev. 5:5)

Chapter 15

Translating Unknown Ideas

Often, translators are confronted with unknown ideas due to the time, geographical, cultural, and socio-economic gaps between the biblical world and the world of the translator. The most common unknown ideas are names of plants and trees (like fig, sycamore, hyssop, cumin, grapevine, dill); geographical features (such as desert, sea); features of weather (like snow, summer, winter, ice); objects related to housing and household (such as upper room, scales, millstone, cornerstone); clothing (such as crown, tunic, cloak, breastplate); names of animals (like bear, camel); money and measurements (such as mile, denarius, shekel, cubit, talent, bushel); Jewish religious terms (such as synagogue, priest, temple, altar) and others. This chapter will deal generally with these unknown ideas and later on pick up issues related to weights and measurements, and names in different chapters.

Principles for Translating Unknown Ideas

Determine the meaning of the term in the source language. This may require the use of a dictionary or a Bible dictionary and other aids. Contextual analysis of the term may also yield the desired result. Afterwards, re-express the meaning of the expression in the receptor language using one of the following means. First, one may use a functionally equivalent term, that is, a referent in the target culture whose function is similar to that of the referent in the original language. Another method is to use word-for-word translation. Further, instead of using a single word, it may be necessary to use a descriptive or self-explanatory phrase to convey the meaning of the idea in the source language into the receptor language. For example, the term yeast or leaven (Matt. 13:33) may be translated as "substance that makes bread increase in size." Similarly, "altar" may be translated as "place/table where sacrifices are made to God." Since this solution has the tendency of producing a long and clumsy translation, the translator should try as much as possible to use only the part of the meaning that will fix neatly into the translation. If the term appears severally in the same passage, the second and subsequent references may not take the full descriptive phrase. In the case of an altar, for instance, the first occurrence may be "table where sacrifices are made to God" while the subsequent ones appear as "that table for sacrifice." When the descriptive phrase is a compound word (such as money-house for bank [Luke 19:23] or sheep-watcher for shepherd [1 Sam ...]), it is important to follow the natural pattern of the receptor language. This approach is appropriate when formal equivalence is considered insufficiently clear.

Secondly, in a situation where the idea to be translated is unknown to the speakers of the receptor language, the translator may use something similar to what is to be translated and well-known to the speakers of the receptor language. For example, the statement, "Go and tell that fox for me" (Luke 13:32) is a metaphor that (when studied in its context) means Jesus is comparing Herod to a fox. Jesus' point is that Herod is cunning as the fox is. In a context where foxes are unknown, but another cunning creature is known or where the fox is known but not considered cunning, another well-known and considered cunning creature can be used. For example (as noted earlier), in most Ghanaian folktales, the spider (Akan: *ananse*) is more often than not cunning. Substituting the spider for fox within the Ghanaian context would enhance understanding without compromising the source message. This approach is more appropriate for texts in which a teaching illustration is being given or where a comparison is made.

Borrowing or transcription is also another way of dealing with unknown ideas. This is done by reproducing or transliterating the original term. If transparent or explained in the context, a borrowed term may be used alone; otherwise, transcription is followed by an explanation or a translator's note.

Some situations may require the use of foreign words (words taken from another language). A foreign word differs from an adopted word in that, even though both have their source in another language. An adopted (loaned or borrowed) word has become part of the receptor language while a foreign word has not. Words are usually adopted from major languages that are spoken in an area to refer to ideas that have recently emerged. The major disadvantage of the use of foreign words is that it is difficult for ordinary readers to understand since they are not likely to be familiar with them. For this reason, the translator must reduce the use of foreign words to the barest minimum. Where it has to be used, it must be used either together with a descriptive phrase that explains its meaning or together with a general word that explains what the foreign word stands for. The use of words like "Christ" and "anti-Christ" in the Fante Bible are examples of borrowing from the English language. Borrowing is also seen in the Kiswahili version of "And by him we cry, Abba, Father" (Rom. 8:15) as "*ambayekwa hiyo twalia, Aba, yaani Baba*" ("in which we cry, Abba, that is, Father"). In this text, the word "Aba" is the Kiswahili transliteration of the Aramaic *Abba* (in the Greek text).

Conclusion

Unknown ideas are not uncommon to the Bible translator. Unknown ideas are due to the huge gap that exists between the biblical world and ours. Yet, it is the duty of the translator, acting as a cultural mediator, to bridge this gap by making what is "unknown" known to his/her audience. The term needs to be understood well and then translated using a suitable strategy.

Review Exercise

1. Why are some ideas unknown to the Bible translator? List some biblical terms that are unknown to your language group.

2. How are you going to translate the following terms: Satan, bride, sacrifice, saints, church, Heaven?

3. What key biblical terms do you think your community needs to adopt from another language (say English, French. Hebrew, Greek, Aramaic, or a local dialect) into your mother-tongue translation? Explain your answer.

4. A foreign word is not the same as a borrowed word. Do you agree? Explain your answer with relevant examples.

5. Translate 3 John into your mother-tongue. Comment on the translation theories used and how you have mediated between the biblical world and yours.

Chapter 16

Translating Measurements

At the early stages in human history, trade was done through the barter system. However, in the later development, societies developed means to measure, weigh, and exchange goods. The need for standardization of trade values became obvious. The system was, however, confusing because different cities developed their own standard of measurements. In biblical terms, weighing (pounds) and measuring (volume, length, and area) are two different functions.

One of the most difficult areas in Bible translation is the translation of biblical measurements. These units are about forty. The difficulty arises because most modern readers and translators are not familiar with those measurements. In fact, many of these measurements do not fit into our system of measurements. More so, there are differing systems existing side by side, making it difficult to pinpoint which system is to be followed. Again, ancient Hebrews actually lacked precision in Mathematics; Biblical metrology is far from being an exact science, and consequently, no reliable or coherent system has been established. For this reason, there is no scholarly consensus as to what value to assign to each of these units on the modern scale. The result is that modern translators do not follow the same system of conversion.

Translation of Time

Time systems differ from place to place. I, however, give the following table as a guide for dealing with time.

Biblical Time	Modern Equivalence		Reference
	12-hour system	24-hour system	
Sunrise	6 am	06:00	Mark 16:2
First hour	7 am	07:00	
Second hour	8 am	08:00	
Third hour	9 am	09:00	Matt. 20:3; Acts 2:15
Fourth hour	10 am	10:00	
Fifth hour	11 am	11:00	

Sixth hour	Noon	12:00	Matt. 27:45
Seventh hour	1 pm	13:00	John 4:52
Eighth hour	2 pm	14:00	
Ninth hour	3 pm	15:00	Acts 3:1
Tenth hour	4 pm	16:00	John 1:39
Eleventh hour	5 pm	17:00	Matt. 20:6-9
Sunset	6 pm	18:00	Luke 4:40
First watch of night	6 pm - 9 pm	18:00 - 21:00	
Second watch	9 pm – midnight	21:00 - 00:00	Luke 12:38
Third watch	Midnight - 3 am	00:00 - 03:00	Luke 12:38
Fourth watch	3 am - 6 am	03:00 - 06:00	Matt. 14:25

Length and Distance

Initially, body parts like figure, arm, hand, foot, finger, palm, span, and the distance between the tip of the middle finger and the elbow were used to measure length. Distances were related to the distance a person could walk in a day, or the distance traveled by an arrow and so on.

Cubit: The cubit is the main unit of linear measurement used in the Bible. It is the distance between the elbow/forearm to the tip of the middle finger. The variation between the length of the human arm from person to person leads to the fact that there was no absolute cubit standard. Usually, it varied from seventeen to eighteen inches. The cubit determined a measure for many aspects of life in ancient Israel. For example, a Sabbath day's journey measured 2,000 cubits (Exod. 16:29). It was used in reference to the height of a man (1 Sam. 17:4), the depth of water (Gen. 7:20), and approximate distances (John 21:8), the ark (Gen. 6:15-16), the Tabernacle (Exod. 26-27), the Temple and its furnishings (1 Kings 6:7), and the walls of Jerusalem (Neh. 3:13). Two different cubits were used, namely, the long or royal (architectural) cubit and the short (anthropological) cubit. Scholars believe the long cubit is approximately 52.5 centimeters (7 hands), and the short cubit is about 45 centimeters (6 hands).

Rod/reed: These are units of measurements equivalent to six cubits. They appear to be interchangeable (see Ezek. 29:6; 40:5)

Span. The span is the distance between the tip of the stretched-out extended thumb and the tip of the little finger. It was half the common cubit (Exod. 28:16; 1 Sam. 17:4). The ephod (Exod. 28:16) and the breast piece (Exod. 39:9) were a square span. Goliath's height was six cubits and a span (1 Sam. 17:4).

Handbreath/palm is the width of the hand at the base of the four fingers or the breadth of the palm at the base of the fingers (1 Kings 7:26; 2 Chr. 4:5). It is equivalent to a sixth of a cubit.

Fathom refers to the length of the outstretched arms (about 6 feet or four cubits) (see Acts 27:28). A fathom was a standard measurement of the depth of an ocean. It is the distance between one's hands when the arms are fully stretched.

Stadion (Furlong): The stadion (pl. stadia) (RSV) or furlong (KJV) refers to a length of four hundred cubits (Luke 24:13; John 6:19; Rev. 14:20).

Mile: A Roman measurement of one thousand paces (five feet to a pace), equaling about 1477.5 meters or 1,616 yds. (Matt. 5:41).

Principles for Translating Weights and Measurements

In a culture where words like cubit, span and handbreadth already exist, the translator must use them.[1] If, however, these technical terms are non-existent in the receptor language, a descriptive word or phrase could be used to translate it.[2] In the case of the cubit, for instance, one may render it as an "arm-length." One may also convert it into meters and centimeters and give the equivalent in the metric system. More often than not, the conversion will yield fractions that the translator may have to round up or down. In doing so, he/she needs to reconcile two needs, namely "the need for precision and a true rendering of corresponding references in the Bible" and "the need to create a smooth text that does not distract readers by being unduly precise, where the measurement is not in focus."[3] I use the dimensions of Noah's Ark (Gen. 6:15) to illustrate this point. The dimensions of the Ark are 300 cubits (length), 50 cubits (breadth) and 30 cubits (height). Converting these measurements assuming a long cubit of 52.5 centimeters gives 157.50 X 26.25 X 15.75 meters. In this case, the translator does not need to put the exact measurement (that is, the decimals) in the text since this may lead the reader to focus attention on the figures rather than the actual message the text

---

[1] Peter Schmidt, *Biblical Measures and their Translation: Notes on Translating Biblical Units of Length, Area, Capacity, Weight, Money and Time* (np: SIL International, 2014), 6.

[2] Schmidt, *Biblical Measures and their Translation*, 6.

[3] Schmidt, *Biblical Measures and their Translation*, 6.

carries. Rounding them up and down individually gives 158 X 26 X 16 meters. This is problematic because one loses the original ratios between them. It is, therefore, better to work with round numbers like 150 / 25 / 15 meters. A footnote explaining the basic premise for these values may be necessary. Numbers 7:13 gives us an example involving weights where two vessels are said to weigh 130 and 70 *shekels,* respectively.

The issue of whether the translator is required to distinguish between short and long cubits needs to be looked at. Three main options exist.[4] The first option is to use a term which is equivalent to a cubit in the receptor culture and maintain it for every occurrence of cubit, whether long or short. A clarifying note may be attached in the form of a footnote or something added to the introduction or glossary, which may be useful in explaining that the standard for the cubit varied in its value in biblical times. The modern equivalents of each standard can be added to the notes. The second approach is to use modern equivalents, assuming the same cubit everywhere. Except in Ezekiel 40:5, where the text specifies that the long cubit was the standard, this method seems more appropriate for translating the cubit. In the third approach, the translator uses modern equivalents and distinguishes between the two standards using their respective modern equivalents 45 centimeters (or 17.5 inches) for short cubit and 52.5 centimeters (or 20.5 inches). This approach also needs some explanatory notes. The translator should decide which method is appropriate and adapt it.

Conclusion

Translating measures wrongly has a negative effect on the understanding of a passage. It, therefore, behooves every translator to do well to give an accurate rendering of biblical measurements. Yet, certain detailed equivalents may have to be avoided else the attention of the reader will be distracted unnecessarily.

Review Exercise

1. What difficulties arise when one tries to translate biblical measures into modern cultures? Illustrate your answer with examples.

2. How would you convert the following measure into your mother tongue?

---

[4] I have gleaned what follows from Schmidt, *Biblical Measures and their Translation,* 7-8.

a) 4 cubits

b) 10 fathoms

c) A Sabbath-day's journey

d) A reed

Chapter 17

Translating Real and Rhetorical Questions

All languages use questions, though different languages use them differently. Questions are commonly used to seek information; for example, who do people say the Son of man is? (Matt. 16:13) or "How many loaves do you have?" (Mark 6:38). These are real or literal questions. Apart from this use, questions may be used for other purposes. For example, "Your daughter is dead. Why trouble the Teacher any further?" (Mark 5:35) or "God is treating you as sons; for what son is there whom his father does not discipline?" (Heb. 12:7). A question of this nature which does not demand information is referred to as a rhetorical question. This chapter deals with issues related to the translation of questions.

Functions of Rhetorical Questions

A real question seeks information, but a rhetorical question performs different functions.[1] I outline some of these functions below. First, rhetorical questions may be used to emphasize an obvious fact (see, for example, Matt. 7:22; Mark 3:3, 1 Sam. 4:8). It is important to note that in English, a negative question form implies a positive statement, whereas a positive question form implies a negative statement. For example, "Am I not a Philistine, and are you not servants of Saul?" (1 Sam. 17:8) has two questions, both of which are negative. The first part, "Am I not a Philistine?" is a negative question which implies a positive statement "I am most certainly a Philistine." Similarly, the negative question "Are you not servants of Saul?" means "You are certainly a servant of Saul." On the other hand, Pilate's positive question "Am I a Jew?" (John 18:35) means the negative statement "I am certainly not a Jew." Finally, Paul's positive questions, "Are all apostles? Are all prophets? Are all teachers? Do all work miracles? Do all possess gifts of healing? Do all speak in tongues? Do all interpret?" (1 Cor. 12:29, 30) means the negative statements "All are certainly not apostles. All are certainly not prophets. Surely, all do not work miracles. Surely, all do not possess gifts of healing. Certainly, all do not speak in tongues. Certainly, all do not interpret [tongues]."

---

[1] I have gleaned most of the following discussions from Barnwell, *Bible Translation*, 171ff.

Secondly, rhetorical questions may be used to focus on one out of many conditions listed one after the other. Rhetorical questions of this nature can be changed into an "if" clause without any change in meaning. For example, the three questions, "Are any among you suffering? They should pray. Are any cheerful? They should sing songs of praise. Are any among you sick? They should call for the elders of the church and have them pray over them, anointing them with oil in the name of the Lord" (James 5:13, 14) can be transformed into "if" clauses, as "If anyone among you is suffering, let him pray. If anyone is cheerful let him sing songs of praise. If anyone among you is sick let him call for the elders of the church and have them pray over them, anointing them with oil in the name of the Lord."

The third use of rhetorical questions is to introduce a new topic/theme, an aspect of a topic or catch the reader's attention. For example: Then turning toward the woman, Jesus said to Simon, "Do you see this woman? I entered your house (Luke 7:44). In this text, Jesus uses the rhetorical question "Do you see this woman?" to draw attention to the woman who was mentioned earlier in the preceding passage. Paul shifts to a new topic using the questions, what then are we to say? Should we continue in sin in order that grace may abound? (Rom. 6:1). He does the same in Galatians 3:19: Why then the law?

Another use of rhetorical questions is to express surprise. This use can be found in Mark 6:2, "On the Sabbath he began to teach in the synagogue, and many who heard him were astounded. They said, "Where did this man get all this? What is this wisdom that has been given to him?" The people asked these questions because they were surprised at the kind of teaching Jesus gave.

Rhetorical questions may also be used to rebuke or exhort. Jesus used rhetorical questions to rebuke the disciples "Why are you afraid? Have you no faith?" (Mark 4:40). Another example is found in Jonah 4:11 "And should I not be concerned about Nineveh, that great city, in which there are more than a hundred and twenty thousand persons who do not know their right hand from their left, and also many animals?"

Finally, rhetorical questions can be used to express doubt. This rhetorical question is a form of "thinking aloud.". The person addresses him/herself. An example is found in Luke 12:17, "And he thought to himself, 'What should I do, for I have no place to store my crops?" Here, the man is not sure of what to do, and he is thinking through.

Principles for Translating Questions

Before translating a question, the translator needs to determine whether it is a real question or a rhetorical question. In languages where the forms of rhetorical and real questions differ, attention must be paid to the differences.

First, it is important to note that in a receptor language, rhetorical questions may have different functions from those discussed above. It is possible to have a rhetorical question in the receptor language even when the source language does not have it. The frequency at which rhetorical questions are used for communication varies from one language to another.

More often than not, most questions begin with introductory remarks such as "And he said," "They said," "And Jesus said," and so on. In most languages, it is unnatural for a question to follow such introductory remarks. It may therefore be necessary to translate as "And he asked", "They asked", "And Jesus asked" and so on.

Thirdly, it may be necessary to change a rhetorical question in the source language into a statement in the receptor language in order to bring out the actual meaning of the question in its context. Rhetorical questions in biblical texts have different functions. There are some languages, however, in which all rhetorical questions function to rebuke someone. In such a case, translating all rhetorical questions as questions means that all of these will be interpreted in the receptor language as rebukes, even if they are not rebuking anyone in the source language. For example, Romans 8:35, "Who shall separate us from the love of Christ?" is not meant as a rebuke, but would be interpreted as such if translated literally (in such a cultural context). What needs to be done, in this case, is to transform the rhetorical question into a statement in the receptor language. The above example yields, "No one can separate us from the love of Christ."

Fourthly, in some situations, the translator may use a rhetorical question of different forms to express the exact meaning of a rhetorical question in the source language.

Last but not least, in some cases it may be necessary to supply the implied answer to the rhetorical question in the receptor language if that is the only way by which the natural pattern of the receptor language can be achieved. For example, "Who can forgive sins but God only? There is no one" (Luke 5:21).

Conclusion

Questions are found many times in the bible and everyday communication in all societies. The principles outlined in this chapter are meant to help translators deal effectively with questions when they encounter them in their tasks. Like, other features of the biblical text, the translator needs to examine the question, known its type and the role it plays before attempting a translation.

Review Exercise

1. Explain why biblical writers sometimes use rhetorical questions.

2. Explain how you would translate rhetorical questions.

3. What is the difference between real questions and rhetorical questions?

4. Determine, through a careful contextual analysis, which of the following questions are **real questions**, and which are **rhetorical questions.** Translate each of them into your language.

    i. What has become of the goodwill you felt? (Gal. 4:15)

    ii. Who touched my garments? (Mark 5:30)

    iii. Are grapes gathered from thorns, or figs from thistles? (Mat. 7:16)

    iv. Are not two sparrows sold for a penny? (Matt. 10:29)

    v. "'What have you done?' asked Samuel." (1 Sam. 13:11a)

    vi. Sir, did you not sow good seed in your field? How then has it weeds? (Matt. 13:27)

    vii. Then the disciples came and said to Jesus, "Why do you speak to them in parables?" (Matt. 13:10)

    viii. And they were amazed and wondered, saying, "Are not all these who are speaking

    ix. Galileans?" (Acts 2:7)

    x. For if a man does not know how to manage his own household, how can he care for God's church? (1 Tim. 3:5)

    xi. God is treating you as sons; for what son is there whom his father does not discipline? (Heb. 12:7)

Chapter 18

Translating Section Headings

When the Bible was first written, there were no punctuations, paragraphs, section headings and so on. Today, almost every Bible contains texts arranged in paragraphs and sections. These divisions enhance both public and private use of the Bible as they help the reader to find particular references easily. Section headings serve as a tool in finding pages of an unbroken print, especially for new readers who will face some difficulties without this aid. While this system helps understand the biblical text, it can also be misleading if not properly done. In view of this fact, the present chapter discusses ways by which section heading can be handled effectively in order to avoid obscure translation.

Principles for Translating Section Headings

First, section headings should contain the central theme of the section. In other words, they should give the reader a clue as to what the section is about. They must also correlate with the overall theme of the book in which they are found. I will cite two examples to illustrate how a section heading may be misleading. A section heading like "The Parable of the Good Samaritan" (Luke 10:25-37) may be misleading because it assumes that all Samaritans are bad except the one in the story. Again, it does not reflect the actual message in the passage. Considering the passage, a section head like "The Parable of the True Neighbour" would be appropriate. Another example is "The Parable of Prodigal Son" (Luke 15:11-32) which places undue emphasis on the younger son who went away with his possessions and misused them. The central figure in the text is the father, not the son(s). An appropriate heading could be "The Parable of the Loving Father" or "The Parable of the Forgiving Father." The section heading "The Shipwreck" (Acts 27:39-44) may be more appropriately rendered in some languages as "The Waves Break the Ship" or "The Waves Cause the Ship to Break into Pieces." A common heading for Acts 16:16–40 is "Paul and Silas in prison." One could give a heading that refers to what happens at the peak of the story, such as "A Roman jailer and his household believe in Jesus." My suggestion is based on the fact that the existing heading does not reflect the climax of the events in their respective sections.

The second point is that in order to give a proper heading to a section, it is appropriate that one translates the entire book first to get the general theme and message of the book. Section headings are then given to each section in a way to reflect both the overall theme of the book and the central theme of the section in question. The translator must give the section heading when he/she has the message of the section fresh in his/her mind.

Thirdly, section headings should be a specific, brief, clear and informative statement, reflecting the main message of the section. One should therefore be careful not to introduce new ideas in the section heading.

Fourthly, section headings may be a complete sentence, incomplete sentence or a noun or prepositional phrase. Examples of section headings from the NRSV in these categories include "Paul Sails for Rome" (Acts 27:1-12), "Paul Arrives at Rome" (Acts 28:11-16) and "Paul Preaches in Rome" (Acts 28:23-31).

Fifthly, section headings should be positioned in such a way that they may not be read as part of the main text. To achieve this, it may be proper to place them in the middle of the page, underlined or in bold.

Sixthly, it is advisable to mention people by name when beginning a new section. The reason is that section headings interrupt the sequence of the text, making it difficult for readers to know the antecedents of pronounces that begin new sections.

Next, section headings must be reduced to the barest minimum. They should only be inserted where there is a natural break in the text. Section headings that interrupt the natural flow of the text must be avoided.

There are different ways in which one may capitalize the section heading. These include capitalizing each word in the section heading (such as "The Loving Father"), capitalizing only nouns and verbs (such as "The loving Father") and capitalizing only first words (such as "The loving father"). Any of them can be used; one, however, has to be consistent. In any case, the first word must begin with a capital letter.

Conclusion

Section divisions and headings inform the understanding readers get. Section divisions have been determined in the source language, and so the mother-tongue translator may not have much to do about it. The headings must, however, be done to suit the needs of the receptor community. There are even cases where two or more sections (in the source or model text) can be given one section heading provided it reflects the main theme of the passage.

Review Exercise

1. What is a section heading? How is a section heading supposed to function?

2. What section heading will you give to the following passages?

a) Genesis 1

b) Genesis 4

c) 1 Kings 1:1-27

d) Nehemiah 1:1-4

e) Mark 3:7-12

3. It has been argued that 1 Corinthians 11:1 should be part of 1 Corinthians 10. What is your view?

Chapter 19

Translating Proper Names

The subject of this chapter is proper names. A proper noun is a noun that is used to denote a particular person, place, or thing. The different types of proper nouns encountered in the Bible include names of divinities and spirit beings, such as God: אֱלֹהִים יְהוָה; gods: Ashera, Baal, Dagon, Molech; celestial beings: Gabriel, Michael, Lucifer, Beelzebub; names of people which may include names with explanation, such as Moses "because I drew him from the water" (Exod. 2.10) and Nabal "his name means foolish" (1 Sam. 25: 25); names without explanation, including Melchizedek (Gen. 14: 18-20) and Mary [Matt. 1:18]); names of people groups such as Canaanites, Jubusites, Samaritans, Amorites; names of descendants including Hittites, Moabites, Israelites; names of places with an explanation such as Bethel, or without explanation, like Gethsemane (Matt. 26.36) and Azekah (1 Sam 17); and names of people referring to cities, towns, and countries, including Moab (Num. 21:13) or Israel.

Names and naming play a key role in the Hebrew Scriptures aside from identification. There are, however, some instances where names simply identify a person, place or thing. In some contexts, a name may have no significant role in the narrative or in the description of the character of a person. The names Deborah ("bee" Judg. 4:4), Hadassah ("myrtle" Esth. 2:7) and even Absalom ("father of peace" 2 Sam. 3:3) fall under this category.

Principles for Translating Proper Names

Translation challenges arise with respect to names when (1) a person name refers to territory and descendant at the same time; (2) a person or place has two names (e.g., Jacob/Israel; Saul/Paul); (3) a city has more than two historical names; (4) a name comes across the two Testaments (e.g., Spirit of YHWH (OT) and Holy Spirit (NT) both refer to one entity); (5) they are title or names of kings (e.g., Pharaoh, Christ, Messiah, Herod).

The first strategy is transliteration, which is transcribing the proper noun in the source text in accordance with the pronunciation and the morphology of the target language. According to Roger Ormanson (i) transliteration must be preferred whenever possible and especially when the name appears just once in the Bible and most receptor readers are not familiar with it; (ii) names that are well-known by the receptor readers must also be transliterated, but with a footnote or explanatory notes in the text when it emphasizes the significance of the name.[1] Footnotes to proper names may indicate whether a name has a similar sound to a word that gives the name its meaning (assonance) or whether its meaning is derived etymologically.

This is the most common strategy in African and English versions. The transliteration approach helps to avoid foreignness for readers who are accustomed to seeing transliterated versions. For example, in Isaiah 8:1, the name Maher-shalal-hash-baz appears as a transliteration in most English and African versions (Yoruba: Maha-Ṣalali-Haṣi-Basi; Swahili: Maher-shalal-hash-bazi; Zulu: uMahere Shalali Hashi Bazi), but the GNB opts instead for a translation ("Quick-Loot-Fast-Plunder") which makes the text both odd and meaningless. The Chewa[2] (or Nyanja) translation also followed the GNB and so rendered it Kusakaza-Kwamsanga Kufunkha-Kofulumira ("Quick-Destroy Destroy-Fast-Fast").

Another strategy is addition, whereby additional information (such as connotation associated with the noun) is added to the original proper noun in the target text.

Another strategy is adaptation, whereby the proper noun in the original text has a cultural meaning, and it is adapted to a proper noun in the target text with a similar cultural value.

The translator may also use deletion, that is, delete the proper noun in the source text and replace it with descriptive equivalence, supplementing it with additional information or an explanation in the form of notes or glosses.

The literal translation of each of the elements of the source-text proper noun into the target text may also be an appropriate method.

Transposition, that is, replacing the proper noun in the source text with a common noun in the target text is another strategy for dealing with proper nouns.

There could be influences from other religions in the translation of names. Ekem has demonstrated this fact with examples from the Dagbani Bible (2006), which borrows appreciably "from Islam due to assimilation of Islamic life and thought into the world-view of Dabani communities."[3] Examples of

---

[1] Roger Ormanson, "What's in a name?" in *TBT* 40(1), 1989, 117-118.

[2] Chewa is a Bantu language spoken in much of Southern, Southeast and East Africa, namely the countries of Malawi and Zambia, where it is an official language.

[3] John DK Ekem, "Paper delivered at the Reviewers' Training for Bono Bible Translation Project in Sunyani," 6.

cases of Islamisation of biblical names in the Dagbani Bible include *Nuhu* for Noah, *Yisifu* for Joseph, *Dauda* for David, Sulemaana, *Mariama* for Mary and *Yisa* for Jesus. In addition, *Anabi* was adopted as the rendering of "Prophet" so that Prophet Jeremiah was rendered *Anabi* Jerimia. Hausa-speaking communities of Northern Nigeria are also noted to have used the Islamic term "Allah" for "God".[4]

Another aspect of translation to be considered has to do with the challenges posed by Hebrew or Greek nouns that can be either translated or transliterated. Usually, these are proper names that can be used as common nouns as well. For example, the noun Adamah is both a common noun meaning "a man" and the proper name "Adam." Translators need to determine at what point in the Genesis narrative one should begin to use "Adam" rather than "man." Opinions differ as to how to go about this. Some versions make the change at Genesis 2:7 (Targum), others at 2:16 (LXX), and still others at 2:19 (KJV), 2:20 (NIV), 3:17 (RSV), 3:21 (NEB), or 4:25 (NAB, REB, NRSV). Another example is to decide whether the Greek word *Christos* is to be transliterated "Christ" or translated "anointed one," or "Messiah." Considering the fact that it was only after the Gospel reached Gentiles that the word *Christos* came to be understood as a proper name (Jesus *Christ)*, it may be appropriate to translate *Christos* in the Gospels as Messiah (e.g., NEB, NAB, NRSV) and use Christ for it latter in Acts and beyond. Writing on the Swahili translation of Jesus's name, Jean-Claude Loba-Mkole the Greek form "ὁ Ἰησοῦς" (unlike the Hebrew or Aramaic "יְהוֹשֻׁעַ" or "יֵשׁוּעַ" which means "he saves") has no meaning.[5] He argues further that, since Swahili-speaking communities attach meaning to names, "*Yehoshua*" or "*Yeshua*" is a better rendering of Jesus's name than *Yesu/Yezu*. In Africa in general, names have meaning, and therefore, Loba-Mkole's argument applies to all African mother-tongue translations, which adapt a transliterated form of the Latin transliteration "*Iesu*" or the Greek Ἰησοῦς. The suggested approach will enhance readers to appreciate the theological significance of Jesus's name.

Translating the Tetragrammaton (יהוה)

The name יהוה refers to the God of Israel. Biblical scholars refer to this four-letter word as tetragram or tetragrammaton by scholars.[6] The tetragrammaton

---

[4] Ekem, "Paper delivered at the Reviewers' Training," 6.

[5] Jean-Claude Loba-Mkole, "An Intercultural Criticism of New Testament Translations" *Translation* (2013): 95-122, 106.

[6] V. Hamilton, *Exodus* (Grand Rapids, MI: Baker Academic, 2011), 64.

appears more than 6 823 times in the Old Testament.[7] One of the thorniest issues in Bible translation has to do with how God's personal name, YHWH, should be rendered. Translating the word *YHWH*, the name of God in the Hebrew Bible, is a complex matter involving theological, linguistic, and cultural issues. The Jews initially pronounced this name. However, after the time of Ezra, they felt that the name was so holy that it should not be pronounced.[8] After this time, the tetragrammaton was replaced in the aural domain by the title "adonay," "Lord." That is to say, it remained part of written Hebrew but not part of spoken Hebrew. Hebrew readers substituted it with Adonai when reading their Scripture.

Later, when Hebrew scholars (called Masoretes) added vowels to written Hebrew to preserve pronunciation, the Masoretes added the vowels of adonay as a reminder that people should read it as adonay rather than saying the personal name Yahweh.[9] The Greek version of the Hebrew Scriptures rendered it as κύριος (Lord) to ensure that it (the name YHWH) was kept holy and never pronounced.

In the Hebrew Bible, "adonay" is used to mean master in reference to a human being (Gen. 45:8-9) or God (Josh. 3:11). Most English translators, following the Septuagint tradition, also render this name as "LORD" written in capitals. Human masters are rendered "lord" with small "l" while a reference to God as master is rendered "Lord" with capital "L." The Greek version of the Hebrew Scriptures rendered it as κύριος (Lord). This section considers the issue and suggests some principles for African Bible translators.

Origin and meaning of יהוה (YHWH)

Hebrews regard names as that which reveals the bearer's character. Keith Sherlin observes that in the Ancient Near East, "*names were* thought of as disclosing the attributes and characteristics of a person."[10] Thus, in scripture, a name and the character it represents are one. God, revealing Himself through the Hebrew culture, alluded to his sovereignty by referring to himself as YHWH (Ex. 3:13-15).

---

[7] S. Renn (ed.), *Expository dictionary of Bible words* (Peabody: Hendrickson Publishers, 2005), 439-440.

[8] Katy Barnwell, "Translating the Tetragrammaton YHWH," *Notes on Translation* 11(4), (1997): 24–27, 24.

[9] Barnwell, "Translating the Tetragrammaton YHWH," 24.

[10] Keith Sherlin, *Evangelical Bible Doctrine: Articles in Honor of Dr. Mal Couch Couch* (Bloomington: AuthorHouse, 2015), np.

Moses had some cultural reasons for asking about God's identity. He knew the people of Israel would ask him about the identity of the deity who had sent him and then associated his name with his character. God then revealed his name to Moses "I AM THAT I AM," a name which derives from the word *yah*, meaning "to be." This verb "to be" expresses both "identity" and "existence."[11] The name underscores God's nature as the one who is, who has always been and who will forever be the unchangeable God, that is, the one Who is from everlasting to everlasting. At the same time, it also highlights the mystery of God and how impossible it is to define his name.

In their captivity, the Israelites needed a more powerful being than the Egyptian king, Pharaoh, to free them. This situation made it necessary for God to reveal, through His personal Name, that He is sovereign over all powers. The following quote from Jonathan S. Nkhoma aptly summarizes the discussion so far:

> We have to note that once God revealed [H]imself as a Personal God of the Israelite community (Exodus 3:13-15), [H]e announced [H]is divine freedom to act as [H]e wills. Though [H]e is their personal God, [H]e is not subject to human control or manipulation. This attribute of sovereignty is clearly stated in the context in which Moses demands the presence of God to accompany Israel (Exodus 33:12-23). While God promises [H]is presence to accompany Israel, [H]e announces:
>
>> 'I will be gracious to who I will be gracious and I will have compassion on whom I will have compassion.' (Exodus 33:19).
>
> In line with [H]is divine sovereign character, God also warns Israel against any disrespectful use of [H]is name and makes the point part of the 'Ten Words' (Ten Commandments) given to Israel as a regulating factor for the newly established covenant relationship between [H]im and Israel (Exodus 20:1-17).[12]

This name YHWH stresses existence: I AM the One who always is. All life is contained in God and comes from God, so we call Him "the self-existent

---

[11] David T. Adamo, "Translating the Hebrew Name יהוה into the Yoruba language of Nigeria in the Yoruba Bible," *Die Skriflig* 53(1), (2019), 2.

[12] Jonathan S. Nkhoma, *Significance of the Dead Sea Scrolls and Other Essays: Biblical and Early Christianity Studies from Malawi* (Mzuzu: Mzuni Press, 2013), 165.

one."[13] The term אהיה is the first person imperfect form of the verb היה which means 'I was,' 'I am,' and 'I will be,' and may also mean 'that,' 'what' and 'who.'[14] Hamilton suggests nine possible interpretations for אהיה אשר אהיה could be translated in the following ways: (1). "I who I am" (2). "I am who I was" (3). "I am who I shall be" (4). "I was who I am" (5). "I was who I was" (6). "I was who I shall be" (7). "I shall be who I am" (8). "I shall be who I was" (9). "I shall be who I shall be."[15] The same meaning is expressed differently and in different tenses in the above nine suggestions.

Six Options for Translating YHWH

Biblical writers usually used YHWH to reflect God's ethical character, to express a direct and intuitive notion of God or to present the Deity in his personal character and in his direct relationships to human beings or to nature. Kees F. de Blois has identified six different options for translating YHWH, a summary of which I present below: (1) Translate the meaning of YHWH; (2) Translate the title Lord; (3) Translate YHWH and "Elohim" ("God") the same way; (4) Use a name from the receptor language; (5) Transliterate YHWH using a variant of Yahweh or Jehovah adjusting the spelling to enhance pronunciation in the receptor language, and (6) Use a combination of the above options. I now proceed to examine each option briefly.[16]

Option 1: Translate the Meaning of YHWH

The French translation *L'Eternal* (the Eternal One) falls in this category. The previous section noted that the name YHWH means roughly "he is," and so translating YHWH as "the Eternal One," for example, is not totally out of place. The Ghanaian Nzema Bible (1998) followed this model and rendered YHWH with the traditional religious term *Edenkema* ("Eternal All Powerful Creator and Sustainer"). The 1996 Kiswahili Bible renders YHWH as *Mwenyezi Mungu* (Almighty God, the One who controls and is in charge of human fate and destiny). Similarly, the Malawian Chichewa Common Language Bible also uses the descriptive term *Chauta* ("God the Great One of the Bow"). The problem with this approach, however, is that in most of its appearances, this meaning is not in focus. Nico Daams argues he sees this meaning only in Exodus 3:14–15 and possibly in Hosea 1:9.[17] In this light, translating YHWH

[13] Nkhoma, *Significance of the Dead Sea Scrolls and Other Essays*, 166.
[14] Hamilton, *Exodus*, 64.
[15] Hamilton, *Exodus*, 64.
[16] The presentation here draws heavily from Nico Daams, "Translating YHWH," *Journal of Translation* 1(1), (2005):47-55, 49-51.
[17] The presentation here draws heavily from Daams, "Translating YHWH," 49.

with a term that reflects part of the meaning of the name will not help receptor language readers have the real meaning that the Hebrew people had.

Option 2: Translate the Title "Lord"

Many recent non-Western translations translate YHWH with the local name for Lord or master. Usually, the adoption of this strategy is premised on the assumption that the receptor language readership will understand the "equivalent" title in the local language as referring to the sacred name, YHWH.[18] Based on this assumption, the first Kiswahili Bible translated by Anglican missionary Bishop Edward Steere in Zanzibar and published in 1890, adopted the local term *Bwana* (meaning, "Sir," "Mister," "Monsieur," Master," "Husband," "Boss") for YHWH.[19] Mojola considers this approach as inaccurate in the Swahili culture.[20] Yet one finds this same approach exemplified in the use of such terms as *Bwana* (Kiswahili Neno Biblia Takatifu, 2009), *Routh* (Luo Bible, 1977), *Mwathani* (Gikuyu Bible, 2007), *Mukama* (Luganda Common Language Version, 2003), *TUHAN* (Malay Common Language, 1996), among others.[21] This approach is inaccurate and misleading even if capital letters are used throughout, as in the case of Malay Common Language, because the name conveys the meaning "YHWH the name of the God of Israel," which "Lord" fails to convey.[22] The actual meaning of YHWH is lost, and a new meaning with nuances of lordship is introduced. This approach to translating YHWH into African languages is informed by the many English versions that adopt it with some typographical modifications. This translation fails to explore the African cosmogony and the nature of the Hebrew verb forms in the search for a translation principle to handle YHWH. Baal also means lord/master, and this raises the question of how YHWH is to be differentiated from Baal if both are rendered by the same term "Lord." In the context of Exodus 3, where the name was revealed to Moses, one finds it hard to see how the term "lord" suggests that YHWH is a commitment to help Israel, the slave or that YHWH is someone the servant can rely upon.

The problem with this approach is explained by Adamo in his discussion of "Oluwa". Most Yoruba versions of the Bible translate YHWH as "Oluwa", with the exception of *Bibeli Yoruba Atoka* (1980), which has *Jehofa*. "Oluwa" is a title meaning "master", "owner," or "lord;" it is not a name. This makes it

---

[18] Mojola, *Issues in Bible Translation*, 108-109.
[19] Mojola, *Issues in Bible Translation*, 109.
[20] Mojola, *Issues in Bible Translation*, 109.
[21] Mojola, *Issues in Bible Translation*, 109.
[22] Daams, "Translating YHWH," 50.

unsuitable for translating YHWH, which is God's personal name and which means far more than "master" or "lord." Adamo observes that "Oluwa" can be applied to highly dignified humans or as a descriptive name for any god.[23] "Oluwa" lacks the divine element embedded in YHWH. The inadequacy in the use of "Oluwa" to translate YHWH justifies Adamo's proposal of *Olodumare*— which means "splendor, majesty-light and glory which God wears as king"[24]— as the most appropriate word for YHWH. *Olodumare* is the Supreme Being who is superior and incomparable to any other deity.

Option 3: Translate YHWH and Elohim "God" in the same way

Another approach uses the same word to translate both YHWH and *elohim*. This is, however, done after serious considerations about what YHWH actually means in the text in question. Advocates consider the word "God" as the main meaning component of the phrase "YHWH the name of the God of Israel" and the words "YHWH", "name", and "Israel" as the associated components.[25] This method is used in cases where the term YHWH is used simply to refer to "God." That is, YHWH is translated as "God" when it does not signify any of its associated component meanings. YHWH is translated Yahweh (or a variant) when not used in reference to God. Examples of such usage can be found in Genesis 6:6–7a (**God** was grieved that he had made man on the earth, and his heart was filled with pain.), Genesis 6:8 (But Noah found favor in **God's** eyes.), and Exodus 4:2 (Then **God** said to him, "What is that in your hand?"). This principle is not applicable if YHWH refers to one of its associated component meanings, for example, when it is used together with a descriptive phrase that includes "God" as in Micah 4:4 (where YHWH is used together with the phrase "our God").[26]

Option 4: Use a Name from the Local Culture

Another approach is to use the name of a local god. It may be argued that since the Hebrew knew God as YHWH, YHWH must be translated with the name for a local creator-god in the receptor culture. Applying this principle may be difficult in polytheistic cultures where the question of which local

---

[23] Adamo, "Translating the Hebrew Name יהוה into the Yoruba language of Nigeria in the Yoruba," 5.

[24] Idowu cited in Adamo, "Translating the Hebrew Name יהוה into the Yoruba language of Nigeria in the Yoruba Bible," 5.

[25] Daams, "Translating YHWH," 50.

[26] Daams, "Translating YHWH," 50.

deity should have its name used to translate YHWH will be difficult to answer. This approach has some missiological significance of helping the receptor text readership to easily identify with YHWH. However, it reduces the incomparable and infinite God to one of the local deities. Since no local deity matches YHWH, to adopt the name of any deity for YHWH is both misleading and confusing. YHWH is not a local God; he is the God of all the universe and must not be localized through translation.

Option 5: Transliterate YHWH, using a Language-Friendly Variant of either Yahweh or Jehovah

The use of a language-friendly variant of either Yahweh or Jehovah for translating YHWH is adopted by 1952 Kiswahili Union Bible (*Yehova*), the 1970 Lingala Bible (Yawe), 1905 Tagalog Bible (Yahweh), and the 1907 Tongan Moulton Bible (Sihova).[27] This approach deals with most of the inadequacies associated with options 1-4. For example, it removes the tendency of limiting YHWH's nature to that of a local deity. It also deals with the possible introduction of a new meaning with connotations of lordship.

Considering the challenges associated with the first four options outlined above, I agree with Daams that the transliteration approach offers the best way for rendering YHWH, at least, under the following three conditions: (1) where the name YHWH is in special focus (cf. Exod. 3:14–15), (2) where YHWH is joined to 'elohim or 'adonay (cf. 2 Sam. 7:25 and 1 Chron. 17:16–17) and (3) where YHWH is in a descriptive phrase (for instance, "YHWH the God of Israel" [cf. Judg. 8:33–34]).[28] Mojola, supporting this view, argues that it is not proper to replace a proper noun with a descriptive term/title or phrase.[29] In his view, it is more appropriate to transliterate the proper name and then issue a footnote for any additional information needed.[30]

The major challenge with this approach is that it may not be accepted by communities who are used to existing translations that render YHWH in another way (say "Lord"). However, this should not prevent translators from adopting this approach if they are convinced that it is the best option for their project. The right thing can be done, and the receptor text readership must be taught why their translation is different from those they are familiar with.

---

[27] Mojola, *Issues in Bible Translation*, 108.

[28] Daams, "Translating YHWH," 51.

[29] Aloo O. Mojola, *Bible Translation and Culture: Critical Intersections & Conversations* (Nairobi: Tsaifiri Printing Press, 2018), 105.

[30] Mojola, *Bible Translation and Culture*, 106.

Option 6: Use a Combination of the above Options

Another approach is to combine two or more of options 1-5. A classic example of the combination strategy is used in the Kapingamarangi Old Testament, which adopted a combination of option 5 (*Yihowah*, a transliteration of YHWH) and option 3 (*Dimaadua*, an honorific for "God"). With the exception of cases where the name YHWH is in special focus, joined to *elohim* or *adonay* or is in a descriptive phrase (where YHWH is used), all other appearances of YHWH were rendered *Dimaadua*.

This approach is a good one, but the translator has to determine rightly when the name YHWH refers to "God" and when it signifies one or more of the associated meanings "YHWH," "name," and/or "Israel." This approach, when applied to Exodus 15:3, yields: God (YHWH) is a warrior; Yahweh (YHWH) is his name. Here, the first YHWH refers to "God," and so it is translated as "God.". In the second appearance, YHWH is translated Yahweh (or a variant) because it signifies "name."

Conclusion

Names are very important in every culture; therefore, they must be translated in the best possible ways. An appropriate philosophy regarding proper names must be determined at the beginning of a translation project and adhered to. Experience has shown that there can be no one strategy for all cases. Each case has to be treated on its own merit.

Review Exercise

1. Should the Tetragrammaton (YHWH) be translated or transliterated? Explain your position.

2. Will you translate Christ or transliterate it in your work? Why?

3. What influence can other religions have on the translation of proper names? Give relevant examples from your community.

4. Can a proper name be replaced by a descriptive phrase or title? Explain your answer.

5. What is the difference between a generic term and a personal name?

Chapter 20

African Sign Language Bible Translation

A considerable number of people in Africa are deaf and need Sign Language Bibles to access the word of God. In recent times Sign Language translation has become a field of growing interest to major translation agencies, despite the numerous challenges facing the success of such projects. There are over 70 million deaf people in the world who use sign language as their first language and equally need the word of God. Over 400 sign languages exist worldwide, out of which only 40 have portions of the Bible translated into them. With the exception of the American Sign Language, no sign language has a full Bible translation.[1] Some Bible Societies have been working hard for many years to translate the Bible into a sign language, and now many more are responding to this challenge. I have dedicated this chapter to the examination of the need, challenges and prospects of sign language Bible translation.

What is Sign Language?

Sign Language refers to "a visual-gestural system with its own rules and regulations where hand and body movements form signs that represent concepts."[2] In sign language, the movement of hand and arm, the face and upper body are the main sources of communication. Different hand shapes/hand forms are used to represent the letters of the alphabet of a spoken language. This process, referred to as **Finger-spelling**, is employed to convey concepts with no existing signs. Sign language has "intellectual, expressive and social functions as spoken language" and is in no way inferior to spoken language.[3] Sign language has dialects, just as spoken language does. Like spoken language, sign language not only communicates information but also identifies its speaker and transmits culture across generations.

There are three different kinds of deaf persons: hard-of-hearing people, deafened people and people born deaf. The expression "deaf" is used in this book to refer to hearing-impaired persons who cannot use oral-aural modes of communication with or without sound amplification. The deafened people

---

[1] This was as in 2020.

[2] S. Lombaard and J. A. Naudé, "Towards an Indigenous Bible (In SASL) For Deaf Persons," *Acta Theologica Supplementum* 12, (2009): 172-194, 176.

[3] Lombaard and Naudé, "Towards an Indigenous Bible (In SASL) For Deaf Persons," 176.

are those who become deaf after acquiring spoken language. A Deaf community is not like an ethnic community where the members have distinctive features and usually live in a particular place. Deaf people belong to the deaf community and have deaf clubs and church groups. Sign language develops independently amongst communities of deaf people wishing to communicate. For this reason, sign languages differ from place to place.

> Sign languages aren't structured like text-based or spoken languages [and] they require their own processes for passages of Scripture to be told visually through sign. Chronological Bible Translation (CBT) translates the Bible by stories, while Book-by-Book (BBB) translation uses the chapter and verse structure, the Deaf Bible Society explained.[4]

Methods of Communication among the Deaf

Sign Language has its own lexicon and grammar, which do not relate to any spoken language. Sign language is the first language for the deaf; written language is a second language. Studies have shown that there are at least three ways by which one can communicate with the deaf. The first method is oralism, where deaf people are taught to use spoken language through oral language by using lip reading, speech, and mimicking the mouth shapes and breathing patterns of speech. The second method of communication and instruction, total communication, combines signs and the structure of spoken language to enhance communication among the deaf. This approach makes use of a number of modes of communication such as signed, oral, auditory, written and visual aids, depending on the particular needs and abilities of the child. Also known as simultaneous communication, total communication was developed when people discovered that sign language could not be a fully-fledged language and could therefore not be used as a medium of instruction in the classroom.

The third method used for communication with deaf people is sign language. Sign language is a system of communication that uses visual gestures and signs. Sign languages are expressed through manual articulations in combination with non-manual elements. Sign languages are full-fledged natural languages with their own grammar and lexicon. Sign language, like spoken languages, has different forms and even in some countries, there are several sign languages in use. Therefore, a Bible in sign language produced in one country can only be

---

[4] No Sign Language in the World Has Its Own Bible Translation" *Christianity Today* (2019) [Accessed online on 21/02/2021 at: https://www.christianitytoday.com/ct/podcasts/quick-to-listen/deaf-bible-translation-sign-language.html?utm_medium=widgetsocial]

fully and easily understood and well-comprehended by the deaf in that country alone. In sign language used by deaf people, hands and body gestures are the forms of morphemes and words. Sign language has its own lexicon, grammar and linguistic structure, which is different from those of spoken languages. Linguistically, both spoken and signed communication are to be regarded as types of natural language, meaning that both emerged through an abstract, protracted aging process and evolved over time without meticulous planning. Sign language is not in any way inferior to a spoken language.

Deaf Education in Africa

No one knows when sign language started; it is logical to believe that sign language has been around since pre-historic times. One of the earliest written records of a sign language is from the fifth century BCE, in Plato's Cratylus, which quotes Socrates as saying, "If we hadn't a voice or a tongue, and wanted to express things to one another, wouldn't we try to make signs by moving our hands, head, and the rest of our body, just as dumb people do at present?"[5] The use of sign language is also found in Luke 1 in the story where the people communicated to Zacharias, the father of John the Baptist, whose unbelief had made him unable to speak: "Then they made signs to his father, to find out what he would like to name the child" (NIV). The Greek word translated "sign" is *enneuo* which means "to nod at" that is "beckon or communicate by gesture—making signs."[6]

The history of the use of sign language is traced to France, to one French educator Abbé Charles-Michel de l'Épée, who is credited with the invention of the French Sign Language in the sixteenth century.[7] He observed deaf people in France communicating using signs, refined the signs and adopted them to become Sign Language for instructing the deaf. Abbé Charles-Michel de l'Épée developed sign language for the French deaf, and from France, it spread to other schools for the deaf in Europe.[8] American educator, Thomas H. Gallaudet, adopted the French method of deaf education and, together

---

[5] H-Dirksen L. Bauman (ed.), *Open Your Eyes: Deaf Studies Talking* (Minneapolis: University of Minnesota Press, 2008), 134.

[6] Other recorded references of a similar Greek word (*neuo*) found in John 13:24 and Acts 24:10.

[7] Florence B. Pakata, *Factors Influencing Use of Sign Language in Teaching and Learning in Public Primary Schools in Kiambu County, Kenya* (Master Education in Curriculum Studies: University of Nairobi, 2015), 2.

[8] Beatrice Aletta Prinsloo, *An introductory South African sign language grammar for the beginner sign language student* (Unpublished MA dissertation. University of the Free State, 2003), 12.

with Laurent Clerc, established the first American school for the deaf in 1817.[9] Accepting the use of sign language opened classrooms to a natural language of the deaf. From this time on, different countries began to organize formal sign language classes. Today sign language is widely used throughout the world for educating the deaf.

Deaf education came to Africa mainly through missionary activities and colonialism. In South Africa, for example, sign language education was introduced by missionaries (the Irish Dominican Catholic order of nuns and the Dutch Reformed Church) in the nineteenth century. The first South African school for deaf education was established in Cape Town in 1863 under the leadership of Irish Dominican nun Thomas Grimley.[10] The school was known as the Dominican Grimley Institute for the Deaf, and it was for deaf people of all races. Another school was established at Kingwilliamstown in 1884 by German Dominican nuns, which used oralism as the main mode of instruction. Unlike the first school which was for all races, the second school was for white deaf only.

In Zimbabwe, deaf education was introduced by a Dutch Reformed missionary who in 1947 came across a deaf child and was moved to establish the first Zimbabwean school for the deaf in 1948 for deaf education.[11]

In Kenya, the history of deaf education dates back to the founding of the Kenya Society for Deaf Children in 1958. Later, in 1961, the first two schools for the deaf, Nyangoma and Mumias primary schools for the deaf in western Kenya, were established. Since that time, deaf education has taken place at different levels of education. Today sign language has developed into a well-structured Kenyan Sign Language (KSL), which is recognized as the mother tongue for children who are deaf.[12] Deaf education in Kenya falls under the ministry of education, special education division. KSL is also used to instruct hearing impaired children in both pre-school and lower primary levels. Beyond the primary level of education, Kenyan Sign Language and Signed English are used interchangeably together with other aspects of Total Communication.[13]

---

[9] Prinsloo, *An introductory South African sign language grammar for the beginner sign language student,* 12.

[10] Samuel Frimpong Amoako, "Sixty Years of Deaf Education in Ghana (1957-2017)," *Journal of Communication Disorders, Deaf Studies & Hearing Aids,* 2019, 7:1-11, at 2.

[11] Amoako, "Sixty Years of Deaf Education in Ghana (1957-2017)," 2.

[12] Pakata, *Factors Influencing Use of Sign Language in Teaching and Learning in Public Primary Schools in Kiambu County, Kenya,* 15.

[13] Pakata, *Factors Influencing Use of Sign Language in Teaching and Learning in Public Primary Schools in Kiambu County, Kenya,* 15.

In Ghana, deaf education was first introduced by Andrew Jackson Foster (1927-1987) in 1957. Forster's school was established at Osu, Accra and was called the Ghana Mission School for the deaf. Foster was an American black deaf graduate of Gallaudet University, and so the Ghanaian Sign Language he taught was a variety of American Sign Language. The school employed manual communication and started with 24 students, including 13 deaf children and 11 deaf adults. It is important to note that before Forster came, Ghanaian deaf people were using some signs to communicate. According to Samuel Frimpong Amoako, "[t]he deaf people in Ghana in a village called Adamorobe had their sign language before Foster's arrival in 1957."[14] One may therefore say that Forster's work was to refine the already existing signs and to introduce more signs toward establishing a well-developed Ghanaian Sign Language. Today, Ghana has well-established schools for deaf people from basic to tertiary levels of education. Key institutions that cater for deaf education include the Akropong Presbyterian University/College of Education (APCE) at Akropong-Akuapem, the University of Ghana, Legon (UG), the University of Education (UEW), the Winneba and Kumasi campuses, and the Institute of Education of the University of Cape Coast (UCC).

About 1.9 million Nigerians are hearing-impaired.[15] The Nigerian Sign Language developed independently within the Nigerian deaf community, and so it does not resemble those of countries like America or Australia.[16] Consequently, when hearing teachers who have studied American Sign Language at school come back to their community, they find it difficult to teach or interpret Nigerian Sign Language.[17]

Why the Need for Sign Language Bible?

There are good reasons why the Bible needs to be translated into sign language. The first reason is that sign language is the best way by which the Gospel can be understood by the deaf. Thus, sign language speaks much more accurately to the heart of the deaf because that is the language they know. Since God's word is meant for the salvation of the entire humanity, of which the deaf is a part, it is the mandate of the church to ensure that the word entrusted in her hands reaches the deaf as well through sign language

---

[14] Amoako, "Sixty Years of Deaf Education in Ghana (1957-2017)," 3.

[15] Ruth M. Oyeniyi, "Bible for the Deaf: Implication for Sign Language Bible Translation," *Journal of Mother-Tongue Biblical Hermeneutics and Theology* 2(1), (2020): 35-41, 38.

[16] Oyeniyi, "Bible for the Deaf: Implication for Sign Language Bible Translation," 37.

[17] Oyeniyi, "Bible for the Deaf: Implication for Sign Language Bible Translation," 37.

translations. Most deaf lack a literate worldview hence are not abstract thinkers. Clinton explains this point as follows:

> A passage like 1 John 1:6-7 which instructs believers to walk in the light and not darkness is easy to translate into sign but might be confusing for literal thinkers. Focus is on translating and recording signed versions of key Bible stories rather than verse by verse or chapter by chapter translations. Even passages from Paul's epistles may be turned into stories by framing his teachings with details from the book of Acts which tell the stories of the churches he planted and then continues to train.[18]

The lack of abstract worldview among the deaf necessitates the use of the sign language Bible to make biblical concepts concrete and meaningful among the deaf.

The second reason for the need for a sign language translation is that it has the potential of promoting a sense of belonging and independence among deaf Christians. Without sign language Bibles, the deaf depend on others to get access to the word of God. They depend on the interpretation of others to understand God. When the deaf have their own Bible in their mother tongue, they can "read" (watch) it daily by themselves and understand it. They will be in a position to have their own Bible study classes without having to depend on hearing people. This will go a long way to enhance their spiritual growth and evangelism.

Third, embarking on a sign language Bible translation project will help develop sign languages in various communities, most of which have been neglected. Such a move will give the deaf a sense of belonging.

Deaf Opportunity OutReach (DOOR) and African Sign Language Translation

Many African societies lack sign language Bible translation. There are a lot of translation projects sponsored by various Bible Societies for various African communities. The focus is on the written Bible, not the signed Bible. Ireland rightly posits that "African countries do not have a Sign Language Bible translation for local deaf individuals."[19] There is a Deaf Bible Training and Translation Center in Nairobi, Kenya, called Deaf Opportunity OutReach (DOOR), where Deaf Bible translations are carried out, and deaf pastors,

---

[18] Clinton cited in Oyeniyi, "Bible for the Deaf: Implication for Sign Language Bible Translation," 39.

[19] Ireland cited in Oyeniyi, "Bible for the Deaf: Implication for Sign Language Bible Translation," 37.

evangelists, and church planters are trained. DOOR partners with groups like the United Bible Societies and Wycliffe Bible Translators to bring Scripture to deaf communities in Africa. The President of DOOR, Rob Myers, once stated: "Hearing organizations have been doing Bible translation for hundreds of years, but it is only within the past 20 or 30 years that Sign Language Bible translation has even been considered, or even begun to take place."[20] Myer shares that the need for Scripture and discipleship in local sign languages is desperate, saying, "Out of 70 million deaf people worldwide, less than about 15% of them have Deaf-led church presence within their own communities – and only about that same number have access to Scripture."[21] He explains, "So, many times when we approach a Deaf community, this is some of the first time that they've ever had access to the Gospel."[22] Some countries have responded positively to the call to have the Bible translated into sign languages. In 2017, the Bible Society of Nigeria became the first Bible Society to establish a Deaf Translation Centre.[23] DOOR began work on sign language Bible translation in 2006.

My training as a Bible translator once took me (together with other African translators) to DOOR, which was established in Kenya in 1983 for the translation of the Bible into sign language. Apart from translation works, DOOR also empowers and enables deaf adults, giving them a purpose and a sense of pride. We met deaf translators, videographers, editors & graphic designers who work in the computer/video labs. We were taken through various lectures related to sign language translation. One of DOOR's sign language Bible translation consultants, Shadrack Kakui, took us through the various steps involved in the production of the sign language Bible. Sign language Bible translation consultants are experts in linguistics, biblical exegesis, sign language fluency, and Deaf culture. There were deaf translators from various African countries (including Kenya, Ghana, Zimbabwe, Uganda, Nigeria and Tanzania) all living there in the dormitories and working full time on translating the Bible into their own country's sign language. It was interesting to note how all these people from different countries communicated using Kenyan Sign Language as the common sign language. I got to know that the sign languages of Uganda, Ghana

[20] Myers cited in Oyeniyi, "Bible for the Deaf: Implication for Sign Language Bible Translation," 39.
[21] Myer cited in Anna Deckert, DOOR celebrates new fellowships and Christian workers in East Africa, 2020 [Accessed online from https://www.mnnonline.org/news/door-celebra tes-new-fellowships-and-christian-workers-in-east-africa/ on 29th March, 2021].
[22] Myer cited in Anna Deckert, DOOR celebrates new fellowships and Christian workers in East Africa, 2020.
[23] Oyeniyi, "Bible for the Deaf: Implication for Sign Language Bible Translation,", 37.

and Kenya are all similar to the American Sign Language, the Ghanaian version being the closest. DOOR uses Chronological Bible Storying (CBS) method in its translation. In 2009, DOOR 2009 Translation work started in BEGUT (Burundi, Ethiopia, Ghana, Uganda, and Tanzania) sign languages. In 2013, DOOR started the Nigerian Sign Language translation project and in about three years completed 110 Chronological Bible Stories [CBS] for the Deaf in Nigerian Sign Language.[24] The stories were released in series, and concerning one of the efforts, Olayinka Latona states:

> Determined to make the Bible available to ... Nigerians with hearing impairment, the Christian mission for the deaf church, Nigeria in collaboration with Door International, the Presbyterian Church of Nigeria and the Bible Society of Nigeria recently launched 77 Chronological Bible Translation for the Nigerian Sign Language Bible. 77 Bible stories were added to the previous translation that contained 32 stories which were launched in 2014, adding that with the Bible, the Deaf would be able to read and understand the word of God.[25]

In 2014 DOOR launched a new website to distribute completed Bible projects in several sign languages. The same year, DOOR had 110-passage Chronological Bible Translation completed in Burundian, Ethiopian, Ghanaian, Ugandan and Tanzanian (BEGUT) sign languages. In 2015 DOOR began translation projects in South Sudanese, Mozambican, and 2 Eurasian sign languages. By 2016, DOOR had worked with teams from 16 language groups. Each Chronological Bible Translation consists of 110 biblical narratives from Genesis to Revelation. The narratives are accompanied by an introduction to give context and a section giving more information about the passage. These 110 narratives are divided into three overlapping sets:

    i.   Evangelism ("Know God How?") consisting of 32 narratives from Genesis 1 through Acts 2

    ii.   Discipleship ("Follow God How?") consisting of 77 narratives from Genesis 1 through Acts 2

---

[24] https://biblesociety-nigeria.org/new/bs-nigeria-set-to-dedicate-deaf-translation-centre/
[25] Olayinka Latona, "BSN launches 77 Nigerian Sign Language Bible." Vanguard, December 17, 2016, https://www.vanguardngr.com/2016/12/bsn-launches-77-nigerian-sign-langua ge-bible [Accessed 20/12/2020].

    iii.   Church Planting ("Serve God How?") consisting of 35 narratives from Acts 1 through Revelation[26]

The evangelism training involves DOOR staff teaching national deaf believers and sign language translators how to lead Bible studies for the deaf, sharing the Gospel using evangelism DVDs, teaching and discipling believers using Chronological Bible Storying, and forming Deaf Believers' Fellowships whose members are trained to disciple others.

DOOR has also been involved in church planting among deaf communities since 2005. This program, dubbed DOOR's 2-by-2 program, involves training pairs of Deaf leaders to plant churches that are Deaf-led, reproducible, and sustainable.[27] DOOR provides the deaf churches and evangelism teams with sign language translations of the Bible to enable the deaf communities to access the word of God. DOOR's tagline is "Deaf reaching Deaf for Christ", and that value is evident in the training portion of our ministry, where almost all of our deaf leaders are trained by fellow deaf leaders. The training and the material support to the deaf community are meant to:

    i.   build relationships with local deaf

    ii.   share God's Word in the local sign language

    iii.   disciple new believers

    iv.   help form local deaf believers' fellowships

    v.   identify and train deaf evangelists, teachers, and leaders

    vi.   help the deaf form their own national Deaf Christian association[28]

This program has had a huge impact in East African countries like South Sudan and Mozambique. DOOR reports that a deaf missionary from Kenya, Edward Obaga, travelled from Kenya to South Sudan to support South Sudanese deaf leaders in missionary work and training.[29] Obaga is

---

[26] https://doorinternational.org/what-we-do
[27] https://doorinternational.org/what-we-do
[28] https://doorinternational.org/what-we-do
[29] Anna Deckert, "DOOR celebrates new fellowships and Christian workers in East Africa," 2020 [Accessed online from https://www.mnnonline.org/news/door-celebrates-new-fellowships-and-christian-workers-in-east-africa/ on 29th March, 2021].

commended for moving his family to South Sudan amid the COVID-19 pandemic for the sole purpose of expanding God's Kingdom.

Challenges Associated with Sign Language Translation

First, there is a low level of education among people in deaf communities than that of the general population due to challenges like lack of access to education. Consequently, there is a lack of qualified deaf people to help in sign language translation.

Secondly, most sign language translations available today are published solely or predominantly in video format, a situation that makes the choice of signers a complex issue. Mark Penner asserts that "the visual presence mandated by the media, like voice in recorded texts of spoken languages, makes it all the more imperative that translators be native speakers. This, however, presents a challenge to the translation team, as only 5-10 percent of the deaf population have deaf parents, drastically reducing the pool of potential translators."[30] A problem arises if well-known signers are not believers, as this situation further reduces the pool of prospective translators.

A third challenge is the difficulty associated with the acquisition of exegetical materials to deaf translators in a form they can understand is a major issue. It is very difficult for signers to have full access to an exegetical guide related to the text they are translating and to other various resources that help to decipher the meaning of that text. Ideally, these materials are to be prepared by the deaf themselves in their sign language with accompanying pictures or videos. However, such resources are not readily available today.

Fourthly, there is currently a lack of qualified TCs to check sign language translation. As a matter of fact, TCs for sign language translations are expected to be part of the deaf community because such people, rather than those who learn sign language as a second language, have what it takes to ensure accuracy, naturalness and clarity in the project. The lack of deaf people who have been trained as TCs is a major hindrance to sign language Bible translation projects.

---

[30] Mark Penner, "Issues in Sign Language Translation, with Special Reference to Bible Translation," *Work Papers of the Summer Institute of Linguistics, University of North Dakota Session*, vol. 49 (2009) at 4. Accessed from http://arts-sciences.und.edu/summer-institute-of-linguistics/work-papers/_files/docs/2009-penner.pdf

Steps in Sign Language Bible Translation

Sign language translation is not well developed, and not much scholarly attention has been given to it. Before considering the key steps, let me outline few standards that must be followed to achieve an accurate sign language Bible translation.[31] First, the on-screen signing must be done by a deaf and the translation style must be approved by the receptor deaf community. Secondly, a person who is not deaf but was born by a deaf person and bred within the deaf community and is conversant with their parents' Sign Language can be part of the translation. Also, the TC for a sign language Bible translation project must be a person who understands and is fluent in the receptor sign language. With this background, I now outline some key steps in undertaking a sign language Bible translation project.

i. The sign language project must begin with a socio-linguistic survey of the deaf community for which the translation is to be made. Then, attempts should be made to produce an accurate and dynamic visual translation from the original Greek, Hebrew, and Aramaic languages to serve as the source text for sign language translation.

ii. After putting together a team of (about 5) deaf translators, a first draft based on the source text should be made.

iii. The TC must then view the translation with a person who was raised by one or more deaf parents or guardians (that is, child of deaf adult, CODA) who serves as an interpreter. Together with the translators, the TC checks the draft for accuracy, naturalness and clarity.

iv. Suggestions for change and points for discussion are sent to the translation team for necessary revision(s). After revisions are agreed upon, they are often recorded using the previous draft as a cue, with the signer replacing flawed portions with new material. The on-screen signer must be deaf, and the signer and translation style must be approved by the community for which the translation is done. This means that the community will watch the signer and engage with the translation style, thus preventing the output of a product the community will not use.

---

[31] For a more comprehensive treatment consult Oyeniyi, "Bible for the Deaf: Implication for Sign Language Bible Translation," 40.

v.   The TC must then check the new draft to see if there is a need for further review.

vi. Steps iv and v may be repeated until a final draft is approved. At the same time, others on the team and the translator himself should check the work for naturalness and understandability, and changes are recorded and edited into the working draft.

vii. The final draft is then recorded in a professional studio with blue-screen technology to allow for the insertion of various backdrops into the final product later using the computer. Final video editing, including voice-over, backdrop insertion, subtitles, and verse references, are then done to complete the task.

Conclusion

Nothing is evident in this chapter other than the fact that written Bibles do not meet the needs of deaf people, and therefore a signed Bible for the deaf would make the Bible more accessible to this section of the community. I encourage various Bible translation agencies to begin a project as soon as possible to translate the written Bible into sign language. In this project, deaf people should be selected, trained and used as translators together with a team of Bible experts who will help in the translation from the source language. Different signers must be identified from the different parts of the country. The signers, who are expected to work hand-in-hand with the team of translators, must be natural and spontaneous, and should be trained in the skill of signing in front of a camera.

Review Exercise

1.   What is sign language?

2.   Why is sign language Bible translation important?

3.   Explain the processes involved in the translation of a text into sign language.

4.   What are the various ways in why deaf people can communicate?

5.   In what ways can we develop sign language as a discipline?

6.   Write a comprehensive proposal to a Bible translation funding agency to sponsor sign language Bible translation project in your community.

Afterword

In this book, I have introduced the reader to the basic principles of Bible Translation, challenges, strategies and prospects in the African context. This has been achieved through well-researched presentations and practical examples offered in various chapters. I have affirmed the need for a close relationship between the theory and the practice of translation. In this concluding section, I wish to, first of all, offer a summary of our findings and then move on to offer some suggestions for developing Bible translation further.

I have argued that Bible translation should be done based on the original language of Scripture texts, not on a translated version of it. The use of reliable Bible translations in other languages as intermediary source texts may be allowed for translators who lack source language proficiency. Again, the translator should aim at transferring the source text into the receptor language accurately, without loss, change, distortion or embellishment of the meaning. This principle requires sound exegesis of the text, and hence the translator is required to develop good exegetical skills. Furthermore, there is the need to transfer not only the informational content, but the feelings and attitudes of the original text as well. For example, the use of sackcloth and ashes to show repentance or sorrow should be communicated in such a way as to evoke that same feeling in the readers of the receptor text (Isa. 58:5). This, however, does not mean that the translator should necessarily maintain sackcloth and ashes. Rather, it may be necessary for many African societies to use a funeral cloth to replace sackcloth and ashes, and yet have the same impact on the readers. In addition, I have shown the need to maintain the literary forms employed in the original text (such as poetry, prophecy, narrative and exhortation) as much as possible or the need to use corresponding literary forms with similar communicative functions in the receptor language. Further still, the translator must aim to faithfully represent the original historical and cultural context as well as political, ideological, social, cultural, or theological agenda. This requires adequate historical and cultural background study of the source text. Finally, Bible translation may require adjustments and restructuring in the receptor language in order to achieve accuracy, naturalness and comprehension.

The procedure begins with a careful linguistic and sociolinguistic study of the specific target audience for the translation to determine the kind of translation appropriate for them. Next, a team of translators is formed. The translation should be done by trained and competent translators into whose mother tongue the translation is being done. If prevailing conditions do not allow this, then mother-tongue speakers should be involved to the greatest extent possible in the translation process. More so, translators must be given training in translation principles and practice and to providing appropriate technical support. Further to this, every text must be tested as extensively as possible in the receptor community to ensure that it communicates accurately, clearly and naturally, keeping in mind the sensitivities and experience of the receptor audience. Feedback from the audience should be noted and used for the improvement of the translation. Media such as audio, visual, electronic, print, or a combination of these can be used in the process of reaching out to the community of the receptor text. After the translation is done and published, there is a need to have a periodic review of translations to ascertain when revision or a new translation is required.

Translation Studies, as stated in the book, is still a young academic discipline and therefore has a long way to go. There is a need for a more general theoretical discussion as to the nature of translation in Africa. I, therefore, charge various higher institutions to join hands in developing courses in Bible Translation. Translation is a skill, inextricably bound up with modes of reading and interpreting the source text, which is the proper source material for the writer to draw upon as he thinks fit. Therefore, the study of the source biblical languages (Hebrew, Greek and Aramaic) must be taken seriously and developed further within the academy. Elsewhere I have argued that all forms of theological education, no matter their duration, must have something to do with knowledge about biblical source languages.

It is my hope that the discussions in this book will foster the development and promotion of Translation studies in and beyond Africa. In the end the church will be developed and equipped to raise people of resilient and contagious faith, the glory will be God's and the blessing ours.

Bibliography

Adamo, David T. "Translating the Hebrew Name יהוה into the Yoruba language of Nigeria in the Yoruba Bible." *Die Skriflig* 53(1) (2019).

Agbeti, J. Kofi. *West African Church History: Christian Missions and Church Foundations 1482-1919*. Leiden: E. J. Brill, 1986.

Agyekum, Kofi. *Linguistics: Ethnography of Speaking*. University of Ghana, Accra: Institute of Continuing and Distance Education, 2010.

Amoako, Samuel Frimpong. "Sixty Years of Deaf Education in Ghana (1957-2017)." *Journal of Communication Disorders, Deaf Studies & Hearing Aids* 7 (2019):1-11.

Anderson, T. David. "Perceived Authenticity: The Fourth Criterion of Good Translation." *Notes on Translation* 12(3) (1998): 1-3.

Archer, Gleason L. Jr. *A Survey of Old Testament Introduction*. Chicago, IL: Moody Press, 1974.

Ashcroft, Bill, Griffiths, Gareth and Tiffin, Helen. *Post-Colonial Studies: The Key Concepts*. New York: Routledge, 2007.

Baker, Mona. *In Other Words: A Coursebook on Translation* Third Edition. London and New York: Routledge, 2018.

Bandia, Paul. "Translation Matters: Linguistic and Cultural Representation." *Translation Studies in Africa* edited by Judith Inggs and Libby Meintjes, 1–20. London: Continuum, 2009.

Barnwell, Katharine. *Bible Translation: An Introductory Course in Translation Principles*. Third edition. Texas: SIL International, 1999.

Barnwell, Katy. "Translating the Tetragrammaton YHWH." *Notes on Translation* 11(4) (1997): 24–27.

Bassnett-McGuire, Susan. "History of Translation Theory." *BBT Book Production Series Volume 2: Readings in General Translation Theory*, pp. 5-29. Stockholm: np, 1997.

Bauman, H-Dirksen L. (ed.), *Open Your Eyes: Deaf Studies Talking*. Minneapolis: University of Minnesota Press, 2008.

Baur, John. *2000 years of Christianity in Africa: An African Church history*. Second edition. Nairobi: Paulines Publications Africa, 2018.

Bediako, Emmanuel Owusu. *History of the Bible*. Accra: Advocate Publishing Limited, 2008.

Bediako, Kwame. *Jesus in Africa: The Gospel in African History and Experience*. Akropong: Regnum Africa, 2000.

Berman, Sidney K. *Analysing the Frames of a Bible: The Case of the Setswana Translations of the Book of Ruth*. PhD Dissertation: Stellenbosch University, 2014.

Biney, Moses O. *From Africa to America: Religion and Adaptation among Ghanaian Immigrants in New York*. New York: New York University Press, 2011.

Bruce, F. F. *History of the Bible in English.* Cambridge: The Lutterworth Press, 2002.

Cathcart, Kevin, Maher, Michael and McNamara, Martin (eds.). *Targum Neofiti 1: Genesis.* Collegeville: The Liturgical Press, 1992.

Chafer, Lewis Sperry. *Systematic Theology Vol. 1.* Dallas, TX: Dallas Seminary Press, 1947.

Cheung, Andy. "Foreignising Bible Translation: Retaining Foreign Origins When Rendering Scripture" in *Tyndale Bulletin* 63(2), (2012): 257-273.

Collins, Raymond F. "The Canon of the Old Testament." *The New Jerome Biblical Commentary.* Englewood Cliffs, NJ: Prentice-Hall, 2011.

Conybeare, Frederick C. and Stock, George. *Grammar of Septuagint Greek.* Eugene, OR: Wipf&Stock, 2014.

Craig L. Bloomberg and Jennifer Foutz Markley, *A Handbook of New Testament Exegesis.* Grand Rapids, MI: Baker Academic, 2010.

Cyrus, L. Old Concepts, New Ideas: Approaches to Translation Shifts. *MonTI,* 87-106, 94. Retrieved from http://hdl.handle.net/10234/11973 on 10th January, 2021.

Daams, Nico. "Translating YHWH." *Journal of Translation* 1(1) (2005):47-55.

Deckert, Anna. DOOR celebrates new fellowships and Christian workers in East Africa, 2020 [Accessed online from https://www.mnnonline.org/news/door-celebrates-new-fellowships-and-christian-workers-in-east-africa/ on 29th March, 2021].

Di Giovanni, Elena and Dirar, Uoldelul Chelati. "Reviewing Directionality in Writing and Translation: Notes for a History of Translation in the Horn of Africa." *Translation Studies. Routledge* 8(2) (2015): 175-190.

Dolet, Etienne. "The Way to Translate Well from One Language to Another." *Translation Theory and Practice: A Historical Reader.* Eds. Daniel Weissbort and Astradur Eysteinsson. Oxford: Oxford University Press, 2002.

Dube, Musa W. "Consuming A Cultural Bomb: Translating *Badimo* into 'Demons' In the Setswana Bible." *Postcoloniality, Translation, and the Bible in Africa* edited by Musa W. Dube and R. S. Wafula, pp. 3-25. Eugene, OR: Pickwick Publications, 2017.

Ekem, John D. K. "Interpreting the Lord's Prayer in the Context of Ghanaian Mother-Tongue Hermeneutics," *Journal of African Christian Thought* 10 (2007): 48–52.

Ekem, John D. K. "Jacobus Capitein's Translation of 'The Lord's Prayer' into Mfantse: An Example of Creative Mother Tongue Hermeneutics." *Ghana Bulletin of Theology* Vol. 2 (2007): 66-79.

Eusebius, *The Church History: A New Translation with Commentary* translated by Paul L. Maier. Grand Rapids, MI: Kregel Publications, 1999.

Fee, Gordon D. and. Stuart, Douglas K. *How to Read the Bible for All Its Worth: A Guide to Understanding the Bible.* Grand Rapids, MI: Zondervan, 1982.

Foucault, Michel. *The Archaeology of Knowledge* translated from the French by A.M. Sheridan Smith. London: Tavistock Publications, 1972.

Frajzyngier, Zygmunt, and Shay, Erin. *The Afroasiatic Languages.* Cambridge: Cambridge University Press, 2020.

Geisler, Norman L. and Nix, William E. *A General Introduction to the Bible.* Revised edition. Chicago, IL: Moody Press, 1968.

Genette, Gérard. *Palimpsests: Literature in the Second Degree* Translated by Channa Newman and Claude Doubinsky. London: University of Nebraska Press, 1997.

Gentzler, E. Contemporary translation theories. Second edition. Clevedon: Multilingual Matters Ltd, 2001.

Glassman, Eugene H. *The Translation Debate.* Downers Grove, IL: InterVarsity Press, 1981.

Goddard, Burton L. *The NIV Story.* New York: Vantage Press, 1989.

Green, Benjamin Stephen. *A Skopos-Based Analysis of Breytenbach's Titus Andronicus.* MPhil Thesis: University of Stellenbosch, 2012.

Gundry, Robert H. *A Survey of the New Testament.* Fifth edition. Grand Rapids, MI: Zondervan, 2012.

Hamilton, V. *Exodus.* Grand Rapids, MI: Baker Academic, 2011.

Hariyanto, Sugeng. *Website Translation: with special reference to English – Indonesian language Pair.* Malang: CV Transkomunika Kencana, nd.

Hatim, Basil and Munday, Jeremy. *Translation: An Advanced Resource Book.* London: Routledge, 2004.

Jakobson, Roman. "On Linguistic Aspects of Translation" In *Language in literature.* Eds. Pomorska, Krystina and Rudy, Stephen. pp. 428–435. Cambridge, MA: Belknap Press, 1987.

Jakobson, Roman. *Selected Writings: Poetry of Grammar and Grammar of Poetry* edited by Stephen Rudy. New York: Mouton Publishers, 1981.

Johnson, Elliott. *Expository Hermeneutics: An Introduction.* Grand Rapids, MI: Zondervan, 1990.

Josephus, Flavius. *The Complete Works of Flavius Josephus.* Translated by William Whiston. Nashville: Thomas Nelson Inc., 1998.

Kerr, G. J. "Dynamic Equivalence and Its Daughters: Placing Bible Translation Theories in Their Historical Context." *Journal of Translation,* 7(1) (2011):1-19.

Klaudy, Kinga. "Explicitation." *Routledge Encyclopedia on Translation Studies* second edition edited by Mona Baker and Gabriela Saldanha. London: Routledge, 2011.

Klaudy, Kinga. *Languages in Translation: Lectures on the Theory, Teaching and Practice of Translation.* Budapest: Scholastica, 2003.

Köstenberger, Andreas J. and Kellum, Leonard Scott. *The Cradle, the Cross, and the Crown: An Introduction to the New Testament.* Nashville: B&H Publishing, 2009.

Larson, Mildred L. *Meaning-Based Translation: A Guide to Cross-Language Equivalence.* New York: University Press of America, 1984.

Lensch, Christopher K. "The Morningstar of the Reformation: John Wycliffe." *WRS Journal* 3(2) (1996): 16-22.

Loba-Mkole, Jean-Claude. "An Intercultural Criticism of New Testament Translations" *Translation* (2013): 95-122.

Lockhart, Clinton. *Principles of Interpretation,* 2nd ed. Fort Worth: S. H. Taylor, 1915.

Loewen, Jacob A. The *Practice of Translating: Drills* for Training Translators. New York: United Bible Societies, 1981.

Lombaard, S. and Naudé, J. A. "Towards an Indigenous Bible (In SASL) For Deaf Persons." *Acta Theologica Supplementum* 12 (2009): 172-194.

Marais, Jacobus. "The Language Practitioner as Agent: The Implications of Recent Trends in Research for Language Practice in Africa." *JNGS* 6/3 (2008): 35-47.

Martin, Robert P. *Accuracy of Translation and the New International Version.* Edinburgh: The Banner of McNamara, Martin and Flesher, Paul V.M. "Targum" (Retrieved on 15th June, 2021 from https://www.oxfordbibliographies.com/view/document/obo-9780195393361/obo-9780195393361-0187.xml).

McNamara, Martin. *Targum and New Testament: Collected Essays.* Tubingen: Mohr Siebeck, 2011.

Metzger, Bruce M. *A Textual Commentary on The Greek New Testament: A Companion Volume to the United Bible Societies' Greek New Testament.* Fourth revised edition. Deutsche Bibelgesellschaft: D-Stuttgart, 2002.

Metzger, Bruce M. *The Bible in Translation: Ancient and English Versions.* Grand Rapids, MI: Baker Academic, 2001.

Miller-Naudé, Cynthia L. and Naudé, Jacobus A. "The Translator as an Agent of Change and Transformation: The Case of Translating Biblical Proverbs." *OTE* 23/2 (2010): 306-321.

Mojola, Aloo O. "Bible Translation in Africa: What Implication does the New UBS Approach Have for Africa? An Overview in the Light of Emerging New UBS Translation Initiative." *Acta Theologica Supplementum* 2 (2002): 200-213.

Mojola, Aloo O. and Wendland, Ernst R. "Scripture Translation in the Era of Translation Studies." *Bible Translation: Frames of Reference* edited by T. Wilt, pp. 1-25. Manchester: St. Jerome, 2003.

Mojola, Aloo O. *Bible Translation and Culture: Critical Intersections & Conversations.* Nairobi: Tsaifiri Printing Press, 2018.

Mojola, Aloo O. *Issues in Bible Translation: Navigating Troubling & Tempestuous Waters.* Nairobi: Tafsiri Printing Press, 2019.

Mothoagae, Itumeleng Daniel and Semenya, Boshadi Mary. "The Operation of Memory in Translation: On Moffat's Desecration of the Batswana Linguistic Heritage in The Production of the 1857 English-Setswana Bible." *Studia Historiae Ecclesiasticae* 41(3) (2015): 44–62.

Munday, Jeremy. *Introducing Translation Studies Theories and Applications.* London: Routledge, 2001.

Newman, B. M. and Nida, Eugene A. *Translator's Handbook on Paul's Letter to the Romans.* New York: United Bible Societies, 1973.

Newman, Barclay M. and Stine, Philip C. *A Handbook on The Gospel of Matthew.* New York: UBS Handbook Series, 1988.

Newman, Barclay N. and Nida, Eugene A. *A Translator's Handbook on Paul's Letter to the Romans.* New York: United Bible Societies, 1973.

Newmark, Peter. *Approaches to Translation.* Oxford: Pergamon Press, 1981.

Ngodji, Martin. *The Story of the Bible among Ovakwanyama: The Agency of Indigenous Translators.* Master of Theology Thesis: University of KwaZulu-Natal, 2004.

Nida, Eugene A. "Principles of Correspondence." *The Translation Studies Reader*, Edited by Lawrence Venuti. London and New York: Routledge, 2004.

Nida, Eugene A. *Towards a Science of Translating*. Leiden: Brill, 1964.

Nida, Eugene A. and Taber, Charles Russell. *The Theory and Practice of Translation*. Leiden: Brill, 2003.

Nida, Eugene A. *Toward a Science of Translating: With Special Reference to Principles and Procedures involved in Bible Translating*. Leiden: Brill, 1964.

Nkhoma, Jonathan S. *Significance of the Dead Sea Scrolls and Other Essays: Biblical and Early Christianity Studies from Malawi*. Mzuzu: Mzuni Press, 2013.

Nord, Christiane. "Function + Loyalty: Theology Meets Skopos," *Open Theology* 2 (2016): 566–580.

Nord, Christiane. *Translating as a Purposeful Activity: Functionalist Approaches Explained*. Manchester: St. Jerome, 1997.

Nord, Christine. "Functional Translation Units." *Translation - Acquisition - Use: AFinLA yearbook* (1997): 41-50, 43.

Obeidat, Adham Mousa, Ayyad, Ghada Rajeh and Mahadi, Tengku Sepora Tengku. "The Tension Between Naturalness and Accuracy In Translating Lexical Collocations In Literary Text." *Journal of Social Science and Humanities* 17(8) (2020):123-134.

Omanson, Korger L. *A Textual Guide to the Greek New Testament*. Stuttgart: German Bible Society, 2006.

Orlinsky, H. and Bratcher, R. G. *A History of Bible translation and the North American contribution*. Atlanta, GA: Scholar Press, 1991.

Ormanson, Roger. "What's in a name?" *TBT* 40(1) (1989): 117-118.

Oyeniyi, Ruth M. "Bible for the Deaf: Implication for Sign Language Bible Translation." *Journal of Mother-Tongue Biblical Hermeneutics and Theology* 2(1) (2020): 35-41.

Pakata, Florence B. *Factors Influencing Use of Sign Language in Teaching and Learning in Public Primary Schools in Kiambu County, Kenya*. Master Education in Curriculum Studies: University of Nairobi, 2015.

Pattermore, S. "Framing Nida: The Relevance of Translation Theory in the United Bible Societies." *A History of Bible Translation* edited by P. A. Noss, pp. 217-263. Rome: Edizioni di Storia e Letteratura, 2007.

Pawlikova-Vilhanova, Viera. "Biblical Translations of Early Missionaries in East and Central Africa. I. Translations into Swahili." *Asian and African Studies*, 15 (2006): 80-89.

Penner, Mark. "Issues in Sign Language Translation, with Special Reference to Bible Translation." *Work Papers of the Summer Institute of Linguistics, University of North Dakota Session*, vol. 49 (2009). Accessed from http://arts-sciences.und.edu/summer-institute-of-linguistics/work-papers/_files/docs/2009-penner.pdf

Pfeiffer, Robert H. *Introduction to the Old Testament*. New York: Harper and Brothers Publishers, 1948.

Powell, Mark Allan. *Introducing the New Testament*. Grand Rapids, MI: Baker Academic, 2009.

Poythress, Vern Sheridan. "Gender in Bible Translation: Exploring a Connection with Male Representatives." *Westminster Theological Journal* 60(2) (1998):225-253.

Prinsloo, Beatrice Aletta. *An introductory South African sign language grammar for the beginner sign language student.* Unpublished MA dissertation. University of the Free State, 2003.

Renn, S. (ed.), *Expository dictionary of Bible words.* Peabody: Hendrickson Publishers, 2005.

Robinson, D. "Literal translation." *Routledge Encyclopedia of Translation Studies* edited by Mona Baker. London: Routledge, 2003.

Robinson, D. *Western translation theory from Herodotus to Nietzsche.* Manchester and Northampton, MA: St. Jerome, 1997.

Rohrbaugh, R. L. *The New Testament in Cross-Cultural Perspective.* Eugene: Cascade, 2007.

Salano, Telejumba Kennedy. *An Analysis of Semantic and Lexical Errors of Translating the New Testament from English into Kiswahili: A Case Study of biblia Ya Mafunzo Ya Uzima.* Masters of Arts Thesis: University of Nairobi, 2018.

Sanneh, Lamin. *Translating the Message: The Missionary Impact on Culture.* New York: Orbis Books, 2002.

Schaff, Philip. *History of the Christian Church Vol. 1.* Grand Rapids, MI: Wm. B. Eerdmans Publishing Company, 1910.

Schmidt, Peter. *Biblical Measures and their Translation: Notes on Translating Biblical Units of Length, Area, Capacity, Weight, Money and Time.* np: SIL International, 2014.

Sherlin, Keith. *Evangelical Bible Doctrine: Articles in Honor of Dr. Mal Couch Couch.* Bloomington: AuthorHouse, 2015.

Shuttleworth, Mark. *Dictionary of translation studies.* Manchester: St Jerome, 1997.

Smith, Kevin G. *Bible Translation and Relevance Theory the Translation of Titus.* Unpublished Doctorate Dissertation: University of Stellenbosch, 2000.

Snell-Horby, Mary. *Translation Studies: An Integrated Approach.* Amsterdam-Philadelphia: John Benjamin Publishing Company, 1988.

Snell-Hornby, Mary. *The Turns of Translation Studies: New Paradigms or Shifting Viewpoints?* Philadelphia: John Benjamins Publishing Company, 2006.

Spronk, Klaas. *Beatific Afterlife in Ancient Israel and in the Ancient Near East.* Neukirchen-Vluyn: Neukirchener Verlag, 1986.

Stamps, Dennis L. "Interpreting the Language of St Paul," *Translating Religious Texts Translation, Transgression and Interpretation Edited by David Jasper.* London: The Macmillan Press Ltd, 1993.

Sundkler, Bengt and Steed, Christopher. *A History of the Church in Africa.* Cambridge: Cambridge University Press, 2000.

Tate, W. Randolph. *Handbook for Biblical Interpretation: An Essential Guide to Methods, Terms, and Concepts.* Grand Rapids, MI: Baker Academic, 2012.

Thiong'o, Ngugi wa. *Decolonising the Mind: The Politics of Language in African Literature*. Nairobi: East African Educational Publishers, 2004.

Togarasei, Lovemore. *The Bible in Context Essay Collection* edited by Joachim Kügler, Lovemore Togarasei and Masiiwa R. Gunda. Bamberg: University of Bamberg Press 2009.

Tov, Emmanuel. *Textual Criticism of the Hebrew Bible*. Minneapolis: Fortress Press, 2001.

Tymoczko, Maria. *Enlarging Translation, Empowering Translators*. Manchester: St Jerome, 2007.

United Bible Societies. "Global Scripture Access Report." *2015 Annual Progress* (2015). (Accessed from https://www.unitedbiblesocieties.org/wp-content/uploads/2016/03/GSAR15_A4_ENG_12pages.pdf, on 23/03/2020).

Vanderauwera, R. Dutch *Novels Translated into English: The Transformation of a "Minority" Literature*. Amsterdam: Rodopi, 1985.

Venuti, Lawrence. *The Translator's Invisibility: A History of Translation*. New York: Routledge, 2008.

Vinay, J. and Darbelnet, Jean. *Comparative Stylistics of French and English: A Methodology for Translation* translated by J.C. Sager and M. J. Hamel. Philadelphia: John Benjamins, 1995.

Waddington, C. "Different Methods of Evaluating Student Translations: The Question of Validity." *Meta: Translators' Journal* 46(2) (2001): 311-325.

Walter C. Kaiser and Moises Silva, *An Introduction to Biblical Hermeneutics*. Grand Rapids: Zondervan, 1994.

Wendland, Ernst R. "Theology and ministry in Africa through Bible translation: 'How firm a foundation?'." *The Bible Translator* 57(4) (2006): 206-216.

Zogbo, Lynell. "Bible, Jewish and Christian," *Routledge Encyclopedia of Translation Studies* edited by Mona Baker, pp. 21-27. London: Routledge, 2003.

Zuck, Roy B. *Basic Bible Interpretation*. Colorado Springs, CO: Victor, 1991.

Index

S

Sahidic, 73
section headings, 31, 185, 186
Sign Language, 199, 200, 201, 202,
  203, 204, 205, 206, 208, 209, 217
sign language translation, xv, 204,
  205, 208, 209
simile, vi, xv, 37, 165, 166, 167, 168,
  169
Skopos theory, 96, 98
socio-linguistic survey, 23, 134,
  138, 209
Stadion, 177
sufficiency of Scripture, 38
Swahili, 5, 18, 79, 80, 102, 136, 150,
  157, 162, 190, 191, 195, 217

T

Tanak, 37
Targums, 54, 55, 114, 117
Tetragrammaton, 191, 192, 198,
  213
Textual criticism, 107, 114, 118
theological exegesis, 126
translation brief, xiv, 23, 26, 33, 34,
  36, 99

Translation Consultant, iii, xii,
  xvii, 24
translator, iii, vi, xii, xiv, xv, 5, 7, 10,
  11, 12, 13, 15, 17, 19, 20, 25, 28,
  30, 31, 32, 33, 35, 36, 37, 40, 47,
  49, 50, 51, 58, 59, 62, 68, 77, 78,
  83, 88, 89, 90, 91, 92, 93, 94, 96,
  98, 99, 101, 102, 104, 105, 106,
  107, 114, 117, 119, 120, 122, 123,
  124, 126,129, 134, 135, 136, 138,
  139, 141, 143, 144, 145, 148, 149,
  151, 152, 154, 157, 162, 163, 167,
  171, 172, 173, 177, 178, 182, 183,
  186, 190, 197, 198, 205, 210, 211
transliteration, 107, 172, 189, 190,
  191, 197, 198

V

Vulgate, xi, 54, 59, 62, 63, 66, 114

Y

Yahweh, 194
YHWH, 189, 192, 193, 194, 195,
  196, 197, 198, 213, 214
Yoruba, 81, 190, 193, 195, 196, 213

www.ingramcontent.com/pod-product-compliance
Lightning Source LLC
Chambersburg PA
CBHW072103020426
42334CB00017B/1611